THE SIGN OF THE WITCH

Carolina Academic Press
Ritual Studies Monograph Series

Pamela J. Stewart and Andrew Strathern
Series Editors

❧

Exchange and Sacrifice
Pamela J. Stewart & Andrew Strathern

Religion, Anthropology, and Cognitive Science
Harvey Whitehouse & James Laidlaw

Resisting State Iconoclasm Among the Loma of Guinea
Christian Kordt Højbjerg

Asian Ritual Systems
Syncretisms and Ruptures
Pamela J. Stewart & Andrew Strathern

The Severed Snake
Matrilineages, Making Place, and a Melanesian Christianity in Southeast Solomon Islands
Michael W. Scott

Embodying Modernity and Post-Modernity
Ritual, Praxis, and Social Change in Melanesia
Sandra C. Bamford

Xhosa Beer Drinking Rituals
Power, Practice and Performance in the South African Rural Periphery
Patrick A. McAllister

Ritual and World Change in a Balinese Princedom
Lene Pedersen

Contesting Rituals
Islam and Practices of Identity-Making
Pamela J. Stewart & Andrew Strathern

The Third Bagre
A Myth Revisited
Jack Goody & S.W.D.K. Gandah

Fragments from Forests and Libraries
Essays by Valerio Valeri
Janet Hoskins & Valerio Valeri

The Sign of the Witch

Modernity and the Pagan Revival

David Waldron

University of Ballarat
Australia

Carolina Academic Press

Durham, North Carolina

Library of Congress Cataloging-in-Publication Data

Waldron, David.
 The sign of the witch : modernity and the pagan revival / by David
Waldron.
   p. cm. -- (Ritual studies monograph series)
 Includes bibliographical references and index.
 ISBN 978-1-59460-505-5 (alk. paper)
 1. Witchcraft. 2. Wicca. 3. Neopaganism. I. Title. II. Series.

 BF1562.5.W35 2008
 299'.94--dc22

                                                    2008002577

Carolina Academic Press
700 Kent Street
Durham, North Carolina 27701
Telephone (919) 489-7486
Fax (919) 493-5668
www.cap-press.com

Printed in the United States of America.

For Jasmine, Talia and Rowan.

Witchcraft is a word that frightens many people and confuses many others. In the popular imagination, Witches are ugly, old hags riding broomsticks, or evil Satanists performing obscene rites. Modern Witches are thought to be members of a kooky cult, primarily concerned with cursing enemies by jabbing wax images with pins and lacking the depth, dignity and seriousness of a true religion.[1]

1. Starhawk (Simos, Miriam). *The Spiral Dance: 10th Anniversary Edition.* San Francisco: Harper Press, 1989. p 16.

CONTENTS

Acknowledgments

I would like to thank my partner Jasmine and my family for much needed support and patience in the course of writing this book. I would also like to thank my parents Bruce and Sharn for their assistance in editing and personal support.

I would like to thank my supervisors Jeremy Smith and Janice Newton for much needed theoretical commentary, advice and inspiration in the course of my research.

I would like to thank Dr Rod Blackhirst of Latrobe University and Dr Elizabeth Kent of the University of Melbourne for assistance in understanding the context of the English experience of Early Modern Witchcraft and general inspiration and support in my research.

Thanks go to the Australian Pagan Information Centre in Woodend Victoria for access to source material. Thanks also to Caroline Tully, Linda and Michel Marold, Anne Harper, Andrew and Julie Daws and Sian Reid for access to much needed, and hard to find, texts, manuscripts, surveys and papers relating to the neo-Pagan movement in Australia and the US.

Finally, thanks go to the University of Ballarat for supplying the resources and facilities required to complete my work.

IDEAS AND THEIR TRANSFORMATIVE PERMUTATIONS IN HISTORY

Andrew Strathern and Pamela J. Stewart

We are happy to include David Waldron's work, "The Sign of the Witch", in our Ritual Studies Monograph Series with Carolina Academic Press. Waldron's study is remarkable in that he traces a history of his topic that runs into the contemporary sphere, taking us from seventeenth century to twenty first century Europe, showing the twists and turns of ritual practices and reformative ideas that have given shape to the notion of witchcraft through these centuries. Contemporary ideas and actions attempt to reach back in time, beyond the religious and political conflicts of the seventeenth century, to the much contested realms of pre-Christian practices in the "folk" domain of Europe: practices that are linked to animism, nature worship, goddess figures, and the like, all of which spring into life in the imaginative worlds of the neo-pagan practitioners of Wicca. Carefully, and at times entertainingly, Dr. Waldron guides his readers along the historical pathways and into the labyrinthine worlds of the so-called "post-modern" times, with their emphasis on eclecticism and bricolage, including the eco-feminist strands of affiliation. We ourselves enthusiastically encouraged Dr. Waldron to revise his manuscript in relation to a number of topics as he prepared the work for inclusion in our Series with Carolina Academic Press.

In some ways these experimental activities represent both a response to contemporary forms of social alienation in people's lives, to which Charismatic and Pentecostalist forms of Christianity can also be seen as counteractive responses or types of therapeutic renewal. Jone Salomonsen has perceptively grouped together two studies she has made in the USA, one of the neo-pagan Reclaiming Witchcraft community in San Francisco, the other of the First Church of Christ in Connecticut. Unconnected to each other, and one defined as "pagan" while the other is "Christian", the two show similar el-

ements of attempts at creative renewal through initiation rites for young people. The Reclaiming movement, founded by Starhawk, centers such rituals on
girls at the time of their first menstruation. The First Church rituals center on
the entrance into sexuality by both boys and girls. Both lay some stress on the
theme of "visions" to be attained by initiands. And both movements drew on
anthropological writings stemming from the time of Arnold van Gennep in
order to create their ritual forms. Gennep's work, of course, in turn drew on
the historical and cross-cultural records of his day. Streams of "tradition" and
its reformulations thus feed into these practices (see Salomonsen 2003).

Returning to the seventeenth century and to the highly specific locality of
Essex County in England, two further things are of note in Dr. Waldron's
treatment of the materials. Building on Alan Macfarlane's pioneering work on
the historical study of witchcraft in this area, Waldron also brings in a brief
discussion of our own comparative work on the importance of rumor and
gossip in the genesis of witchcraft accusations (Stewart and Strathern 2004)[1].
The crucial concept here is the idea of social fluidity and uncertainty. Uncertainty breeds suspicions, and suspicions lead to accusations if they are mobi-
lized to do so. Theological ideas and agents of government may become attached to such a populist trend if it reaches a certain crescendo and has to be
dealt with. Local community life is always full of suspicions as well as soli-
darities (see Møhl 1997 on a village community of central France), and forms
of talk, as Møhl stresses, are the media in which such conflicts are primarily
expressed. An application of our theory of the role of gossip and rumor to the
spread of witchcraft accusations generally is hinted at in Waldron's presentation (see our own discussion in Stewart and Strathern 2004: 152–156).

Another work which we recommended to Dr. Waldron while he was
preparing his manuscript in response to our overall comments is the book by
Emma Wilby on "Cunning Folk and Familiar Spirits" (Wilby 2005). Wilby's
study was notable not only for its detailed anatomy of folk and popular practices but also because it employed the term "shamanic" in relation to ritual
practitioners of the seventeenth century and earlier. The use of the term may
remind us of the element of "vision" entering into both neo-pagan and what
we might call neo-Christian practices referred to above. Wilby has drawn attention to the fact that in an "enchanted world" these popular practitioners
gave people the perceived opportunity to communicate with the "supernatural" world: the witches' journey thus becomes comparable to the idea of the

---

1. For further reference to works by Strathern and Stewart, including works on witchcraft and sorcery see (www.pitt.edu/~strather).

shaman's journey that informs so much classic literature on that topic. (See also discussions in the *Journal of Ritual Studies* 16(2), 2002, on the topic of shamanism and its definitions, e.g. MacDonald 2002 a & b; also on neo-shamanism and performance Blain and Wallis in *Journal of Ritual Studies* 20(1), 2006. These references indicate that we have been taking a close interest in the topic in recent years. We are also engaged in working with colleagues at the Institute of Ethnology, Academia Sinica in Taipei, Taiwan, where we have been situated as Visiting Research Scholars for periods of time from 2002 to 2007, on the topic of Shamans and Ritual Performance.)

These two perspectives, the perspective of gossip and the perspective of shamanic practice, can both help to enrich the kinds of materials Dr. Waldron ably covers in his own analytical discussions.

The "sign of the witch" can thus be seen as like a multivocalic or polyvalent symbol that can take on various colors and contrasts and incorporate alternative analytical viewpoints over time. Dr. Waldron has made an ingenious and substantial contribution to this semantic and historical tapestry.

Cromie Burn Research Unit
October 8th, 2007

References

Blain, Jenny and Robert J. Wallis 2006. Ritual reflections, practitioner meanings: disputing the terminology of neo-shamanic 'performance'. *Journal of Ritual Studies* 20(1): 21–36.

MacDonald, Mary N. 2002a. Introduction: shamans, scholars, and seekers. *Journal of Ritual Studies*, spec. issue, 16(2): 60–62.

___ 2002b. The study of shamanism: local and universal dimensions. *Journal of Ritual Studies* 16(2): 88–107.

Møhl, Perle 1997. *Village Voices: Coexistence and Communication in a Rural Community in Central France*. Copenhagen: Museum Tusculanum Press.

Salomonsen, Jone 2003. The ethno-methodology of ritual invention—two Pagan and Christian cases. *Journal of Ritual Studies* 17(2): 15–24.

Stewart, Pamela J. and Andrew Strathern 2004. *Witchcraft, Sorcery, Rumors, and Gossip*. New Departures in Anthropology Series, no. 1, Cambridge: Cambridge University Press.

Wilby, Emma 2005. *Cunning Folk and Familiar Spirits: Shamanistic Visionary Traditions in Early Modern British Witchcraft and Magic*. Brighton, UK: Sussex University Academic Press.

INTRODUCTION

When I first wrote the dissertation that was reconstructed as this book, the arena of Pagan Studies and Wicca, as one of a plethora of New Religious Movements emerging into the cultural mainstream during the 1980s, was still somewhat a fringe area of study. Indeed, neo-Pagan revivalist movements, of which Wicca is the most predominant, were still very much the target of vitriol and scare mongering particularly by religiously inspired political conservatives. Republican congressman in the United States for example, after discovering that many self-proclaimed Witches served in the U.S army at a military base in Fort Hood made the claim, "We believe they are Satanic and that they do not deserve to have any place in Fort Hood". Republican politician Storm Thurmond asked in the senate "What's next? Will armored divisions be forced to travel with sacrificial animals for satanic rituals?"[1]

Since working on my dissertation however, the wide dissemination of ground breaking and original research by pioneering historians, such as the superb research by Professor Ronald Hutton of Bristol University in an extremely detailed local history approach to British Folklore and the history of Wicca, and that of the many social theory, cultural studies and feminist analysis of the Pagan revival have shifted the field into, if not the mainstream, then a least out of the fringe of respectable scholarship. Similarly, the numerous anthropological studies of pagan revivalist communities, festivals and ritual groups have shifted neo-Pagan studies to the forefront of much urban anthropological and women's studies research. In terms of popular culture neo-Pagan and Wiccan inspired characters are now extraordinarily common in fantasy and science fiction stories. Pagan and Wiccan characters and scenarios are not uncommon in television and cinema and they are commonly represented in a positive manner. There are several television serials predominantly featuring neo-Pagan characters and witches in a positive light, Charmed, Hex

---

1. Gynne, S.C. "I Saluted a Witch: An Army base in Texas becomes the hotbed for earth goddess worshipers called Wiccans." *Time Magazine*. Time Warner Publications. 5 July, 1999. p 41.

and Buffy the Vampire Slayer and its spin offs, are perhaps the most significant examples. So while some degree of antipathy and ridicule exists neo-Paganism in both scholarly and popular circles has now come in from the cold, as it were, and entered the forums of popular representation and academia with unprecedented respectability.

In any case, representations of Witchcraft are capable of stirring strong emotions and the image of the Witch has a uniquely resonant psycho-symbolic impact in Western culture. Most of us are aware of the image of Witchcraft illustrated by the image of the wrinkled, malevolent Old Crone as described by a wide array of fairy tales, literature and films such as Disney's "Snow White and the Seven Dwarfs" or MGM's famed musical "The Wizard of Oz". Similarly, as illustrated above, most of us are aware of the representations of Witchcraft by many conservative Christian movements, such as New Christian Right in the United States, who construct their image of Witchcraft as a manifestation of Satanism or amoral Paganism. Representations of Witchcraft are often utilized by the mass media, keen to link images of Witchcraft with cults, mass murderers and anti-humanist behavior, as part of a moral panic linked to the contemporary mythology of Satanic Ritual Abuse. These images have a strong symbolic impact in Western culture and subsequently impact on popular representations of those who have constructed their identity as Witches or Pagans.

As previously discussed, there have been a variety of new forms of Witchcraft representation coming to prominence in Western popular culture. Many feminist and eco-feminist scholars, such as Mary Daly, Andrea Dworkin, Robin Morgan and Miriam Simos (Starhawk), have utilized the image of the Witch as a powerful symbol to metaphorically represent the oppression of women in contemporary post-enlightenment patriarchal and technocratic society. Many of these writers also argue that Witchcraft, construed as a matrifocal belief system rooted in connection with the natural world and feminine identity, offers a new and unique capacity for women to find their own spiritual identity and source of spiritual experience beyond the limitations of patriarchal religion.[2] As one coordinator of the feminist organization "Women's Spirit" writes,

> Feminism tells us to trust ourselves. So feminists began experiencing something. We began to believe that, yes indeed, we *were* discrimi-

---

2. Brooke, Elizabeth. *A Woman's Book of Shadows: Witchcraft: A Celebration.* London: Women's Press, 1993; Daly, Mary. *Gyn/Ecology.* London: Women's Press, 1979; Dworkin, Andrea. *Women Hating.* New York: Dutton, 1974; Starhawk (Simos, Miriam). *Dreaming the Dark.* Chicago: Llewellyn Publishers, 1986.

nated against on the job; we began to see that motherhood was not all it was advertised to be. We began to trust our own feelings; we began to believe in our own orgasms ... Now we are beginning to have spiritual experiences and for the first time in thousands of years, we trust it. We say, "Oh, this is an experience of mine, and feminism tells me there must be something to this, because it's all right to trust myself!" So women began to trust what they were experiencing. For example, a woman has a dream about stones and she goes to the library to see what there is about stones. Then she finds Stonehenge. Then she gets interested in the Druids and discovers that people do ceremonies and that is often called Witchcraft. Then this woman becomes interested in Witches and goes to them to find out what has been going on."[3]

Another form of Witchcraft representation is that of Witchcraft being a more authentic and natural form of religion located in an idealized pre-industrial past. This particular perspective is well illustrated by prominent neo-Pagan and feminist author Miriam Simos (Starhawk),

But Witchcraft is a religion, perhaps the oldest religion extant in the west. Its origins go back before Christianity, Judaism, Islam—before Buddhism and Hinduism as well, and it is very different from all the so-called great religions. The Old religion, as we call it, is closer in spirit to Native American traditions or to the Shamanism of the Arctic. It is not based on Dogma or a set of beliefs, nor on Scriptures or a sacred book revealed by a great man. Witchcraft takes its teachings from nature, and reads inspiration in the movements of the sun, moon and stars, the flight of birds, the slow growth of trees and the cycle of the seasons.[4]

In contrast, historians, writing in the context of nineteenth century Enlightenment narratives of teleological progress, have tended to define the Witch trials of the Early Modern period as a conflict between the terror and barbarity of ignorance and superstition, and the civilizing power of an Enlightenment crusade against irrationality. Some prominent examples of this encapsulation of Witchcraft and the Early Modern Witch trials are Arthur Miller's

---

3. Adler, Margot. *Drawing Down the Moon: Witches, Druids, Goddess worshipers and other Pagans in America Today.* 2nd Edition. New York: Penguin Group Publishing. 1986. p 183.

4. Starhawk. *The Spiral Dance.* p 16.

play "The Crucible" and historian Norman Cohn's attempt use of Witchcraft persecutions as a model to explain Europe's long history of persecuting minority groups which, he argues, culminated in the Nazi persecution of Jews and Gypsies, amongst others, the during Second World War.[5] Enlightenment historians utilized Witchcraft representations as a means of illustrating the dangers of religion, superstition and irrationality in contrast to the humanist ideals of logic, science and reason. An example of this is André and Lynette Singer's comment that,

> Although we find it hard to accept that a rational person accepts these events, rationality hardly came into it. Witchcraft was a belief—and the role of the Devil was declared by the Church. Not to believe it was heresy. If the belief was accepted there was nothing unusual about the trials themselves. For people who believed in covens, Devils and flying Witches the trials brought few inconsistencies. As the belief waned, it became acceptable to condemn the trials and even to ridicule the belief itself.[6]

Another example of this approach is historian Trevor-Roper's commentary on the reasons for the decline of Witchcraft trials and the concomitant belief in diabolism and sorcery in 17th century Europe,

> What ultimately destroyed the Witch-craze on an intellectual level was not the argument of the skeptics but the new philosophy, a philosophical revolution which changed the whole concept of nature and its operations. It was the Enlightenment in which the duel in nature between a Hebrew God and a medieval Devil was replaced by the benevolent despotism of a modern scientific deity.[7]

What these representations illustrate is that the Witch is a powerful and culturally significant symbol in contemporary Western culture. Furthermore, the means by which images of Witchcraft and Witches are represented in contemporary Western culture, are indicative of a wide range of social and cultural structures representative of differing sectors of Western society and models of cultural identity. Similarly, the divergent manner in which different sectors within the Western culture appropriate a particular historical con-

---

5. Cohn, Norman. *Europe's Inner Demons.* London: Sussex University Press, 1975.

6. Singer, Andre & Lynette. *Divine Magic: The World of the Supernatural.* London: Boxtree Publishing, 1995. p 110.

7. Trevor-Roper, Hugh. "Witches and Witchcraft: a Historical Essay." *Encounter,* Vol 28. No 6. 1967. pp 29–30.

struction and its related cultural symbols, gives insight into the relationship between historicity and cultural identity in contemporary society. These points of divergence and symbolic representation are exacerbated by the strong emotive impact of Witchcraft symbols in Western culture, and the fact that these representations of Witchcraft are generally aligned with the socio-political agendas of particular sub-cultures and their corresponding socio-economic circumstance and ideologies.

With regards to the terminology used to describe the various Pagan and Witchcraft revivalist movements, I have decided to use the term neo-Pagan over other possibilities for several reasons. The commonly used term Wicca or Wiccan originated with the strand of neo-Paganism linked to a representation of witchcraft as a pagan survival as initially propagated by Gerald Gardner and other progenitors of the 1950's Pagan revival and is thus only used by certain sectors of the neo-Pagan movement. As such it tends to exclude many antiquarian neo-Pagans, ritual magicians and members of the Goddess spirituality movement who may use a wide array of alternative titles to describe their construction of Pagan identity. Similarly, I have declined to use the term Witch to describe neo-Pagans as it refers to an incredibly wide variety of historical and cultural phenomenon that are labeled under the one term (Witch), originating in medieval England yet used to describe a plethora of social forms. Similarly, its etymological heritage is extremely complex and made problematic through its indiscriminate and intensely politicized usage across cultures, civilizations and history.[8] This problem is exacerbated by the fact that there is little evidence directly linking today's neo-Pagan movement with those individuals tried for Witchcraft in the Witch crazes of the Early Modern period. In this light, I have come to feel that the very diversity of the word "Witch", as applied in Western culture, is so broad and fragmented as to divest the term of useful descriptive meaning in categorizing the neo-Pagan movement.

The term neo-Pagan appeared in the late nineteenth century and was used to refer to Romantic discourses that supported the ideal of a Pagan revival as an antidote to the ills of industrialization and the perceived restrictive nature of conservative Christian morality.[9] It has been criticized within the contemporary neo-Pagan movement as singling out its discontinuity with the past and its lack of homogenous rituals, symbols and practices as a means of dele-

---

8. Clifton, Chas. *Her Hidden Children: The Rise of Wicca and Paganism in America.* Alta Mira Press: New York, 2006. pp 79–83.

9. Hutton, Ronald. *Triumph of the Moon: A History of Modern Pagan Witchcraft.* Oxford: Oxford University Press, 1999. p 28.

gitimating neo-Pagan beliefs in comparison to mainstream religions such as Christianity, Islam and Judaism. It was argued that since Christianity has also gone through substantive revision and contains many breaks and discontinuities, the singling out of Paganism as a discontinuous, constructed and revivalist movement was unfair. This perspective is illustrated by the comment "This 'neo' label keeps popping up. Graham Harvey was just saying how he does not like it on the grounds that we have had many varieties of Christianity, for instance, but we don't call the ones today 'neo-Christians'".[10] However, whilst sympathetic to this perspective I am inclined to agree with the response posed by Michael Strmiska of the History and Comparative Religion Department of Miyazaki International College in Japan when he states that,

> For most religions, Oldness is important. The Old Ways were and hence are Good Ways; that feeling or experience is part of what makes religion powerful and appealing. The nice part about being "neo" is that you are not limited by the weight of past tradition, but are more free to explore and invent. There are pluses and minuses both ways, but one of the tests for neo-Paganism, as I see it, will be whether neo-Pagans will ever be able to agree on enough to allow common, definable ground which can unite people across geography and time, or whether neo-Paganism will remain an experimental, experiential grab-bag blissfully free of authority-structures and fixed dogma.
> For myself, I will reserve the word Pagan for past (or present) traditions that can claim an unbroken line of transmission, like Hinduism and Shinto or religions of First-world people that have survived the persecutions andoppressions concomitant with Christianisation, and use neo-Pagan for modernday movements like Asatru and Wicca.[11]

In initiating a study of Witchcraft representations and historiography in the neo-Pagan movement, I have divided up the myriad of different forms of neo-Paganism into four general areas which I believe are indicative of the main approaches to cultural and ideological construction within the neo-Pagan movement. In a movement as diverse and fragmented as neo-Paganism there is, by necessity, a certain degree of overlap, however, they are not meant to be used in an exclusivist way. In this sense, they are not meant to be categories of neo-Pagan practitioners but are instead patterns of approaching belief, identity and

---

10. Personal communication Fritz Muntean. Editor of the *Pomegranate* Journal of Pagan Studies. "Natrel-L" newsgroup. 29-11-2000.

11. Personal communication Michael Strmiska. Lecturer in History and Comparative Religion, Miyazaki International College. "Natrel-L newsgroup". 29-11-2000.

historico-cultural identity that are indicative of general trends within the contemporary manifestation of the neo-Pagan revival.

Antiquarian or Reconstructionist: Antiquarian or reconstructionist approaches to neo-Pagan identity tend to rely on empirical approaches to historical identity and the legitimacy of ritual and symbolic expression in creating a contemporary neo-Pagan identity. Antiquarian or reconstructionist oriented neo-Pagans tend to follow an indexical relationship to the past by orienting rituals, symbols and cultural representations according to historical findings on the Paganism of antiquity and medieval Witchcraft.

Traditionalist: The groups derived from the ritual magic intensive Witchcraft such as Gardnerian and Alexandrian Wicca. This approach evolved out of the ritual magic, spiritualist and theosophical movements of nineteenth century Europe. Integrated with this spiritualist and theosophical basis of religious practice were the romanticist histories and comparative anthropological analysis of the Folklore Society via historians and folklorists such as Margaret Murray and Sir James Frazer which worked to create a specific cultural identity based in the notion of authentic pagan revivals buried in folklore, spiritualism and ritual magic. The term "Traditionalist" is occasionally used to describe those neo-Pagans claiming to have a hereditary background to their Witchcraft or magical beliefs, however, here the term is used to refer to those groups originating in the spiritualist and theosophical movements of the late 19th and early 20th centuries as linked to the notion of an authentic religious practice rooted in folklore and esoteric magical practice.

New Age/Eclectic: New Age/Eclectic neo-Pagans are particularly concerned with the psychological impact and universality of symbols. They posit the psychic truth of symbolic representations manifested in history and other cultures as the ultimate source of authenticity in ritual, as opposed to the empirical veracity of truth claims. The development of New Age eclecticism amongst neo-Pagans, particularly in the US, is intrinsically linked with the development of the sixties counter culture and is typically heavily indebted to the work of Carl Jung in interpreting and constructing neo-Pagan symbols, mythology and ritual.

Eco-feminist: I have used this term to represent groups that are particularly concerned with the plight of women and utilize the symbol of the Witch as an ultimate expression of the persecution of women within patriarchal culture and society. The fundamental historical concern of the eco-feminist branches of the neo-Pagan movement is the ability of historical representations to empower women, irrespective of empirical arguments regarding the historical validity of their truth claims. Of particular significance within the eco-feminist variants of neo-Paganism are the attempt to utilize the Witch trials of

1480–1680 and the persecution of Pagans by Christians as a model for the contemporary persecution of women. This model, heavily influenced by the Romantic episteme in Western culture, tends to perceive femininity as integrally linked with nature and thus perceive a natural conjunction between deep ecology and radical feminism.

Whilst these four areas of Witchcraft history have different structures of legitimating historical interpretation and ideological/cultural perspectives, there are several elements that link them together. The first is a belief that the advent of the Enlightenment and industrialization represent a distancing of humanity from its more authentic and natural existence uncorrupted by the influence of Western civilization. Secondly, the neo-Pagan movement is generally unanimous in the belief that Western Christianity is guilty of suppressing much of what is free, creative and autonomous in human nature in favor of static, oppressive and patriarchal systems of morality and social control. Thirdly, the Witch crazes of the early modern period are taken as representative of a conscious attempt to oppress and destroy the vestiges of pre-Christian nature religions. Finally, the reclaiming and recreating of the pre-Christian agrarian past is perceived as the most authentic and successful path to transcend the ills perceived to be caused by the oppressive aspects of Christianity, the Enlightenment and Western modernity.

The purpose of this book is to examine the construction of Witchcraft images, histories and identities within the neo-Pagan movement. Of particular significance is the relationship between the various approaches to historiography and the means by which these historical constructions are utilized in the creation of a contemporary neo-Pagan identity. Underlying this analysis is an examination of the interaction of Enlightenment and Romantic epistemes within Western modernity in relation to the construction of Witchcraft symbolism and cultural representations within the neo-Pagan movement. A central focus of this study is the shift from modernist to post-modernist forms of historical legitimation and symbolic appropriation in the post-sixties era. Critical to this analysis is the extent to which the intense commercialization of Witchcraft by the New Age industry and mass media during the 1990s has impacted on the social and cultural structure of the neo-Pagan movement and the corresponding constructions of Witch and Pagan identity.

In this context I have analyzed a broad range of materials in order to bring into focus the historical antecedents and socio-historical context of the many symbolic constructions of "Witches", "Witchcraft" and Paganism. At base, it is these symbolic constructions that form both the cultural and socio-political basis of the Pagan revival and inform the public representations of these New Religious Movements. In this light, I begin with a discussion of the context and end of the witchcrazes in Early Modern England and discuss their legacy and cultural, social and political import in the rise of the English Enlightenment. I move on through the Romantic inspired Pagan revivalist movements of the 19th Century and the influence of the closely linked Rosicrucian and Occult revivals of the same period. I move on to a discussion of the rise of Wicca and concomitant movements in the early 1950s and parallel movements in the United States. This leads to a discussion of the impact of the 60s and 70s feminist movements and the appropriation of the witch as the quintessential symbol of women's historical oppression by Patriarchy. In this context I also review the influence of the New Age based New Religious Movements of the 60s and 70s and the rise of American neo-Pagan movements. I finish with an examination of the impact of popularization and commodification of Witchcraft and Paganism and the issues facing the Pagan revivalist movements today. Through this process I closely link the neo-Pagan revival to developments in philosophical and ideological structures in academia and the broader social context such as the influence of the Enlightenment, Romanticism, Feminism, Post-Modernism and particularly influential scholars such as Carl Jung, Margaret Murray, Robin Morgan, James Frazer and Friedrich Schlegel amongst others.

Chiefly I have aimed this book at the student who desires an overarching perspective on the social, cultural, political and philosophical context of Pagan revivals and its broader influence on society and culture. I also hope this book will serve as an easily readable excursion into the field of Pagan studies for the general public and neo-Pagans themselves so that they may better situate the revivalist movements historically, culturally and ideologically within the broader spectrum of Western society and culture.

Ultimately, the primary focus of this book is to trace the historical and cultural patterns by which representations of Witchcraft and Paganism have been formed since the end of the witch trials of the early modern period. The primary ideological correlation between contemporary neo-Paganism and romanticism, is the belief that it is necessary to gaze inwards and to appropriate images from the past to find forms of identity and symbols of meaning perceived as natural, culturally authentic and in opposition to the forces of the Enlightenment and industrialism. Conversely, this also involves a belief in the veracity of symbols, images and feelings over empirical experience and logic. In this sense, neo-Paganism is fundamentally dominated by a reification of beliefs and images. Symbolically antiquarian but historically contemporaneous ideological and symbolic socio-cultural formations are reinforced by interpretations of a past that are perceived to give a sense of authenticity and a sense of place. Thus the Witch serves as a symbolic focal point of many of the issues facing modern society and our ambivalent and multifaceted interaction with the impact and legacy of the enlightenment and modernity.

THE SIGN OF THE WITCH

THE HISTORICAL CONTEXT OF WITCHCRAFT: PROGENITORS AND ANTECEDENTS

To begin this story we start with the rise of the English notion of Witchcraft and the role of supernaturalism in English politics and society during the English reformation and the lead up to the Puritan revolution of the following century. This might seem an odd place to start, given the well documented contemporary origins of the Pagan revivals and the tenuous nature of the links between historical Witchcraft and its manifestation in recent traditions such as Wicca. However, It is during the rise of what would become the English nation state that the foundations of the English experience of Enlightenment, and thus the construction of supernaturalism and the Witch's iconic role as the epitome of the superstitious and anti-rational came to be formed. In this light the early modern construction of witchcraft and its associated folklore became the focal point of Witchcraft as defined by Enlightenment, Christian and later Romantic discourses and thus served as the cultural and folkloric wellspring of its redefinition as the remnant of Pagan survivals and an antidote to the ills of Christian traditionalism, Enlightenment rationalism and industrialisation in the 19th and 20th centuries. I've taken a specifically Anglo-centric focus in this approach due to the fact that whilst colonial interpretations of witchcraft were important in defining Enlightenment approaches to the supernatural and romantic counter discourses, they played a less direct role in the formation of the English model of Witchcraft rooted in English folklore and nationalism in 19th and mid 20th century revival movements that a reconstruction of the uniquely English experience. Similarly, the Scottish and Irish Experience, whilst again central in the formation of the idea of the "Celtic" was less important in the early stages of the formation of "Witch" identity and symbolism than the Anglo-centric orientation of Saxon inspired Wicca until the later half of the 20th Century. The influences of these other sources will be discussed in more depth later in this book.

In the Anglo-Saxon cultural milieu however, the image of the "Witch" as a cultural signifier underwent a massive transformation during the formation of what would become the English nation state. This reconfiguration of Witch identity in official and popular discourse in the sixteenth, seventeenth and eighteenth centuries played a critical role in forming the image of Witchcraft associated with Paganism, rural life and folklore. This occurred through several stages. Firstly, the attempt of Henry VIII to separate England from the Catholic Church and its corresponding political and cultural break from the continent led to the increased politicisation and centralization of Witchcraft related cases under the secular authority of the English monarch. This was exacerbated by various attempts to bring the spiritual and moral authority of the Church in line with the interests of English secular authority. Similarly, in the aftermath of the Protestant based mass Witch-hunts of the civil war, religious and political authorities perceived the outbreak of popularist religion and supernaturalism to be threats to the maintenance of government and social cohesion. Additionally, the rise of secularist ideology, combined with an increasing anti-supernaturalist and deist orientation on behalf of the English Protestant Churches, led to a climate in which belief in Witchcraft was no longer intellectually tenable and government acted to discourage Witchcraft beliefs and the persecution of suspected Witches. In this light, belief in Witches came to be associated with either foreign papist superstition or mob violence by superstitious rural peasants and the accused victims as innocents to be saved by an Enlightenment crusade against irrationality.

From the late sixteenth century onward, official discourse on Witches and Witchcraft gradually shifted from a perception of Witchcraft practitioners as individuals accused of *maleficium*, consorting with the devil or malevolent use of magic against a local community, to a perception of Witches being the hapless victims of primitive and rustic superstition. At least this was the representation of magic and Witchcraft that came to dominate the official discourse of the state, Church and intellectual elite of England. There was more to this than simply the rise of science and rationality dispelling old superstitions. Indeed, the issue of prosecuting Witches was fundamentally within the preserve of the intelligentsia until the late seventeenth century and demonology remained a significant component of natural science and philosophy amongst the intelligentsia until the early 1700s.[1] Similarly, profound as the influence of experimental reasoning on intellectual life in seventeenth century England was,

---

1. Clark, Stuart. *Thinking With Demons: The Idea of Early Modern Witchcraft in Early Modern Europe.* New York: Oxford University Press, 1997. pp 299–300.

it is difficult to argue why, for example, Isaac Newton's *Principia Mathematica* should make Assize judges less likely to convict Witches, let alone why rural villagers far removed from the discussions of the English intellectual elite would be less likely to launch Witchcraft accusations at each other. The development of the scientific tradition was part of a much broader shift in the social, cultural and ideological basis of English society which occurred concurrently with other developments across continental Europe.

In the case of England, the rise of the secularist and scientific rationalist tradition was preceded by the rise of secular nationhood in the aftermath of the Reformation in the reign of King Henry VIII and its corresponding tradition of anti-Catholicism and alignment of Christian teachings in the Anglican Church with the interests of government. This movement towards the secularisation of government, the domination of the Anglican Church by the monarchy and the formation of the bureaucratic infrastructure was also profoundly influenced by the English civil war and the last great outbreak of Witch-crazes in Sussex and Kent in the late sixteenth and early seventeenth century. Whilst the rise of Enlightenment ideology and rationality definitively ended the intellectual credibility of belief in magic and Witchcraft, the period of persecution and the status of demonology and Witchcraft beliefs were already in sharp decline by the end of the eighteenth century. Central to this process was a paradigmatic shift in the nature of English government, society and culture that radically transformed the social, political, economic and cultural context in which Witchcraft accusations occurred.

Anti-Catholicism and the Reformation

Underlying the massive transformation of the English political and intellectual landscape in the sixteenth century was a profound shift in the political relationship between the English political elite and continental Europe. While a full and detailed study of the formation of the English nation state is far beyond the scope of this book several key issues involved in the process of state formation had a massive impact on the configuration of Witchcraft and magic in early modern English society and culture.[2] Of central importance in the process of state formation and the redefining of Witchcraft were the Eng-

---

2. This topic has been extensively studied and a full analysis is far beyond the scope of this thesis. For more information please see, Hill, Christopher. *Puritanism and Revolution.* New York Schocken Books, 1964; Jones, Edwin. *The English Nation: The Great Myth.* Gloucestershire: Sutton Press, 1998; Rex, Richard. *Henry VIII and the English Reformation.*

lish Reformation and the corresponding political and religious break from Europe in the mid sixteenth century.

From the time of the Roman occupation until the end of the sixteenth century the English political and intellectual orientation was firmly fixed on continental Europe. A major component of this was the political, economic, social and cultural influence of the Catholic Church which played a central role in establishing the political legitimacy of the monarchy and thus profoundly shaped the development of English social, cultural and political structures and formations. Through the extensive and increased influence of the Catholic Church on English political, economic, social and cultural activity throughout the Middle Ages, Renaissance England was brought into increasingly close contact and integration with continental Europe via the political and economic influence of the papacy.[3]

The English Reformation played a pivotal role in the re-orientation of the English political landscape towards secularisation and to a large extent laid the groundwork for both the future development of the nation state and the English experience of the Enlightenment. Henry VIII, ostensibly over his inability to gain papal acquiescence for his divorce from Catherine of Aragon, attempted to create a break between the English throne and the Catholic Church, the source of moral and political authority for most of the Kingdoms on the continent. In its place, Henry reconstructed the English Church so that its institutions and teachings would be directly under the control of the English throne. Thomas Cromwell, Henry's chief minister and noted secularist, was commissioned as the chief architect of the move and he worked to enact, via legislation, propaganda and force, a political and religious break from both the Catholic Church and continental sources of authority, particularly the kingdom of Spain. The anti-clerical majority in the House of Commons, representing the merchants and landed gentry, who wished to break from the financial burden and political restrictions of the Catholic Church, enthusiastically supported this move. Additionally, many among the gentry and merchant classes of England looked eagerly forward to gaining access to the lands and wealth of the English Church. The initial means of affecting the break with the Catholic Church, as a source of moral, political and legal authority, were the government acts of *The Restraint of Appeals*, *The Act of Supremacy* and the seizure of monastic property and holdings.[4]

London: Palgrave, 1993; Sommerville, C. *The Secularization of Early Modern England.* London: Oxford University Press, 1992.

3. Jones, E. *The English Nation.* pp 1–2.

4. Jones, E. *The English Nation.* pp 31–32. Rex, R. *Henry VIII and the English Reformation.* pp 863–881.

The act of the *Restraint of Appeals* in 1533 made it illegal for English citizens to make an appeal to a Papal or any other external court regarding any decision made by the King's court. This act effectively began a massive drive towards political severance between the Church and the English state. The *Act of Supremacy* reaffirmed this in 1534, for the first time proclaiming the English monarch as the supreme head of the English Church. This was perhaps the second most significant element of the political revolution that was the English Reformation. Not only was England legally severed from the apparatus of political authority of the continent and the Catholic Church, but also the head of the secular authority, the sovereign, was made the spiritual head of the nation via government control of the Church of England. This trend was solidified with the *Ecclesiastical Appointments* Act of 1534 which gave the King the right to appoint Bishops and Archbishops without reference to any other authority beyond the divine right of the "Supreme Head on Earth of the Church of England, called Anglicana Ecclesia".[5] The apparatus of government and the state controlled Church of England became the sole basis of authority over the newly formed sovereign state of England. These acts were soon followed with the political and legislative union with Wales, the dissolution and government appropriation of monasteries and convents and the overall strengthening of the machinery of government. This last feature became increasingly significant as the English government learned to apply new forms of authority and social control over the population now bereft of the authority of the Church.[6]

The *Act of Supremacy*, in particular, gave legal force to the exaltation and glorification of the monarchy. It served to legitimise the concept of absolute authority being located in the hands of the apparatus of the secular intitutions of government and served to directly link the power and moral authority of the Church with the assertion of power by the apparatus of government. The separation of the English Church and state from both the continent and Papal authority also led to the adoption of Protestant theology and the obedience theology of William Tyndale, associating moral rightness with obedience to the Church and state by the political apparatus of the English government. The issue of establishing the moral authority of the state became increasingly important as the apparatus of the English government faced a crisis of legitimacy amongst the English population, particularly in the rural sector.[7]

---

5. Jones, E. *The English Nation.* p 34.

6. Jones, E. *The English Nation.* pp 14–15; Sommerville, C. *The Secularization of Early Modern England.* pp 34–36; Hill, Christopher. *Puritanism and Revolution.* pp 41–43.

7. Rex, R. *Henry VIII and the English Reformation.* pp 863–884.

The adoption of obedience theology and the subjugation of the power of the Church to that of the king and secular government led to the assertion that the Word of God was manifested in the apparatus of Church and state. Consequently, obedience to the will of the king and state controlled Church was the primary and paramount claim of religious moral obligation. Thomas Cromwell worked extensively throughout the apparatus of Church and state to promote the idea of the divine right of sovereignty through constructing a wide range of plays, sermons, festivals and tracts designed to associate the power of government with the social and moral authority of the Church in the popular imagination. Other notables took part in this process; of particular importance were Thomas Starkley, Richard Sampson and John Bale who also wrote plays and dissertations that supported the authority of government as inherently linked to the moral authority of the Church in their teachings, as well as pressuring local clergy and government officials to support Cromwell's agenda.[8]

The regime of Henry VIII had embarked on an extensive ideological and propaganda enterprise designed to solidify and propagate the idea of the divine right of Kingship amongst the English population. This was to have significant repercussions upon the nature of government and the political, social, religious and cultural landscape of English society. The English people were taught by the instruments of government and the Church to give absolute authority, both spiritual and temporal, to the one authority and symbol of the nation, the King. Allegiance to the Church and state as political entities was taught to the English people as "The first claim of their conscience".[9]

Another aspect of this revolution in the ideological orientation of the newly burgeoning nation state was the encouragement of xenophobia and hostility to those outside of the territorial and cultural boundaries of the nation. In the statutes and legislation introduced under the Henrican regime the Pope and most foreign powers were described as the "Hated foreign enemy of the English people". This response, which was quickly adopted by the English political and intellectual elite, was applied to almost all Catholic countries and Catholic symbols of authority in Europe. The English people were also encouraged by the apparatus of government to adopt this perspective in their dealings with foreigners. Localised basis of prejudice and conflict within the burgeoning nation state of England were further discouraged by the institu-

---

8. Jones, Edwin. *The English Nation.* pp 15–16; Rex, R. *Henry VIII and the English Reformation.* p 863.

9. Rex, R. *Henry VIII and the English Reformation.* p 863.

tions of religious and political authority in an attempt to inspire and consol-
idate a sense of unity and solidarity for the people of England.[10]

A critical component of the drive towards a secular nation in the English
Reformation was the economic weakening of the Catholic Church as an institution. The seizure of the monasteries and land previously owned by the
Church brought the government a net annual income of 136,000 pounds
whilst the seizure of gold, plate and other assets brought in approximately 1.5
million pounds which was largely handed over to the merchants and propertied classes of England. When one considers that government income from
land tenure had never exceeded 40,000 pounds prior to 1542 the economic
significance of the Reformation can hardly be exaggerated. The political and
economic structure of England was radically transformed with the power and
wealth of the secular institutions of authority gaining a distinct economic and
political advantage over ecclesiastical authority.[11]

The Church was weakened by the loss of systems of patronage via the government seizure of land and assets. The Church had long relied on its wealth
as a significant means of obtaining popular support in the community via employment for laypersons and labourers. This method of patronage also served
as a means of gaining influence over the economic life of local villages and
towns to further strengthen the Church's political power.[12] Consequently, as
the Church lost financial power it also lost political power and economic influence over English society; a situation compounded by the removal of the
Abbots from the House of Lords, which saw its previous majority become a
minority, leaving control of the institution largely in the hands of the landed
nobility. Similarly, the Bishops became almost completely dependent on the
will of the crown for land, finance and survival, which ensured their loyalty
to the will of the sovereign. This combination of political and economic assault served to substantially weaken the political role of the Church and placed
increased significance on the secular institutions of authority, eventually sub-
ordinating the Church under the control of the monarchy and the interests of
both the landed nobility and merchant sectors of society.[13]

Overall, the effect of the Reformation on Witchcraft beliefs was to weaken
and discredit the validity of Catholic based demonological and supernaturalist interpretations of Witchcraft and reconfigure them as a predominantly sec-

---

10. Collinson, P. "No Popery: The Myth of a Protestant Nation." *The Tablet*. March 25.
1995. pp 280 & 384–386.
11. Hill, C. *Puritanism and Revolution*. pp 40–45.
12. Hill, C. *Puritanism and Revolution*. p 42.
13. Hill, C. *Puritanism and Revolution*. p 42.

ular crime against the authority of the sovereign or local community. Attacks on supernaturalism became increasingly common throughout the period after the Reformation and these attacks were largely configured as veiled attacks on the Catholic Church and its perceived links with Paganism, superstition and continental authority. In this light, individuals who associated themselves with Catholicism, even figures amongst the intellectual elite such as Sir Thomas More, could be configured as rude, superstitious and even treasonous.[14]

This radical change in England's political structure in the aftermath of the Reformation had a substantial impact on Witchcraft beliefs and trials during King Henry VIII's regime. England's secular institutions of authority had essentially assumed responsibility for the law with regards to Witchcraft that led to a significant reorientation of the focus and penalties of Witchcraft trials. Whilst belief in the traditions of *maleficium* and demonology as Witchcraft were somewhat suppressed and discredited by the English government, King Henry VIII was particularly concerned about the practice of fortune telling and soothsaying and acted to legally define their practice as forms of unlawful magical activity. In particular, it was a treasonable offence to use magical means to speculate on the length of King Henry's regime or his inability to produce an heir. Many nobles sympathetic to the Catholic Church, in particular The Duke of Buckingham and Lord Hungerford, were executed for treason on charges that included Witchcraft via the use of fortune telling to speculate on the length of the King's reign and the future of the English monarchy without an heir apparent. This shift in the government's and legislature's ideological position towards Witchcraft accusations was paralleled by an increasing political antagonism to supernatural belief and the practice of magic in general. This was particularly significant where Witchcraft and magical belief in popular culture was perceived by the apparatus of government to legitimate the intellectual and moral authority of the Catholic Church. The occult practices of hermeticism, scrying and alchemy were especially singled out for attack by the English government as intellectual and spiritual traditions that were doctrinally based in Catholic mysticism and were consequently believed to lend intellectual credibility to the Catholic Church.[15]

An especially pertinent aspect of this growing particularization of Witchcraft accusations at the official level was the shifting of Witchcraft legislation and prosecution, from a matter of religious or ecclesiastical concern under the control of the church, to the secular realm under the control of the govern-

---

14. Jones, E. *The English Nation*. pp 12–13 & 148.
15. Jones, E. *The English Nation*. pp 46–54.

ment and judiciary. Subsequently, the focus of Witchcraft legislation and policing moved from local outbreaks and specific accusations of *maleficium* (supernatural evil doings) to suppressing the practice of magic and other supernatural activities in general. Similarly, features prominent in Witchcraft beliefs of the Catholic and continental intelligentsia such as the night Sabbatts, cannibalism and most other features of demonological lore were not incorporated into the Witchcraft legislation of 1542 and tended to be ignored in subsequent government records of Witchcraft accusations. In the legislation of 1542, the moral authority of God was directly equated with the political authority of the sovereign and Witchcraft trials and accusations became a matter to be resolved predominantly by secular institutions of judicial or political authority as a crime against the king. This amalgamation of Church and sovereign as the ultimate source of authority in Witchcraft trials and legislation was made particularly apparent in the trials for both treason and Witchcraft of nobles and dignitaries hostile to England's break with Catholicism. In particular, charges of the use of magic relating to speculation on the sustainability of the Sovereign State of England were particularly singled out for prosecution.[16] This process was continued in the Witchcraft edict of 1563 where the definition of magical crimes was broadened to include a wider variety of *maleficium*. Perhaps most significant of all, the practice of illegitimate magic and supernatural activities were defined offences against God's law and therefore a crime against the King rather than simply a crime of harming others by magical means or heresy linked to accusations of devil worship.[17]

England, prior to the outbreak in Sussex and Kent during the 1640s, largely escaped the massive Witch-hunts of continental Europe and had few serious writings on demonology and Witchcraft published. This was not for lack of popular belief in magic or Witchcraft beliefs, but rather due to the unique nature of the English legal, religious and political system, particularly with regards to the relationship between Church and state. The break with the Catholic Church effectively ended the influence of continental ecclesiastical and inquisitorial authority on English law. Similarly, post-Reformation Eng-

---

16. Frere, Howard. *Visitations, Articles and Injunctions of the Period of the Reformation.* Vol 2. London: Aluin, 1963. pp 58, 111, 353 & 372; Kelly, Andy. "English Kings and the Fear of Sorcery." *Mediaeval Studies.* 39, 1977. p 236; Lehmberg, Stanford. *The Later Parliament of King Henry VIII.* London: Cambridge, 1977. pp 156–157; MacFarlane, Alan. *Witchcraft in Tudor and Stuart England: A Regional and Comparative Study.* London: Harper and Row, 1970. pp 14–15; Sharpe, J. A. *Instruments of Darkness: Witchcraft in Early Modern England.* Pennsylvania: University of Pennsylvania Press, 1996. pp 27–29.

17. Sharpe, J.A. *Instruments of Darkness.* pp 28–30.

land was a large and relatively administratively unified state in which the operations of both Church and secular authority were largely subservient to the will of the sovereign. Additionally, in post-Reformation England the crime of heresy was directly linked to the secular crime of treason against the crown and so the large-scale hunts for heretics, integrated with accusations of demonology, as seen in the German states, France and Spain, never really occurred at the local level in any significant scale. Many political opponents of the sovereign were accused of using Witchcraft to speculate on the sustainability of Henry's regime, but few mass trials linking heresy with Witchcraft and demonology occurred. Similarly, the isolation of the English intellectual elite, particularly after the Reformation, meant that the most current ideas of demonology and Witch hunting never permeated English intellectual writings to the same extent as it did the writings of continental scholars who maintained much closer linked with Europe's intellectual centres. The primary effect of this was that the nature of crimes attributed to Witchcraft remained focused on localised beliefs of *maleficium*, relating to alleged physical harm to property, or the health of individuals in their community, or threats to government. Even English demonologists tended to regard the orgiastic demonic Sabbatt, common in continental Europe, as "prurient fantasies engendered by the popish imagination". The features common to the demonologically oriented trials of the continent, such as orgiastic rites, Witches Sabbatts, satanic pacts and cannibalism, were largely absent from English trials until the rise of Puritanism and the onset of the civil war.[18]

Underlying the changes in Witchcraft legislation and the process of Witchcraft accusation was an overall decline in the acceptance of Witchcraft beliefs at the official level, supported by the transformation of the role of religious belief in maintaining the social and political order of English society. The substantial transformation of political, economic and legal processes in post-Reformation England aided this process. After bringing much of the apparatus of government under the centralised control of the sovereign and secular government the Assize judges in England were recruited from the legal profession in London and sent out to investigate accusations across the countryside. The power of ecclesiastical courts was reduced to extremely minor charges of Witchcraft in which the penalty involved performing acts of penance before the congregation on Sunday.[19] This distancing of the judiciary from the local

---

18. Ankarloo, Bengt & Henningsen, Gustav. *Early Modern European Witchcraft: Centres and Peripheries.* Oxford: Clarendon Press, 1990. p 2; Sharpe, J.A. *Instruments of Darkness.* pp 76, 85 & 214.

19. Sharpe, J.A. *Instruments of Darkness.* pp 214–215.

social, cultural and political issues that underlined most Witchcraft accusations ultimately acted to constrain the outbreak of Witchcraft accusations from growing into large-scale Witch crazes. Similarly, the fact that the Assize judges operated strictly on the guidelines of Witchcraft legislation developed by the apparatus of central government had the effect of making many of the popular beliefs of Witchcraft and *maleficium* legally outside of the specific violations of the Witchcraft legislation as defined by the crown.[20]

The Impact of the English Civil War

The onset of the English Civil War saw a large outbreak of Witchcraft accusations in East Anglia, particularly in the counties of Sussex and Kent between 1640–1650. For the first time, large-scale mass Witch hunts and trials were conducted, professional Witch-hunters appeared on the scene and the normal legal process of Assize courts were abandoned in favour of local Puritan religious authorities and local law enforcement. Of particular significance in these trials was the centrality of demonological texts and beliefs in the work of Satan that had previously played only a peripheral role in English Witchcraft trials and accusations.[21]

The Civil War was for many observers and participants a war fought on ideological terms. Many of the conflicts raging between the forces of Parliament and Charles I were, to some extent, manifested in localised conflicts between supporters and detractors of Parliament at the regional level. These conflicts had a substantial impact on Witchcraft beliefs and practices due to the tendency, on the part of legal and ecclesiastical authorities who supervised the trials, to gain legitimacy in the eyes of the general populace via their ideological affiliation with one or another side of the conflict.[22] Similarly, the 1640s saw a massive outpouring of new ideas and a previously unheard of level of social discourse on a broad variety of topics. The ruling classes of England were placed into new and radical positions in which issues like religious tolerance, gender relations, class relations, lay preaching, the role of the military in public and religious affairs were able to be discussed with relative openness by the general populace. The development of a relatively free press during the conflict, increased access to reading material amongst the general population and the move towards the vernacular in printing legal, religious and scientific

---

20. Sharpe, J.A. *Instruments of Darkness.* p 92.
21. MacFarlane, A. *Witchcraft in Tudor and Stuart England.* pp 135–142.
22. Sharpe, J.A. *Instruments of Darkness.* pp 140–145.

texts during the previous century acted to encourage public discourse on social and political issues.[23] Many of the traditional institutions previously considered inviolate, such as the Bible, marriage, the family, male superiority, class and government, came under serious scrutiny by the general public. Similarly, the mechanism of government and the Anglican Church's interpretation and administration of Witchcraft beliefs and accusations also came under public criticism. The circumstance of new ideas and debates in relation to Witchcraft beliefs led to the strengthening of Puritan models of Witch hunting and demonology in Puritan dominated areas like East Anglia. The incorporation of new ideas and theories into public discourse on Witchcraft beliefs also led to the incorporation of concepts regarding Witchcraft beliefs from the continent such as the myth of the Sabbatt, belief in Satanic pacts and the employment of professional Witch hunters. The weakening, and in some cases collapse, of the apparatus and authority of centralised government over this period meant that the application of these concepts, which were gaining currency in a society undergoing the stresses of war and massive politico-economic change, could be effectively implemented at the local level.[24]

East Anglia, the centre of England's only large scale Witch craze, was not a front line area of the conflict but many of the social, political and economic issues of the conflict had a profound effect on daily life within that community. Whilst many of the features of government administration were still in place during the Civil War, a significant proportion of the normal processes of government infrastructure, particularly those relating to centralised political authority, were absent at this time.[25] With regards to accusations of Witchcraft, one of the most influential results of the breakdown of centralised government authority was the absence of London based Assize judges to handle accusations of Witchcraft and *maleficium*. The initial figures to preside over the Essex investigations, in lieu of Assize judges, were the Earl of Warwick and Sir Thomas Bowes, neither of which had any previous experience of Witchcraft trials. Similarly, the delegation sent from parliament to try Witches in Suffolk in 1645 consisted of two clergymen and a Sergeant-at-law with little to no experience in Witchcraft accusations or trial procedures. By the time Assize judges arrived to take over the Witchcraft trial proceedings in 1645 the

23. Hill, Christopher. *Some Intellectual Consequences of the English Revolution*. Madison: University of Wisconsin Press, 1980. pp 7–8.

24. Nottestein & Wallis. *A History of Witchcraft from 1558–1718*. London: Barnes and Noble, 1968. pp 199–201; MacFarlane, Alan. *Witchcraft in Tudor and Stuart England*. p 142.

25. Sharpe, J.A. *Instruments of Darkness*. pp 140–141.

fervour for Witchcraft accusations had completely run out of control leaving large numbers of people in prison or facing the gallows for the practice of Witchcraft. The local justices and legal authorities, predominantly concerned with maintaining the war effort and popular loyalty to parliament, had ignored and even encouraged local pressures that had enabled Witch hunting to spread across the province of East Anglia.[26]

The Witch trials of East Anglia flared up at a time when the overall frequency of Witchcraft prosecutions was in a state of steady decline. However, the religious fervour and socio-political and cultural divisions across England during the civil war worked substantially to increase social tension and led to a situation where a mass panic against marginalised segments of society could easily occur.[27] The trials began when Mathew Hopkins, a local landed gentleman of Manningtree in the county of Essex, pressed for an investigation into his concerns that Witches were living in his local neighbourhood. The first suspect, an elderly, one-legged widow called Elizabeth Clarke, confessed to keeping familiars. In an unorthodox procedure, probably due to the absence of Assize judges, Elizabeth was interrogated with a process called watching. In this process, the suspect was kept awake indefinitely in the hope of catching spirits and familiars visiting the accused or trying to free her. The use of sleep deprivation, alongside rough handling and mistreatment by guards when allied to questioning, undoubtedly aided the interrogation process and the apparent willingness to confess to Witchcraft accusations.[28] The confessions and interrogation process continued throughout 1645 leading to 36 women being indicted for Witchcraft in Chelmsford. Of these women, 19 were executed on the seventeenth of July and a further 9 died of jail fever shortly afterwards. This pattern of accusation, torture and sentencing began to spread into towns near the border of Suffolk including Shotley, Tattingstone, Bramford, Polstead and Shelly.[29]

Within a few weeks accusations had spread to the neighbouring district of Suffolk and then to Norfolk. Some references suggest that as many as 40 people, mostly women, were tried in the district of Norfolk with approximately 20 being sent to the gallows. Another trial at Huntingdonshire dealt with 8 women accused of Witchcraft of which 5 were executed. Several independent

---

26. Nottstein & Wallace. *A History of Witchcraft.* p 201; Sharpe, J.A. *Instruments of Darkness.* pp 140–141.

27. MacFarlane, Alan. *Witchcraft in Tudor and Stuart England.* p 26; Sharpe, J.A. *Instruments of Darkness.* pp 126 & 146.

28. Sharpe, J.A. *Instruments of Darkness.* pp 128–129.

29. MacFarlane, A. *Witchcraft in Tudor and Stuart England.* pp 135–137.

borough districts also held Witchcraft trials. Of the fate of the accused 1 was hung at Norwich, 5 at Great Yarmouth, 7 at Alderburgh and an unknown number at Stowmarket and Kings Lynn. The Assize court on the Isle of Ely reports a further 17 women were investigated there in 1646-1647 but there are no surviving records of either the conviction or dismissal of the charges. Collectively, Hopkins and his associate John Stearne were involved in the investigation of 250 Witchcraft cases of which 200 were brought to trial and 100 executed. Of the 184 individuals prosecuted whose sex is known, 161 or 87% were women; most were from the poorer sectors of village and small town communities.[30] The impact of the trials was such that, at the height of the accusations in August 1645, an order at the county quarter session admitted that the normal methods of feeding prisoners held in the county jail were inadequate. They requested additional finances and a levy on the parishes from which the accused originated, so as to keep up with the increasing numbers of those accused.[31]

There were many unusual features in the 1645–1647 Witchcraft panics, aside from the obvious substantial increase in the frequency of accusations and high conviction rate. As opposed to the typical English Witchcraft accusations prior to the 1645 outbreak, rooted heavily in neighbourly disputes and social tensions relating to the illegitimate or harmful use of magic, many elements common to continental Witchcraft trials played a significant role in the East-Anglian witchcraze. Of particular significance was the utilization of the continental Witchcraft mythology of demonic pacts with Satan.[32] On occasion, confessions would describe the Devil as appearing as a man in black who would ask the accused to renounce God and Christ, offer money and the potential for revenge against perceived slights and then force the accused to sign their name in blood in a little black book. Alternatively, the devil would appear in the form of an animal, even a pet or farm animal, and offer to do revenge upon the accused's enemies in exchange for signing a pact to serve Satan against the forces of God. Confessions often featured the continental demonic mythology of the accused having an unpleasant sexual intercourse with Satan as a means of sealing a pact. Usually confessions would indicate that the Devil performed this deed in the shape of animal familiars that ranged from horses

---

30. Sharpe, J.A. *Instruments of Darkness.* p 129; Hutchinson, Francis. *A historical essay concerning Witchcraft: With observations of matters of fact, tending to clear the Texts of the sacred Scriptures and confute the Vulgar Errors about that point.* London: AMS Press, 1982 (1712). pp 12–15.

31. Sharpe, J.A. *Instruments of Darkness.* p 130.

32. Sharpe, J.A. *Instruments of Darkness.* p 130.

to ducks and giant crayfish. These confessions tend to imply the integration of learned concepts of demonology from the continent into the processes of interrogation and confession in England.[33] These patterns of accusation and mythology were extremely common in the mass Witch crazes of the continent, especially the German Bishoprics and Duchies. However, many elements of the trials, such as the acts the Witches were supposed to have performed and the strong presence of familiars and animal spirits, were concurrent with popular conceptions of Witchcraft and magic in England. This combination of ideas from continental mythology and local beliefs in the supernatural indicate that the Witchcraft mythology found in the East Anglian trials represented an integration of learned models of demonology from the continent with the quasi-diabolical animal spirits of the mainstream English pattern of Witchcraft accusations.[34]

Another similarity with continental Witchcraft trials lay in the process of forcing a confession. The interrogation process had far more in common with the horrendous tortures used in continental Witchcraft accusations than in the more orthodox judicial proceedings of the English Assize courts. In the Hopkins and Stearne cases the accused was sealed in a room, stripped naked and perched on a stool in the middle of the room with their feet off the ground. Here they would be denied sleep and food for three days and closely watched in the hope that their familiar spirits might come to aid them. In other words, they were subjected to severe psychological and physical abuse and torture. When the interrogation began, Hopkins or Stearne would subject the accused to a barrage of leading questions and then allow verbal abuse or questioning by other interested parties. A local clergyman, Francis Hutchinson, disgusted with the trials in Essex wrote in retrospect of the interrogation process,

> Imagine a poor old creature, under all the weakness and infirmities of old age, set like a fool in the middle of a room, with a rabble of the town about her house: then her legs tied cross, that all the weight of her body might rest upon her seat. By that means, after some hours, that the circulation of her blood would be stopped, her sitting would be as painful as the wooden horse [a form of military punish-

33. Douglas, Mary. *Witchcraft Confessions and Accusations.* London: Cambridge University Press, 1970. p 50; Sharpe, J.A. *Instruments of Darkness.* pp 130–136; Stearne, J. *A Confirmation and Discovery of Witchcraft.* Exeter: University of Exeter Press, 1985 (1644). p 29.

34. Sharpe, J.A. *Instruments of Darkness.* pp 136–137 & 140.

ment]. Then she must continue her pain at least four and twenty hours, without sleep or meat ... what wonder was it, if when they were weary of their lives, they confessed any tales that would please them [i.e. their interrogators], and many times knew what not.[35]

The features described in the interrogation were of vital importance in defining the character of Witchcraft accusations. Operating on the basis of published confessions and convictions, parish after parish came forward with claims of Witch's marks, familiars and demonic pacts that increasingly matched the requirements of the Hopkins/Stearne Witchcraft profile.[36] The popularity and increasing frequency of these claims gave renewed support to Hopkins and Stearne's own writings on demonology and Witchcraft and served to substantially increase their reputations. At the height of the craze they were given the titles of Witchfinder and Witchfinder General and were paid approximately 2 pounds each for their services in finding a suspected Witch. Local "cunning" men and women as well as local midwives, often called for expert advice on evil magic by the Assize courts, also began to develop reputations as Witch hunters and gained income for services in prosecuting suspected Witches. Mary Phillips, a Manningtree widow and cunning woman who was called in for professional advice in the first Essex trails, developed a reputation for finding the Witch's mark and demanded 1 pound 5 shillings expenses for her services. A female "associate" of Hopkins received 4 pounds 7 shillings for "diet and wine" whilst assisting Hopkins in an accusation. Several other local craftsmen also gained significant financial rewards. John Paine received 1 pound and a shilling for hanging seven Witches, William Danielle 1 pound for each erected set of gallows, Henry Lawrence "the roper" received 7 shilling for preparing nooses and a local grave digger received 6 shillings for burying the bodies.[37] These costs, which financed a mini-industry in the district over the course of 1645–47, were a considerable outlay for local government. Similarly, the apparatus of the judiciary and prison system were heavily strained over this period. That local governments and parishes were prepared to meet the burden of these costs indicates the seriousness with which Witchcraft accusations were taken. However, they also indicate the level of financial burden that a Witch craze had on a local community when combined with the loss of a considerable number of individuals from village eco-

---

35. Hutchinson, Francis. *A Historical Essay concerning Witchcraft.* p 63.
36. MacFarlane, A. *Witchcraft in Tudor and Stuart England.* pp 135–139.
37. Sharpe, J.A. *Instruments of Darkness.* p 145; MacFarlane, A. *Witchcraft in Tudor and Stuart England.* p 136.

nomic life, even if most of the accused were taken from the poorest sectors of society.

There were many individuals opposed to the trials, particularly amongst the local Anglican clergy. Francis Hutchinson, for example, writes of his perception of the Witch trials,

> Old women are apt to take such fancies of themselves, and when all the country was full of such stories, and she heard the Witch-finders tell of how familiar the Devil had been with others, and what imps they had, she might think that a beggar boy had been a spirit and mice upon her mother's bed had been her imps; and, as I have heard, that she was very harmless and innocent, and desirous to die, she told the story to any body that desired it; and besides, as she was poor, and mightily pitied, she had usually money given to her when she told the story.[38]

A group of merchants in Colchester worked to have Hopkins, Stearne and forty other individuals outlawed from the town for "Conspiracy for illegal Witch hunting".[39] One particularly prominent individual, a wealthy local merchant, acted to block a Witchcraft accusation and apparently threatened Stearne and any individuals who gave evidence against the accused. As Stearne writes,

> This man with another who is likewise reported to have been fello-agent with him in that businesse, and the two chiefest in it, was the cause that was not questioned in that Town: but for his part, I saw him labour and endeavour all he could to keep this woman, whom he so much held withal from her legal trial, and likewise heard him threaten both me and all that had given evidence against her ... as I have since heard, she was condemned at that Assize, and by his procurement reprieved.[40]

Several clergy were described as regularly preaching and speaking out against the Witch trials in the course of which one cleric was reprimanded and fined by the county committee for preaching against Hopkins and Stearne. In 1646 John Gaule, the vicar of Great Staughton in Huntingdonshire, led a political campaign against the trials arguing that, while Witches may exist, the practice of Witch hunting and the investigative techniques of Hopkins and Stearne encouraged popular superstition and mob rule, divided communities, increased the suffering of the poor and was based in questionable principles

---

38. Hutchinson, F. *A Historical Essay Concerning Witchcraft.* p 69.
39. MacFarlane, A. *Witchcraft in Tudor and Stuart England.* p 138.
40. Stearne, J. A *Confirmation and Discovery of Witchcraft.* p 58.

of justice. Similarly, the steward of the Earl of Warwick was described as extremely sceptical and critical of Witch hunting proceedings and acted to save several accused individuals. A newsletter published in Essex at the time finished the account of a Witch trial with the rebuke, "Life is precious and there is need of far greater inquisition before it be taken away".[41] However, despite the existence of individuals and communities that opposed the Witch hunt and its methods, the solidarity of its practitioners, the strength of the underlying economic, political and social pressures and the persuasiveness of Witch hunting rhetoric amongst the labouring and mercantile classes of East Anglia, meant that systemic concerted opposition never really took place until the area was firmly under control of the Assize courts and centralised government.[42]

Typically, historians have labelled the unique features of the East Anglian Witch trials as products of the demonological background and penchant for demagoguery of Hopkins and Stearne. Many English historians have argued intensively that the uncharacteristic savagery of the East Anglian Witch trials were the result of foreign continental influences introduced by Hopkins and Stearne.[43] However, Hopkins and Stearne specifically denied that their skills in Witch hunting came from "profound learning" or from reading "learned authors on the subject". Instead, they attributed their skills to experience that "though it be meanly esteemed of; yet is the surest and safest way to judge by".[44] Hopkins' texts, aside from a mention of King James I perspective on the outlawed swimming test (a trial in which the accused Witch is dunked in water to see if she floats), makes little mention of any demonological works or Witchcraft judicial proceedings.[45] Stearne however is a little more complex, in that his longer and more detailed treatise contains numerous references to the Lancashire trials of 1612 and the Rutland family case of 1618–19. Stearne also makes references to Thomas Cooper's text *Mystery of Witchcraft (1617)* and extensively plagiarises excerpts from Richard Bernard's *Guide to Grand Jury Men (1627)*.[46] The use of Bernard's work is particularly significant as he incorporated the works of many continental scholars including Bodin and Del Rio as well as Kramer and Sprenger, authors of the notorious *Malleus Malefi-*

---

41. Maple, E. *The Dark World.* pp 83–90; MacFarlane, Alan. *Witchcraft in Tudor and Stuart England.* pp 140–141; Sharpe, J.A. *Instruments of Darkness.* pp 141–143 & 146.

42. Sharpe, J.A. *Instruments of Darkness.* pp 220–221.

43. Sharpe, J.A. *Instruments of Darkness.* p 130.

44. Hopkins, M. *The Discovery of Witches.* Microfilm held at the University of Melbourne. Woodbridge: Research Publications, 1983. p 30.

45. Hopkins, M. *The Discovery of Witches.* p 6.

46. Stearnes, J. *A Confirmation and Discovery.* pp 11–26.

cium which was hitherto largely ignored in English Witch trials. At the same time, Bernard's work focused predominantly on demonological interpretations of English trials, particularly those that had achieved wide publicity.[47] From this perspective and, bearing in mind that very little is known of Hopkins and Stearne prior to the 1645 outbreak, it appears that Hopkins and Stearne's approach to Witchcraft was an amalgam of English demonological ideas, influenced by the continental experience, that were incorporated into the matrix of English folklore of *maleficium* and applied through popularist rhetoric and the pervasive currency of demonological ideas in the predominantly Puritan community.

This material is particularly illustrated in Wilby's study of the role of supernaturalist and shamanic/folk magic traditions with the English experience of witchcraft. Typically historical discourse has attempted to reinforce a mythos of English rationalism against the rampant supernaturalism of the continent, yet for much of the mythology behind the English experience of witchcraft and witch finding there are demonstrated strong currents of magical and shamanic folklore that played a strong influential role in both the trials and the shaping of popular mythology surrounding witches and witchcraft as will be discussed in more detail in the next chaopter.[48] Indeed, as Wilby argues, throughout the Witch trials of East Anglia (and throughout the rest of the British Isles) there was a strangely contradictory mix of both the rational and mundane and examples of overtly sumagical activity prescribed in demonological texts. Throughout the Witch trials, we see examples of the fragmented but endemic milieu of magical and shamanic folklore that shaped the practices of the cunning men and women so pertinent to the prosecution of suspected witches, the beliefs of the general rural populace and thus the discourses of witchcraft and magical practice that informed the trials.[49] Indeed it is much of this folklore, collected by 19th C folklorists that was appropriated to become the cultural and historical foundation of the Wicca and other Pagan revivalist movements of the 19th C. It is also here that we start to see the basis behind the association of Paganism and Witchcraft. For while the practitioners tried for witchcraft would have undoubtedly perceived themselves as Christians there were undoubtedly shamanic and pre-Christian elements involved in the perception of witchcraft and magical activities, albeit

---

47. Sharpe, J.A. *Instruments of Darkness.* p 139.

48. Ankarloo, B & Henningsen, G. *Early Modern European Witchcraft.* pp 2; Wilby, Emma. *Cunning Folk and Familiar Spirits: Shamanic Visionary Traditions in Early Modern British Witchcraft and Magic.* Sussex Academic Press: Brighton, 2005.

49. Wilby, E. *Cunning Folk and Familiar Spirits.* pp 2–53.

incorporated into the world view of a predominantly Christian populace. As Wilby writes,

> While it is difficult for most westerners today to imagine the rigours of the Early Modern environment, it is just as difficult to imagine the mental worlds of the people who struggled within it. To the common people in this period, the harsh and unyielding physical world was also an enchanted one. Powerful occult forces permeated life at every level. The air teemed with supernatural entities which constantly influenced the natural world and the lives of men. A prayer could be answered. A spell could cure. A look could kill. A spirit or deity could be at your ear at any time of the day or night—guiding your spinning hand or your plough arm, charming the crops in the fields or the animals in the barns, bringing good luck or gold, or raining down famine and disease ... While their practical abilities enabled them to deal as best they could with the physical world, it was their beliefs and rituals which enabled them to deal with the invisible forces which lay behind it.[50]

A major issue in understanding the East Anglian Witch trials is the interpretation of the role of Protestantism in creating the cultural, social and religious milieu in which mass accusations of Witches from a demonological perspective could occur. It appears that the Protestantism of the intellectual elite and government authorities was not particularly concerned with the hunting of Witches. Instead, the East Anglian Witch crazes were not supported by the Protestantism of the educated clergy but by a popular form of Puritanism that was reinforced by the war and allowed to flourish due to the weakness of central government and desire to secure popular support for the parliament cause.[51] Many of the local justices, clergy and parish notables of the region were heavily influenced by propaganda portraying Royalists as agents of the Devil and the increasing support, through the reporting of dramatic events of the war, for belief in the literature of apparitions, wonders and revolutionary millenarianism. Essex and Suffolk had also experienced a campaign in 1643–44 to root out scandalous and corrupt clergy which had many parallels with the East Anglian Witch trials.[52] In these campaigns, grass roots Puritanism and propertied classes, led by charismatic individuals like Hopkins and Stearne, had turned on clergy deemed ungodly, royalist or insufficiently en-

---

50. Wilby, E. *Cunning Folk and Familiar Spirits.* pp 9–10.

51. MacFarlane, A. *Witchcraft in Tudor and Stuart England.* pp 186–189.

52. Sharpe, J.A. *Instruments of Darkness.* p 142; Holmes, Clive (ed.) *The Suffolk Committee for Scandalous Ministers 1644–46.* Norwich: Suffolk Publications, 1970.

thusiastic in support for the Parliament cause.[53] In 1644 a yeoman named William Dowsing led a populist campaign against the Anglican Church that vandalised decorations and ornaments in over 150 Churches in the region perceived to be in opposition to the parliament cause.[54] It also appears that the forces of parliament occasionally utilised popular Puritanism as a means of encouraging mass local action and lynchings against potential royalists as well as drumming up support for the Parliament cause for the purpose of recruitment.[55]

Indeed, this pattern of witchcraft linked to broad populism, innuendo and accusation is a well identified aspect of witch crazes and related phenomenon world wide. It was a vehicle noted in Pritchard's ground breaking work in Witch hunting amongst the Azande[56], appropriated and applied to the East Anglian trials by MacFarlane and Thomas[57] and further explored in its English context by Stewart and Strathern.[58] As Stewart and Strathern argue, and is very clearly evidenced in the East Anglian experience of Witchcraft, is the central role of rumour and gossip in the processes leading to accusations of witchcraft or other *maleficium* and also the means by which these patterns serve as a means of psychically attacking people within a community (aka as a vehicle for witchcraft). Thus witchcraft serves both as the manifestation of ideas rooted in supernaturalism, demonology and magical folklore and as a set of structural social processes endemic to the social order of small communities.[59] Similarly, racinating configurations of deviant classes of people rooted in local folklore and Christian inspired demonology serve to further the processes of scapegoating, confession, accusation and counter confession in the bewildering epidemic of accusation that was the East Anglian witchcraze.[60] As in Cohen's theory of moral panics regarding socially construed de-

---

53. Jones, Colin & Newitt, Malyn & Roberts, Stephen. *Politics and People in Revolutionary England: Essays in Honour of Ivan Roots.* London: Oxford University Press, 1986. pp 60–74.

54. White, Evelyn. "The Journal of William Dowsing of Stratford." In Cooper, Trevor (Ed.) *The Journal of William Dowsing: Iconoclasm in East Anglia During the English Civil War.* London: Baydell and Brewer, 2001.

55. Sharpe, J.A. *Instruments of Darkness.* p 140.

56. Pritchard, Evans. "Sorcery and Native Opinion." *Africa,* Vol 4, no 1. 1931. pp 23–28

57. MacFarlane, A. *Witchcraft Prosecutions in Essex, 1560–1680.*

58. Stewart, Pamela J and Strathern, Andrew. *Witchcraft, Sorcery Rumours and Gossip.* Cambridge University Press: Cambridge. 2004.

59. Stewart, P and Strathern, A. *Witchcraft, Sorcery, Rumours and Gossip.* p 9.

60. Schermer, Michael. *Why People Believe Weird Things.* Freeman: New York, 1997. pp 100–105.

vients of 400 years later, "right thinking people" hold the barricades and man the walls of respectability against deviants, social construed deviant behaviour and patterns of gossip and accusation.[61]

In this context, it is hardly surprising that a mass Witch-hunt broke out in Essex during this period, but the actions of Hopkins and Stearne served as a critical catalyst for the mass action that led to the prosecution or persecution of over 250 people. It is known that Hopkins and Stearne were propertied gentleman and it was relatively common, in Parliament dominated areas for men from this social strata to organize localised mass movements for political and economic gain. In other parts of England during the Civil War, men from this social stratum were critical in forming and promoting the goals of the leveller movement, wrote pamphlets and political treatises, supported a variety of radical sects, took control of regiments and companies in the New Model Army and were beginning to make their way into urban and country government. The conditions after 1640 were ideal for individuals from the middle classes to deploy their talents in a wide variety of political activities, Witch hunting among them.[62]

However, despite their prominence, it is clear that the Witch crazes cannot be solely attributed to Hopkins and Stearne. They received widespread support, public funds, and general cooperation and encouragement from both government and the general populace. The two individuals certainly provided an outlet and catalyst for Witchcraft suspicions, but the suspicions, social tensions and the willingness to act on those suspicions, should the opportunity arise, were already present before Hopkins and Stearne took to the stage. In most settlements interested individuals, with the general support of local community and respected community leaders, instigated accusations and the interrogation process against suspected Witches.[63] Trial records indicate that there were a variety of local tensions driving the accusations, particularly the antipathy of wealthy individuals towards paupers (typically aged widows) who asked for charity.[64] Writings from the era also indicate that Hopkins and Stearne were generally encouraged to stay in most townships and were treated as respected figures if not minor celebrities.[65] John Gaule writes of the public response in many villages that, "The country people talk already, and that

61. Cohen, Stanley. *Folk Devils and Moral Panics: The Creation of the Mods and Rockers.* Robertson: Oxford, 1980.
62. Sharpe, J.A. *Instruments of Darkness.* pp 142–143.
63. MacFarlane, A. *Witchcraft in Tudor and Stuart England.* p 138.
64. MacFarlane, A. *Witchcraft in Tudor and Stuart England.* pp 138–141.
65. Sharpe, J.A. *Instruments of Darkness.* pp 136–142.

more frequently, more affectedly, of the infallible and wonderfull power of the Witch finders, then they doe of God, or Christ, or the Gospell preached".[66]

The Witch trials had begun to wind down by 1650 due to the economic strain and social disruption caused by the trials and the onset of the restoration ended the trials permanently. The intellectual and political elites whose status had been restored were antagonistic to what they perceived as plebeian religious enthusiasm and the return of central government placed a major restriction on renewed Witchcraft accusations.[67] The trials of 1645–47 gave post-restoration sceptics substantial ammunition to use against Witchcraft beliefs and the institutions of government adopted this doctrine, as a means of attacking religious authority deemed detrimental to the interests of the state. Witch hunting became associated with extreme sectarian Protestantism, the radicalism of the 1640s and the general instability of those decades which enabled men like Hopkins and Stearne to gain prominence as Witchfinders or through leading mob attacks on Anglican Churches. In official discourse, the Witch trials became symptomatic of the dangers of primitive superstition, the superstitious nature of the English rural sector and the need for religious beliefs and practices to be firmly in line with the interests of government.[68] In a sense, the Witch trials became fundamentally associated, in official and elite discourse, with the dangers of populism, radicalism and the need for strong government under the control of the intellectual elite.

The End of the Witchcraze

By the eighteenth century, legal proceedings and prosecutions against people accused of Witchcraft in England had fallen into steep decline. The damage wrought during the rash of accusations in Essex and Kent, brought on by the chaos of the English Civil War in the mid seventeenth century, had left an increasingly sceptical judiciary and intelligentsia who no longer appeared to give much credence to the veracity of supernaturally based claims of maleficium or satanic pacts. This tradition of scepticism was amplified by the tendency of many judicial and political authorities to demonstrate a distinct antagonism towards the social disruption and chaos that Witchcraft accusations could cause. Additionally, the ideology of Church and state had undergone massive transformation during the Civil War and restoration, leaving a social

---

66. Guale, John. *Select Cases of Conscience Touching Witches and Witchcraft*. London: Oxford University, 1973 (1646). p 93.

67. Sharpe, J.A. *Instruments of Darkness*. pp 142–143.

68. Sharpe, J.A. *Instruments of Darkness*. pp 142–143.

and political establishment in which issues like magic and demonology were no longer as critical to the functioning of society as they were in pre-restoration England. Belief in Witchcraft became predominantly a localised phenomenon based in the rural areas most distant from the apparatus of central government and became increasingly perceived as antithetical to the discourse of the political and intellectual elite. Of particular significance in this transformation of Witchcraft beliefs amongst the intellectual elite was the virtual elimination of successful charges relating to devil worship or satanic sorcery by 1664. Whilst some claims of demonic possession persisted, the mythology of individuals engaged in Sabbatts or making pacts with the Devil became virtually non-existent. The cases that remained palatable to the judiciary were charges of *maleficium* against members of the public engaged in local political or financial disputes. In the aftermath of the restoration and the East Anglian Witch trials, the criteria for conviction became extremely demanding and most Assize judges, magistrates and lawyers became reluctant to frame charges unless the perceived act of malevolent magic resulted in the death, serious illness/injury or economic catastrophe on the part of the victim.[69]

The last known official trial of Witchcraft to receive a guilty verdict occurred in 1712 when Jane Wenham was convicted in Hertfordshire of bewitching her neighbours.[70] A local farmer by the name of John Chapman attributed the death of approximately 200 pounds worth of cattle and horses in the town of Walkerne to the alleged Witchcraft of Wenham. However, "not being able to prove any thing upon her, he did not inform against her, but waited till time should present a favourable opportunity of convicting her".[71] Other locals followed suit in making accusations against Wenham and she was alleged to have been responsible for strange symptoms exhibited by a 16 year old servant girl named Anne Thorne. Thorne had been found stripped to her shirtsleeves, wringing her hands in frustration and she soon began to run wildly around the village in hysterics. She described a strange roaring in her head whenever her mind came across Jane Wenham, that she claimed, forced her to strip and "run some whither".[72]

One of Chapman's servants, Mathew Gilston, had been strangely afflicted with a fever after refusing to give Wenham straw. Chapman, meeting with

---

69. Holmes, Clive. "Women: Witnesses and Witches." *Past and Present*. Issue 140, 1993. p 45–78.

70. Sharpe, J.A. *Instruments of Darkness*. p 229.

71. Guskin, Phyllis. "The Context of English Witchcraft: The Case of Jane Wenham." *Eighteenth Century Studies*. Vol 15. 1981–1982. pp 48–71.

72. Guskin, P. "The Context of English Witchcraft: The Case of Jane Wenham." pp 48–71.

Wenham after this altercation entered into a heated argument in which he reportedly called her a Witch and a bitch. Wenham then applied to the local magistrate, Sir Henry Chauncy, to file a defamation case against Chapman claiming that she expected "not only to get something out of him, but to deter other people from calling her so any more". Unwilling to associate himself directly with Wenham's now soiled reputation Chauncy ordered the case to be arbitrated by any neighbour in good standing that Wenham should choose. She asked the local priest to arbitrate the case and he ordered that Chapman and Wenham must strive to live more peaceably together, and that Chapman should pay Wenham one shilling to compensate for the damage to Wenham's reputation, but he refused to offer Wenham any further satisfaction against Chapman. Wenham reportedly left the hearing in "great heat" saying "if she could not have justice here she would have it elsewhere". However, as Anne Thorne's symptoms became more acute, public sympathy increasingly turned away from Wenham and she was committed to prison and trial for Witchcraft on the 4th of March 1712.[73]

The Assize judge selected to preside over the Wenham trial was Sir John Powell who was extremely sceptical of the veracity of Witchcraft accusations and the supernatural in general. Judge Powell was described as extremely disdainful of the proceedings and demonstrated surprise and disgust when Anne Thorne went into a supposedly supernaturally created fit, attributed to Wenham, during the court proceedings. When the local priest read a prayer for the visitations of the sick over Thorne, Powell was heard to make the sarcastic comment, "I have heard papists and Pagans use exorcism but I have never yet heard it practised in the Church of England". He expressed "extreme dismay" when cakes, feathers and other paraphernalia associated with Wenham's supposed magical practices had been burnt in cleansing rituals rather than be retained as evidence. Powell also rejected the usefulness of evidence, such as regurgitated bent pins and paraphernalia attributed to spell casting and cursing rituals. When presented with eyewitness accounts purporting to have seen Wenham flying at night Powell was heard to caustically remark "I have heard of no laws in England that prohibit the practice of flight".[74] However, despite Powell's scathing attitude the jury found Wenham guilty but the Judge, in an "attitude of extreme disgust", immediately granted a reprieve on her penalty. The case became highly politicised and Jane Wenham was officially pardoned

---

73. Sharpe, J.A. *Instruments of Darkness.* p 230.
74. Guskin, P. "The Context of English Witchcraft: The Case of Jane Wenham." pp 48–71. Sharpe, J.A. *Instruments of Darkness.* pp 229–231.

almost as soon as the case was concluded. A local wealthy, landed gentleman and a Whig magnate, disgusted with an accusation they believed to be derived from primitive and papist superstition, provided Wenham with legal protection, a cottage and a pension.[75]

One of the clearest aspects of English Witchcraft beliefs illustrated in the Wenham case is that the gulf between local beliefs of magic, Witchcraft and *maleficium* and that of learned discourse of Witchcraft and magic had, by the eighteenth century, reached the point where government authorities were almost completely out of sympathy with the beliefs of the local populace. This represented a massive shift from the sixteenth and early seventeenth century where demonology and the finding of Witches were perceived as, if not sciences, then at least intellectually credible. However, by the mid seventeenth century the full weight of governmental and legislative authority had shifted almost completely towards the suppression of Witchcraft beliefs and the discouraging of belief in the supernatural amongst the local populace.

In 1736, the English Parliament repealed the statutes regarding Witchcraft put in place by Mary of Scotland (1563), Elizabeth I of England (1563) and James I and VI (1604) declaring that "No prosecution, suit or proceedings shall be carried out against any person or persons for Witchcraft, sorcery, enchantment or conjuration". The statute of 1736 allowed the prosecution of the *pretence* of magic, but it fundamentally denied the validity of Witchcraft accusations and the reality of supernatural power.[76] Witchcraft accusations at this point in time became officially perceived as the false pretence of the gullible, the irrational and the superstitious. Whilst magical practices, Witchcraft accusations and local magically oriented folklore, ritual and medicines continued to wield an influence on English life, it became essentially confined to low culture, with belief regarding the reality of magic and Witchcraft becoming increasingly divided along class lines.[77]

There had always been prominent differences between educated and localised interpretations of Witchcraft, sorcery, demonology and magic in Europe. Attempts to reconcile the differences between rural village communities,

75. Gijswift-Hoffa, Marijke. "Controversy c.1680–1800." In Ankarloo, Bengt & Clark, Stuart (Ed.) *Witchcraft and magic in Europe: The Eighteenth and Nineteenth Centuries.* Athlone History of Witchcraft. Vol 5. London: Athlone Press, 1999. pp 195–196 & 207; Sharpe, J.A. *Instruments of Darkness.* pp 226–227.

76. Russell, Jeffrey. *A History of Witchcraft: Sorcerers, Heretics, and Pagans.* London: Thames and Hudson, 1980. p 123; Gijswift-Hoffa, Marijke. "Controversy c.1680–1800." p 211.

77. Gijswift-Hoffa, M. "Controversy c.1680–1800." p 195.

where the bulk of Witchcraft accusations took place, and learned discourse within secular and religious institutions of authority have been the focus of a major component of historical research into Witchcraft beliefs and practices.[78] At the height of the Witch crazes of the Early Modern period, this class division of Witchcraft beliefs was manifested in differences between learned theological discourse on demonology, magic and Witchcraft, and the localized indigenous beliefs of Witchcraft that were rooted in folklore, local politics and beliefs in the practice of *maleficium*. As Richard Kieckhefer writes,

> There remained a substantial difference between the educated elite— people who could resurrect through their reading ideas that had lain dormant for centuries in manuscripts, who could easily maintain contact with centuries of intellectual activity remote from their own countries, and who were trained in the arts of speculation and deduction—and the illiterate masses. Though there were no impenetrable barriers between them, the gap was wide enough that the preoccupations of one class can scarcely be assumed to have been shared by the other.[79]

However, by the end of the seventeenth century the focus of class differentiation surrounding Witchcraft beliefs had been somewhat transformed as the intellectual elite wrestled with interpretations of Witchcraft based in demonology and Christian mythology, interpretations that were now challenged by new paradigms of skepticism and secularization that held belief in the supernatural as primitive superstition.[80]

The divergence of Witchcraft beliefs along class lines during the late seventeenth century has had the effect of limiting the effectiveness of trial records and legislative approaches to Witchcraft as indicators of the longevity of supernatural beliefs amongst the general populace. What trial records, pamphlets and legislation reflect are the preconceptions, concerns and beliefs of the educated classes represented by the opinions of lawyers, government officials, clergy and the landed gentry. Even the members of the general public who formed the trial jury itself were required by legislation enacted by Charles II to have an income at least equal to 20 pounds per annum in freehold land

---

78. Kieckhefer, R. *European Witch Trials: Their Foundation in Popular and Learned Culture, 1300–1500.* Berkeley: University of California Press, 1976. p 1–3; Sharpe, J. *Instruments of Darkness.* pp 37–79.

79. Kieckefer, R. *European Witch Trials.* pp 4–5.

80. Gijswift-Hoffa, M. "Controversy c.1680–1800." p 195.

and rent.[81] The ultimate effect of this class based domination of the legislature, judiciary and intellectually credible writings on Witchcraft was to ensure that the Witch trials would remain within the purview of the English political elite so long as centralised government remained intact, in contrast to the outbreak of Witch accusations during the civil war. By the seventeenth century, the political, economic and intellectual elite had become increasingly sceptical of Witchcraft beliefs and popularist religion and as a consequence there was a steady overall decline in successful Witchcraft accusations from the restoration onwards. Even in those cases where belief in Witches was still accepted by educated individuals, such as Joseph Glanvill's attempt to scientifically and syllogistically prove the existence of Witches; there was still a tendency to claim that the crime was almost impossible to prove. After the experience of 1645–47, there was a solid consensus in government and amongst the ruling elite that popularist rhetoric should never be used to secure a conviction. Consequently, despite some notable exceptions such as the case of Jane Wenham, successful Witchcraft prosecutions and convictions entered into a period of steady decline in the aftermath of the restoration and had become virtually non-existent by the early eighteenth century.[82]

According to historian Owen Davies, while belief in Witchcraft had become the target of controversy and often ridicule amongst the English intellectual elite, belief in *maleficium*, demonic interference in worldly affairs and Witches remained a reality of rural life until the latter half of the nineteenth century. The substantial reorientation of intellectual arguments regarding Witchcraft and government policy in urban centres and amongst the intellectual, political and economic elite penetrated rural life, particularly in remote communities, far more slowly than other parts of England. As late as 1870, the magistrate of the Thames police court was petitioned to arrest Biddy Coughlin for Witchcraft following the death of chickens that had layed abnormally shaped and undersized eggs. According to Davies, these kinds of accusations and demands on magistrates remained common throughout the eighteenth and nineteenth century. [83] Underlying the persistence of Witchcraft beliefs in rural England was the fact that until the advent of the industrial revolution the social and cultural context, if not the political and legal structure, of Witchcraft accusations in rural districts had remained relatively unchanged for almost

---

81. Thomas, Keith. *Religion and the decline of Magic: Studies in Popular Belief in Sixteenth and Seventeenth Century England.* London: Penguin Books, 1971. pp 538–539.

82. Thomas, K. *Religion and the Decline of Magic.* pp 539.

83. Davies, Owen. "Witchcraft: The Spell That Didn't Break". *History Today.* Vol 49. Issue 8. Aug 1999. pp 7–14.

two centuries and was little altered by the transformation of the intellectual climate in English centres of government and learning. Witchcraft in England was by and large an economic crime oriented towards damage to livestock, farming and business, with demonology and Church discourse of heresy playing a much more minor role than in the heartland of European Witch Hunts in the German Duchies and Bishoprics. The majority of the population were still living in an agrarian economy and large sectors of the population were reliant on animal husbandry to supplement their diet and income. Other than the faint relief offered by the Poor Law and Christian doctrines of charity, there was almost no safety net for the general public in times of misfortune. Thus the illness of family or friends and/or the loss of livestock or staple foodstuffs, could cause considerable hardship and, in the absence of more readily available explanations, could lead to suspicion of Witchcraft. When people suspected a magical cause to their ills they usually needed to look no further than their neighbours as potential suspect for supernatural foul play. Relations between neighbours in rural communities were often close-knit and intense with little privacy and common frictions regarding begging, borrowing, trespass and moral behaviour. In a society ripe for malicious gossip and where belief in the supernatural was the norm, it is hardly surprising that Witchcraft accusations and beliefs amongst the rural populace continued well into the nineteenth century.[84]

This class-based difference in perceptions of magic and Witchcraft became increasingly prominent from the eighteenth century onwards. Whilst after the Wenham case the securing of a conviction and penalty became virtually impossible, there were numerous cases where the general populace took the law into their own hands in the beating and even lynching of suspected Witches. Despite the fact that injury and death resulting from these cases were treated as assault and murder by the judicial system, and that considerable effort had been made to educate the general public against belief in magic, lynchings and beatings for perceived magical attacks occurred sporadically throughout the English country-side until the nineteenth century.[85]

One case where this conflict over the validity of Witchcraft beliefs is particularly well illustrated is the trial and hanging of Thomas Colley for the lynching of John and Ruth Osborne. In 1751, in the town of Tring, thirty miles north of London, Colley had led a mob that hounded Ruth and John Osborne, claiming they were Witches and were guilty of cursing and en-

---

84. Owen D, "Witchcraft: The Spell that didn't Break". pp 7–14.
85. Thomas, K. *Religion and the Decline of Magic.* pp 540.

chanting the local inhabitants of the village. The lynching of the 70-year-old couple was announced in advance, leading the local overseer to shelter them in his workhouse. When the property was besieged by a mob of local towns-folk, the couple was moved to the local Church for protection. By the end of the night, the church had been overwhelmed by the rioters who dragged John and Ruth Osborne to the village pond, where they were repeatedly ducked under water by Colley and several associates resulting in Ruth's death. Her husband John was then beaten to death by the angry mob.[86]

The educated elite of England responded with outrage against the incident, citing the inherent barbarity of the rabble, the superstitious nature of the peasantry and the need to educate the general populace against the dangers of superstition. The *Gentleman's Magazine* was particularly outraged by the fact that Colley refused to be convinced by the arguments of a local official who came "to reason with him, and convince him of his erroneous opinion, in believing there was any such thing as Witchcraft". He reportedly informed Colley "Witches had no manner of existence but in the minds of poor infatuated people in which they had been confirm'd by the tradition of their ancestors, as foolish and crazy as themselves". The opinion of local villagers and the rural working class of England were markedly different and appear, through surviving records, to be quite supportive of Colley. For example, one local reputedly stated that "It was a very hard case, that a man should be hang'd for destroying an old wicked woman, who had done much mischief by her abominable charms and Witchcraft".[87]

In the Colley trial and other related cases, there are two main features illustrating the transformation that had occurred in the perception of Witchcraft and magic amongst the English educated elite. Firstly, the focus of government policy became the suppression of the Witch hunter and the effects of local indigenous beliefs of Witchcraft, as opposed to the previous emphasis on attacking the actual practice of Witchcraft as either *maleficium* or the illegitimate use of magic. Secondly, the dynamics of Witchcraft accusations and public perceptions of Witchcraft became focused on conflict between the civilised gentleman backed by the institutions of Church and state, against a perceived rustic and superstitious peasantry and working class. This was a radical transformation from the earlier perception of Witchcraft as a conflict between God and the Devil or between secularists and the power of the

---

86. Sharpe, J.A. *Instruments of Darkness.* pp 1–5.
87. Sharpe, J.A. *Instruments of Darkness.* p 4; Gijswift-Hoffa, M. "Controversy c.1680–1800." p 195–196.

Church.[88] Scepticism had come to replace demonology as the official discourse on belief in Witchcraft and magic.

Scepticism over the validity and potential abuse of Witchcraft accusations had been a part of the Witch crazes of the early modern period since the fifteenth century. Similarly, concerns about the validity and necessity of Witchcraft accusations ranged from the abuse of Witchcraft accusations as a potential political tool, the problems of evidence inherent in such an "otherworldly" form of supposed illicit activity and a wide-ranging theological argument over the biblical veracity over the existence of Witchcraft as defined by ecclesiastical and secular courts.[89] Similarly, the role Witchcraft beliefs played in the legitimating ecclesiastical power over the secular instruments of government at the local level heavily influenced the attitude of government towards tolerating Witchcraft beliefs and supernaturalism. This issue became increasingly important in the lead-up and aftermath of the Reformation and the political break between the English throne and the Catholic Church. However, a major transformation of the intellectual, political and economic landscape of England needed to occur for intellectual opposition to Church and government sanctioning of Witchcraft accusations to have significant influence over government policy and legal infrastructure. In essence, for the power of government policy to make a significant impact on Witchcraft beliefs at the local level (indigenous beliefs of Witchcraft and magical folklore remained fragmented, diverse and radically different to that of the intelligentsia throughout the early modern period) major changes in the relationship between social organization, government and religion amongst the bulk of the population also had to occur.

New Perceptions of Witchcraft and Magic

Fundamentally defining the nature of debates over the validity of Witchcraft accusations and magic was a paradigmatic restructuring of power and the relationship between Church, secular authority and society during the eighteenth century. Protestants, Catholics, neo-Platonists and Aristotelians engaged in a wide-ranging ideological debate in relation to perceptions of sorcery, miracles, magic and the supernatural. Underlying this confrontation was

---

88. Gijswift-Hoffa, M. "Controversy c.1680–1800." p 195–196.

89. Briggs, Robin. *Witches and Neighbours: The Social and Cultural Context of European Witchcraft*. London: Harper Collins, 1996. pp 19–21, 406–407; Gijswift-Hoffa, M. "Controversy c.1680–1800." p 196.

a political conflict over the nature of the newly burgeoning nation state, the role of Church in society and the place of the sciences in understanding the radically transforming social, economic and political landscape of England.[90]

The Glanvill/Webster debate of the late 1670s is one example of the kinds of intellectual conflicts regarding the supernatural in seventeenth century England. In 1668 Joseph Glanvill, Anglican and respected member of the Royal Society, wrote "*Sadducimus Triumphatus*" in which he attacked what he believed to be the sceptical conceit that "Witches were merely the creature of Melancholy and Superstition".[91] He argued "the reality of Witches is not a matter of vain speculation but a matter of fact". He then attempted to prove the existence of Witches from a combination of scriptural, eyewitness reports, physical evidence and Aristotelian logic. In conclusion, he argued that denial of the existence of Witches led syllogistically to the denial of supernatural agency and thus to Salvation, heaven, hell and all other principles of religion. Consequently, Glanvill argued that in order to preserve the necessary function of the Church in supporting the social, political and moral order (not to mention the King as head of Church and State), as well as the necessity of a higher good for moral thought to exist, there needed to be a new science of religion that incorporated supernatural elements into the context of experimental and empirical reasoning.[92] Glanvill's respected work in science and mathematics, his high status as a representative of theological studies combined with the overall rational approach to the topic, gave his work considerable influence. In this light, and given his high personal status and reputation it was difficult to simply dismiss his work as representative of either popish or primitive superstition and consequently his work became widely published.[93]

Interestingly enough, the most prominent critique of Glanvill's work did not originate from atheistic or even secularist thinkers like Thomas Hobbes, but from a non-conformist medical practitioner by the name of John Webster. Operating from a Paracelsian perspective and convinced of the reality of both supernatural and occult force, Webster, in *The Displaying of Supposed Witchcraft*, did not argue against the existence of the supernatural, but rather the Devil's supposed causation of them.[94] He drew heavily on his experience as a medical practitioner with a strong focus on the cases where he had been asked to cure instances of possession. He argued that, in his experience, when

---

90. Sharpe, J.A. *Instruments of Darkness.* pp 258–262.
91. Sharpe, J.A. *Instruments of Darkness.* pp 244–245.
92. Gijswift-Hoffa, M. "Controversy c.1680–1800." pp 198–200.
93. Sharpe, J.A. *Instruments of Darkness.* pp 244–245.
94. Gijswift-Hoffa, M. "Controversy c.1680–1800." pp 198–200.

people claimed to have been injured by demonic agency one could usually clearly demonstrate the illness to be disease or a natural ailment. Furthermore, he argued that in the rare occasions when supernatural agency appeared conclusive, proving that the damage was the result of a Demonic intervention in an empirically verifiable way would be an impossibility. He also went on to argue that scriptural and philosophical support for Witches was extremely weak and unsubstantiated and thus proved to be no source of legitimacy in substantiating supposed demonic influence in worldly affairs.[95] What is particularly interesting in the Glanvill/Webster debate is the fact that both writers attempted to draw upon the new mechanical philosophy combined with scripture, demonology and syllogism to argue their respective cases. At the very least these kinds of debates, very common in seventeenth century England, demonstrated that the popularly perceived divide between ignorant superstition and the educated gentry in debates about the existence of Witchcraft was far from universal. However, perhaps the most important aspect of the Glanvill/Webster debate is the fact that by the later half of the seventeenth century it was no longer intellectually tenable to legitimate arguments regarding the natural or supernatural world without at least some reference and support to secular logic, empirical data and scientific method.

Whilst being generally supportive of Witchcraft trials and accusations in the sixteenth and early seventeenth centuries, by the end of the seventeenth century Protestant Church authorities in England had become increasingly opposed to belief in the supernatural interference in worldly affairs, especially with regards to accusations of Witchcraft and demonic agency.[96] Whilst there had always been strong traditions of scepticism with regards to Witchcraft beliefs and practices, it had lacked the popularist and religious support required to strongly influence government and judicial policy prior to the restoration. By the 1660s, scepticism with regards to Witchcraft and magic was becoming increasingly entrenched in the ideology of English secularist or deist oriented intellectuals. However, the strength of the beliefs and demonological doctrine on both public perception and amongst the English ruling elite was such that critique of supernaturalism and Witchcraft beliefs had to be couched in terms that legitimated the established political and religious basis of authority. Hobbes, for example, whilst paying lip service to Christianity and accepting the legitimacy of trying people for Witchcraft was severely critical of belief in the supernatural and demonic agency as Pagan superstitions of the ignorant and the gullible. As he writes,

---

95. Sharpe, J.A. *Instruments of Darkness.* pp 244–246.
96. Sharpe, J.A. *Instruments of Darkness.* pp 237–242.

From this ignorance in how to distinguish dreams, and other strong
Fancies, from Vision and Sense, did arise the greatest part of the Religion of the Gentiles in times past, that worshiped Satyres, Fawnes,
Nymphs, and the like; and now adayes the opinion that rude people
have of Fairies, Ghosts and Goblins; and of the power of Witches. For
as for Witches, I think not that their Witchcraft has any reall power;
but yet that they are justly punished, for the false beliefe they have,
that they can do such mischiefe, joyned with their purpose to do it if
they can: their trade being neerer to a new Religion, than to a Craft
or Science.[97]

Amongst the English intelligentsia there was a groundswell of support for the
burgeoning scientific movement and many early scientists attempted to dis-
tance themselves from the supernatural and occult related claims in favour of
a new version of Protestantism that embraced secularist government and approaches to science. Empirical and experimental styled reasoning, supported
by a faith in objectivity as a means of legitimating research, gained massive
support throughout England during this period, particularly via individuals
such as Hobbes and Bekker who argued in favour of an approach to government founded in natural rather than supernatural law. However, less well supported was the perceived mechanical philosophy of nature that, almost invariably, accompanied the growing influence of scientific rationality.

Meric Causabon published *Of Credulity and Incredulity* in 1668, as a critique of the new mechanistic philosophy and its perceived detrimental effects
on the public order and morality, which became adopted as the Anglican orthodoxy with regards to belief in Witchcraft. Whilst arguing for restraint and
demonstrating his concern with regards to the spread of papal and foreign influence in England, Casaubon believed that the weight of reliable testimony
stood in favour of the existence of Witches. Moreover, to not believe in Witches
and demonic agency in human affairs weakened the position of the Church
and encouraged atheism, which was therefore a threat to the established social,
political and moral order. Similarly, Cambridge scholar Henry More in *Antidote Against Atheism* argued that the acts of Witches and devils could be empirically proven and should easily "silence the quiet scoffing of the sceptics."[98]

These debates as to the role of science, the Church, belief in the supernatural and the new political role for the Church in an increasingly secular po-

---

97. Hobbes, Thomas. *Leviathan*. New York: Viking Press. 1982 (1657). p 92.
98. Gijswift-Hoffa, Marijke. "Controversey c.1680–1800". p 198.

litical arena, dominated intellectual and ideological debate during the eighteenth century. Ostensibly academic debates as to the existence of the supernatural and demonic/angelic interference in human affairs became quickly incorporated into broader debates regarding the role of religion in the new social political order and the impact science and secularist thought would have on the English intellectual climate. Fears as to the lack of belief in the supernatural order encouraging immorality and undermining the role of government as supported by the Church, were met with arguments regarding the social disruption caused by Witch hunts, popularist religion and fears of belief in the supernatural, encouraging fifth columns of Catholic based, continental influence in English society. [99]

Attempting to reconcile the differences between the Protestant Church and the burgeoning scientific community by holding the intellectual middle ground, writers such as Bekker, Locke, Toland, Chubb, Wollaston and Morgan attempted to integrate a faith in reason as the ultimate arbiter of knowledge with the beliefs of the Protestant Church. Balthazar Bekker, in particular, argued that under Calvinist and Cartesian doctrine there was no place in nature for the existence of Witchcraft or the physical manifestations of magic or Satan. He felt that the gospel, when correctly interpreted via philological method, supported the contention that the actions of the Devil were manifested in either the wickedness of human beings or through visions. When this interpretation of scripture was combined with the all-powerful nature of God in Calvinist thought, there was no logical possibility of the independent actions of the Devil manifesting in the physical realm. He also argued that as Satan was, in a scriptural sense, a spirit or supernatural entity then he could not act in the physical world without a body as his medium. Hence, the physical acts ascribed to the Devil would have to be performed through matter and motion, which would thus be dependent on the regular laws of nature and thus the will of God. So unless the Devil was a physical being dependent on the laws of nature, which according to scripture he was not, then his alleged tempting, possessions and supernatural acts were untenable.[100] The conclusion wrought by this line of reasoning was that any actions ascribed to the supernatural, magic, Witchcraft or Satan were in fact the product of deranged, simple, gullible or primitive minds. The fact that these beliefs largely originated within the minds of the uneducated rural populations, indigenous peo-

---

99. Gijswift-Hoffa, M. "Controversy c.1680–1800." pp 197–218. Sharpe, J.A. *Instruments of Darkness.* pp 254–275.

100. Gijswift-Hoffa, M. "Controversy c.1680–1800." pp 200–202 & 225.

ples within the colonies or from within the Catholic Church, gave further evidence that Witchcraft was the product of superstition, gullibility and the primitive mind divorced from the rationality of European Protestantism. In this light, the intelligentsia of eighteenth century England turned increasingly to the idea that education and science were the only reasonable solution to deal with the dangers of superstition and the most effective means of encouraging piety, rationality and wise government amongst the people and apparatus of government.[101]

This form of doctrinal cleansing, the removal of all traces of superstition from religion and the reduction of the influence of religion over government and science, became a central theme of English religious, governmental and social thinking during the eighteenth century. Driving this growing secularisation of religion and government were figures like Hobbes and Bekker, who made extensive attempts to end the influence of "Popish Idolatory" and corresponding doctrines of purgatory, indulgences, invocations of saints, Witchcraft, sorcery and belief in the supernatural intruding into the physical realm.[102] The Puritan critique of transubstantiation, holy water, holy relics, exorcism, rejection of the cult of the saints and virgin Mary undermined the legitimacy of many of the demonological concepts that legitimised Witchcraft beliefs, perceiving them to be impious, papist and unpatriotic. These rituals and beliefs were perceived in the Protestant tradition to be residual Pagan elements left within the corrupt Catholic Church that were both alien to true Christian belief and undermined loyalty to the English Church and state.[103] Supporting this trend was the English "deist" movement that sought to prove that any theological tenet that stood against reason and science was an affront to God, nature and the human mind. Some, such as Locke, sided with Protestant Christianity and Calvinism, arguing that once Christianity was stripped of its popish, irrational and superstitious relics of a Pagan past true faith should support the tenets of reason and scientific rationality, thus developing a solid basis for a rational, ethical and pious social order. Popularist religion and Catholicism in particular, were defined as irreparably superstitious, irrational and it was argued that they utilised phenomena like Witch crazes and heresy trials as tools of the priesthood to control a gullible and uneducated rural population.[104] Belief in the supernatural was perceived to not only undermine the Christian faith, from a Protestant perspective, but also attacked the tenets of reason and good government.

---

101. Gijswift-Hoffa, M. "Controversy c.1680−1800." pp 200−201.
102. Sharpe, J.A. *Instruments of Darkness.* pp 263−264.
103. Hill, Christopher. *Some Intellectual Consequences of the English Revolution.* p 64.
104. Gijswift-Hoffa, M. "Controversy c.1680−1800." pp 201 & 227.

By the later half of the eighteenth century, the respectability of the super-natural in England, under consistent attack from government, Protestant Churches, the intellectual community and deists, was thoroughly on the decline. Even in religious circles there was a consensus that "The age of miracles was past: they had played their role in the founding of the faith, but salvation was now to be sought in works and scripture".[105] This conviction, which had become fundamentally linked to the ideology of English Protestant secularism, had a major influence on the educated perception of Witchcraft and the supernatural. In an age where it was believed that God alone had the power to work miracles and the age of miracles was in the past, a belief in the supernatural and the work of demons and Witches in the physical world was not just irrational but also impious and reeked of Pagan influence.[106]

---

105. Gijswift-Hoffa, M. "Controversy c.1680–1800." pp 199–200.
106. Gijswift-Hoffa, M. "Controversy c.1680–1800." pp 200–201.

2

THE END OF WITCHCRAFT?
THE ENLIGHTENMENT AND
THE SUPERNATURAL

By the nineteenth century, public and institutional perceptions of the Witch trials in England had come to be dominated by what historian Elliot Rose defined as the "bluff" school and the "anti-Sadducee" school.[1] The latter, typified by writer Montague Summers, argued that belief in Witches and demonic agency represented an existent cult of Satanists and Pagans that threatened the social, moral and political order. Alternatively, and much more widely accepted, was the "bluff" school's argument that Witchcraft beliefs were a manifestation of the superstition and destructive tendencies of Catholicism, popularist religion and mob violence that had been countered in all but the most rural and backwards areas by teaching respect for scientific method and anti-supernaturalism through the education system and the Protestant pulpit. According to this model, Witches were the poor misguided victims of superstition and mob rule and only Enlightenment values instilled into the general public via the education system could prevent the gross injustices of the primitive past. This interpretation of the Witch crazes argued that on the continent Witch trials and beliefs were instilled by the Catholic Church, drawing upon established Pagan superstitions as a means of keeping the public fearful and under the control of the Papacy. This model defined the trials of suspected Witches as analogous to the persecution of heretics during the middle ages. In contrast, English Witchcraft was perceived to represent local hostilities and superstitions strengthened by a parliament sponsored popularist Puritanism that threatened to destroy the country prior to the restoration of the monarchy. This perception of the rise and decline of Witchcraft beliefs as a struggle against ignorance, mob rule and Catholic sponsored oppression had, by the

---

1. Rose, Elliot. *A Razor for a Goat.* Toronto: University of Toronto Press, 1962. pp 7–10.

end of the nineteenth century, become the orthodoxy in attempts by Anglo-phone historians to understand the role of Witchcraft beliefs and practices until the late 1970s.[2]

This perspective can clearly be seen in the works of many twentieth century historians. For example, noted Keith Thomas echoes the Anglophone Enlightenment interpretation of the decline of belief in magic and Witchcraft by claiming that the real damage to the legitimacy of Witchcraft beliefs was caused by the development of the mechanistic philosophy of Newton and empirical approaches to the understanding of nature. He argues that the self-perpetuating and circular reasoning of the magical, religious and neo-Platonic forms of thinking that dominated Medieval and Early Modern intellectual life could not compete with the capacity of scientific and empirical reasoning when it came to explaining natural phenomena. As he writes,

> The essence of the revolution was the triumph of the mechanical philosophy. It involved the rejection of both Aristotelian and of the neo-Platonic theory that had temporarily threatened to take its place. With the collapse of the microcosm theory went the destruction of the whole intellectual basis of Astrology, chiromancy, alchemy, physiognomy, astral magic and their associates. The notion that the universe was subject to universal laws killed the concept of miracles, weakened the belief in the physical efficacy of prayer and diminished faith in the possibility of direct divine inspiration.[3]

The perception that Witchcraft beliefs and practices declined as a result of changes in the intellectual climate of England's elite that gradually percolated throughout English society, has become the standard interpretation of the decline of English Witchcraft beliefs. It constructs the image of the Witch as the persecuted victim of irrational superstition who could only be saved by the Enlightenment crusade against clerical authority, papist superstition and rustic brutality, and ignorance by the Protestant aligned intellectual elite of England. Once empirical reasoning and experimentation became accepted as the ultimate and universal basis for legitimate knowledge it is argued that the elaborate metaphysical structures of Aristotelianism and neo-Platonism lost their source of creditability. As Christopher Hill writes,

> The majestic laws of Newton made nonsense of the traditional idea that the earth was the centre of the universe in which God and the

2. Ankarloo, B. & Henningsen, G. *Early Modern European Witchcraft.* pp 1–3.
3. Thomas, K. *Religion and the Decline of Magic.* pp 768–769.

Devil intervened continuously … Witches and parsons, so powerful in 1603, counted for little in the world of rationalism, materialism, science and toleration.[4]

From Hill's perspective, the new philosophy spread via the political upheaval and development of new ideologies that developed in the aftermath of the civil war. Knowledge was no longer separated from the common people in Latin but was instead written in the technical vocabulary of technical sciences. Belief in the possibility of a unifying metaphysical basis for knowledge became supplanted by departmentalized sciences. Theology and religion became fields of research distinct from politics, economics, philosophy and the natural sciences. The development and rise to power of the middle classes led to the adoption of intensified professionalism and specialization on behalf of scholars and artists. In essence, Hill's model postulates a widespread growth of independent secularist thought, originating from the triumph of Newton's mechanistic philosophy, that made knowledge more accessible to the general public and removed many of the ideological restrictions posed by the predominance of theological considerations. In such an environment, many plausible rationales for injustice, illness, disaster and death could be found besides that of supernatural or magical explanations. When combined with the greater stability of the post-revolutionary period, common law's victory over royal prerogative, the end of plague and increased prosperity, the new mechanistic philosophy instilled a greater sense of surety, on the part of the general populace, that social, environmental, health and political conflicts could be resolved through human agency rather than the supernatural.[5]

Another perspective to emerge from this interpretation of Witchcraft beliefs is the notion that the Early Modern Witch crazes were a state/Church sponsored mass persecution of social and religious dissidents as a means of social control. This model of Witchcraft persecutions has had immense influence on popular perceptions of Witchcraft and has gained increased significance in the aftermath of the Nazi holocaust, McCarthyism and the Stalinist purges of suspected political dissidents. Perhaps the most influential exponent of this theory is Norman Cohn, whose model of the Early Modern Witch crazes is heavily influenced by the experience of the mass persecutions of Nazi Germany and other examples of state sponsored anti-Semitism. Cohn argued that belief in Witchcraft, and people's experiences regarding the supernatural, were merely fantasies sponsored by the Catholic Church and were

---

4. Hill, C. as cited in Clark, S. *Thinking with Demons.* p 296.
5. Hill, C. *Some Intellectual Consequences of the English Revolution.* pp 64–66.

drawn from the mythology used to persecute Jews and Christians of ancient Rome. Of particular significance in Cohn's work is his belief that Witchcraft mythology and persecutions were closely linked to anti-Semitism and provided a model for the Nazi persecution of Jews. According to Cohn, the central feature of early modern Witchcraft persecutions was the projection of a fantasy in which marginalized sectors of society are depicted as engaged in rampant anti-human practices such as incest, bestiality, cannibalism, child molestation, human and animal sacrifices and other orgiastic practices. The represented marginalized sectors of society are also assumed to share similar symbolic formations, such as the worshiping of animal/human images with enlarged sexual organs.[6] From Cohn's perspective, the central feature of this construction of ideology and symbolism is that it represents the innermost self of European psychological construction, the inner fears, obsessive desires and unacknowledged needs of early modern Europeans.[7] Many of these images and symbols relate to repressed desires and anxieties experienced during childhood and infancy and are, in their original form, entirely unconscious. The creation of a society of Witches is therefore an unconscious revolt against the existing social order and the response of a society in a state of crisis and transition.[8] As he writes,

> For what we have been examining is above all a fantasy at work in history (and incidentally, in the writing of history). It is a fantasy, and nothing else, that provides the continuity in this story. Gatherings where babies or small children are ceremonially stabbed or squeezed to death, their blood drunk, their flesh devoured—or else incinerated for consumption later—belong to the world of fantasy. Orgies where one mates with one's neighbor in the dark, without troubling to identify whether that neighbor is a stranger or, on the contrary, one's own father or mother, son or daughter, belong to the world of fantasy. And so does the devil or subordinate demon who, in the guise of a monstrous tomcat or goat man, presides over and participates in these performances. Human collectivities, large and small, certainly are capable of grotesque and monstrous deeds ... Nevertheless there is no good reason to think that these particular things ever happened: we have examined case after case, and have found

---

6. Cohn, N. *Europe's Inner Demons.* pp 1–4, 11, 30, 34, 117–122, 262.
7. Cohn, N. *Europe's Inner Demons.* pp 258–261.
8. Adler, M. *Drawing Down the Moon.* pp 50–51.

hardly any where the accusation did not include manifestly impossible features.[9]

From Cohn's perspective, this process of propaganda, marginalization and persecution has its origins in the caricatures of Christians and other dissident religious groups within the Roman Empire. Accordingly, the Christian political establishment after Constantine, as the inheritors of the Roman legal and political system, used this same constellation of propaganda and persecution to persecute Jews and heretical sects like the Waldensians, the Manicheans, the Lollards and the Albigensians. Furthermore, this process of moral panic, backed by the promotion of a propagandic fantasy rooted deeply in Western symbolism, is clearly demonstrated in a long history of persecution and domination against minority groups deemed politically inconvenient or useful as scapegoats.[10]

Cohn's studies of the Witch crazes were completed under the auspices of the Center for Research in Collective Psychopathology, later renamed the Columbus Center, which was established to examine the "Psychological roots of the very urge to persecute or exterminate". The center was established in the early 1960s by David Astor to investigate how persecutions and exterminations originate, and how the impulse to commit genocide is generated and spread throughout a community, leading to its expression in violent action.[11] The research conducted under this institute illustrates a major component of Enlightenment Witchcraft scholarship, that Witchcraft persecutions are indicative of government attempts to persecute dissidents. This attempt to draw comparisons between contemporary instances of mass persecution and the Witch crazes of the early modern period is a major theme in Enlightenment interpretations of Witchcraft and the Enlightenment image of the Witch as the victim of irrationality and religious dogma. Playwright Arthur Miller utilized Witch trials in Salem as a model to represent McCarthyist policies in America. Similarly, Trevor-Roper interpreted Witch persecutions as the domination of the peasantry by a wealthy Church and aristocracy from a functional perspective, as did Jules Michelet from a Romantic approach. The eco-feminist tradition of neo-Paganism, discussed in chapter 6, relies extensively on the model of Witch-hunts as the systemic patriarchal persecution of women perceived to be synonymous with twentieth century feminist struggle.

---

9. Cohn, N. *Europe's Inner Demons*. p 258.

10. Adler, M. *Drawing Down the Moon*. pp 49–52; Cohn, Norman. *Europe's Inner Demons*. pp 1–4, 16–17, 22, 55–58, 229–230.

11. Cohn, N. *Europe's Inner Demons*. Editorial Forward.

These representations of Witchcraft revolve around a narrative of the Enlightenment as a liberation of the human condition from the barbarity, violence and primitivism of religion and superstition. The Witch is construed as the passive victim of domination and persecution that can only be saved by the light of reason and progress. According to Diane Purkiss, this model of Witchcraft interpretation represents a narcissistic form of academic self-fashioning.[12] Those who believe in the supernatural are constructed as ignorant, primitive, violent and savage, whereas those who oppose Witchcraft beliefs are rational, enlightened, scientific and engaged in a crusade against the darkness of ignorance.[13] These approaches tend to ignore the very prominent role played by English intellectuals in the development of Witchcraft beliefs and practices amongst the general public. According to Purkiss this problem in Enlightenment interpretations of Witchcraft is particularly apparent in Cohn's usage of the Witch trials to explain the Nazi persecution of Jews. By focusing on the mythology and irrationality attributed to anti-Semitism, the role played by industrialization, eugenics and systematized tools of oppression and destruction in the Nazi Holocaust can be conveniently ignored in favor of a tale of ignorant barbarism in conflict with enlightened rationalism and tolerance. In a similar fashion, the role of prominent intellectuals, often with strong scientific credentials, and a discourse of Witchcraft configured in terms of natural law, can be ignored in favor of a model of the decline of magic as simply an Enlightenment crusade against barbarism.[14] In Purkiss' view, this construction of the primitivism of the Witch and those who believed in and promoted Witchcraft and demonological lore reinforces historians' self-perceptions as rational, scientific and enlightened and serves to construct the image of the Witch as the "Dark Other" of the Enlightenment historian. As she writes,

> The Witchcraft believer is credulous, where the academic is skeptical; the believer takes word on trust, where the academic is "used to assessing documents for their reliability"; the believer is primitive, where the academic is sophisticated. Those oppositions construct an identity for the believer in Witchcraft which affirms the identity of the academic who recounts those beliefs.[15]

---

12. The themes of romanticist vs enlightenment constructions of Witchcraft will be further elaborated in chapter 2.

13. Purkiss, D. *The Witch in History: Early Modern and Twentieth Century Representations.* London: Routledge. 1996. pp 60–61.

14. Purkiss, D. *The Witch in History.* pp 59–62.

15. Purkiss, D. *The Witch in History.* p 60.

The Witchcraft trials of early modern Europe and the Americas have proven to be an extremely complicated and elusive period of history for historians to understand and interpret. The primary sources that remain are effectively a strange ethnographic record compiled by deponents, court officials, recorders, pamphleteers, demonologists and others who often hated and feared their subjects. Consequently, primary sources have tended to be sparse, opaque and difficult to penetrate and interpret.[16] This inherent difficulty in creating empirically accurate representations of what occurred in Europe and the Americas during this era is compounded by the powerful impact and psychological imagery that the Witch trials and the symbol of the Witch engenders in modern popular understanding within Western society. This is particularly important with regards to the difficulty with which a serious study of Witchcraft can be integrated with the Enlightenment ideology of progress and rationality dispelling ignorance and superstition. As Steve Russell writes,

> Witches are uncomfortable companions for respectable scholars. The smoke from their chimney flies against the wind and their money turns to dung in your pocket. They lack both respect and respectability, are notoriously disordered and undisciplined, and leave confusion and chaos in their wake. They baffle reason and transgress boundaries. The scholars' familiar tools, which include a capacity for rational thought, objective analysis of evidence, careful organization of facts, and logical argument, seem blunter than usual in their presence. Some qualities not always cherished in the academy, those such as intuition, imagination, humor, courage, and a profound respect for, and humility in the face of what is vast, mysterious and strange, are more useful if you want to begin to understand the Witch.[17]

A significant consequence of attempts to understand the phenomena of the Early Modern Witch crazes, as either a model for contemporary atrocity or an affirmation of Enlightenment values, is the tendency for historians to interpret the Witch crazes as if they were an ideologically, culturally and politically homogenous pan-European phenomenon. This assumption that the Witch crazes necessarily related to a specific meta-narrative across Europe has had a profound impact on the historiographical structure of Witchcraft narratives oriented around modernist ideologies of science and progress. The Enlightenment model of Witchcraft history, tied closely to a teleology of progress and

---

16. Russell, S. *Foucault Genealogy and Witchcraft*. School of Humanities. Monash University Gippsland. Obtained via personal communication 31-1-2000. p 3.

17. Russell, S. *Foucault Genealogy and Witchcraft*. p 4.

rationality overcoming superstition, has come under increasing attack since the 1970s by continental European historians who argue that English interpretations of Witchcraft have been designed to reaffirm English difference from Europe and, in particular, been utilized to support an ideology that constructs England as uniquely aligned with Enlightenment values to the detriment of continental Europe. These approaches, pioneered by historians like Bengt Ankarloo, Gustav Henningsen and Maia Maduk, are both localized and intensely empirical focusing on the impact of the trials on local village life and relying on trial records and other legal documents instead of Witch hunter's manuals like the *Malleus Maleficarum*. Whereas Witchcraft on the continent was associated with demonology, papist superstition and the mass persecution of heretics by Catholics, Witchcraft in England was an economic crime associated with localized conflicts driving the accusations. Continental historians have come to criticize this perspective, arguing that whilst England had many differences with the Witch trials of areas like Lorraine, Bamberg and Westphalia, the phenomena of English Witchcraft is far from unique. As Henningsen writes,

> That it (English Witchcraft) greatly differed from Continental tradition is obvious, but England was not a special case. Most of what has been identified as peculiar to English Witchcraft should from now on be considered as characteristic for large parts of Northern Europe ... In other words, while studying the case of England, several generations of Anglo-Saxon historians have unwittingly become engaged in a comparison between central and peripheral variants of a phenomenon common to most of Europe. The English "peculiarities" could furthermore be extended to many lower-court trials on the continent, where the accused were simply tried for *maleficium* and not asked demonological questions by the local judges.[18]

There does appear to be some justification for the contention that Anglocentric based interpretations of Witchcraft beliefs and practices have distorted public and academic perceptions of Early Modern European Witchcraft. Critical elements of the Witch crazes and Witchcraft beliefs, such as the role played by the complicated and somewhat ambiguous relationship between the inquisition, secular authorities, ecclesiastical courts and local village politics, have often been only superficially studied by historians focusing predominantly on the English experience without examining the larger political and

18. Ankarloo, B. & Henningsen, G. *Early Modern European Witchcraft.* pp 1–3.

cultural context of the European situation. The linguistic limitations of many English scholars has led to the bulk of continental Witchcraft studies being confined to researching the Witchcraft history of France and Germany, ignoring the centrality of Spain, Portugal and Italy in the development of early modern learned discourse on Witchcraft practices. This is exacerbated by the almost complete ignorance of Witchcraft beliefs and practices in more remote areas of Europe until the work by local historians on the continent began to be widely recognized in the Anglophone world during the 1980s.[19]

These interpretations of Witchcraft, and the way they have been utilized as a means of academic self-fashioning and the reaffirmation of Enlightenment values, have had an immense impact on popular interpretations of Witchcraft beliefs and practices. Certainly the model of the Witch, as the passive victim of either superstition or an ideological purge of dissidents by the Catholic Church, has formed a common image in literature, art and the neo-Pagan movement. The image of the Witch as the feminine victim of patriarchal Church authorities has been utilized again and again by sectors of the neo-Pagan movement since Jules Michelet in the 1860s. Furthermore, as will be discussed in detail in chapter 6, the model of the Witch as a uniquely feminine symbol associated with nature set against a patriarchal and misogynist Church, is a fundamental component of the eco-feminist branch of the neo-Pagan movement. Similarly, the Witch and those who believe in magic were relegated, in Enlightenment thought and historical interpretations, to the collective association of femininity, indigenous cultures, the natural world, agrarian society and superstition. These were images and associations that would be appropriated, inverted and reconstructed by Romantic writers, artists and philosophers as the antidote to the destructive and alienating components of Enlightenment rationalism, industrialism and the disintegration of English rural society in the nineteenth century. These same associations have formed the staple of representations of Witchcraft and Paganism, from the Hellenist revival and the theosophical society and spiritualist movements in nineteenth century Europe, to the rise of Gerald Gardner's Wicca and the impact of the sixties counter culture and New Age on contemporary representations of witchcraft and paganism.

---

19. Ankarloo, B. & Henningsen, G. *Early Modern European Witchcraft*. pp 1–3.

3

ROMANTICISM AND THE
PAGAN REVIVAL

As an attempt to transcend its own nothingness the Romantic image is doomed in advance because it is always constitutive, able to posit regardless of presence but, by the same token unable to give a foundation as to what it posits except as an intent of consciousness. It is against this knowledge that we must read the Romantic attempt to deny the gap between fiction and actuality through an aesthetic which claims the identity of beauty and truth or mind and nature.[1]

The development of the reconstruction of European history that became critical to the formation of the neo-Pagan movement during the early twentieth century is inherently linked with the development of Romanticism as an artistic, literary and philosophical movement. From its origins in nineteenth century spiritualism and English folklore studies, the development of neo-Pagan historical discourse was fundamentally integrated with the re-appropriation of Pagan motifs and European folklore in nineteenth century Romantic thought and aesthetics. To a large extent, the influence of the Romantic episteme in English society and culture formed the ideological and cultural basis of the neo-Pagan movement that emerged in the early twentieth century. In this light, it is important to begin with the development of Romanticism and its reconstruction of images of nature, femininity and spirituality that were to become the basis of the neo-Pagan movement.

---

1. Rajan, Tilottama. *The Dark Interpreter: The Discourse of Romanticism.* New York: Cornell University Press, 1980. p 14.

What Is Romanticism?

Romanticism is a highly complex and ambiguous term possessing a wide variety of inter-related meanings, interpretations and emphases. It is a term that defies and eludes simple and concise explanation. Partly this is due to the fact that the word "Romantic" has a variety of common meanings in popular culture. Similarly, there is a certain ambiguity in the academic definition of the term. Its usage is variously applied to describe an historical era, a philosophical tradition and a category of art and literature. Consequently, the term Romantic encompasses a wide variety of circumstances and contexts admitting a broad spectrum of possible meanings. Jacques Barzun writes of this difficulty stating that,

> The words "Great Romantics" or "German Romantics" are used as if their meaning is perfectly clear and agreed upon by everybody. That is the impression given by reading books. The truth is that at least half the contradictions come from the tolerated looseness in this use of the term "Romanticism" ... Somebody has said that it is a great convenience to have a number of words which will answer the purpose of ridicule or reprobation without having any precise meaning. "Romantic" is such a word.[2]

A further difficulty in defining the meaning of the word Romanticism is that the term has generally been applied in hindsight to a particular conglomeration of aesthetic, literary and philosophical forms originating in late eighteenth and early nineteenth century across Western and Central Europe. As Beilharz writes,

> Unlike the call for responses to the question, "What is Enlightenment?" there was no such curiosity in the public sphere about Romanticism. Perhaps this is not surprising, for the terms themselves (like so many others) were created after the fact; the enlighteners viewed themselves as philosophers not enlighteners, while the Romantics—if forced—would probably have signed on as poets.[3]

In this context, Romanticism does not describe an actual movement in the classic sense of the term; that is a conglomeration of individuals struggling to-

---

2. Barzun, Jacques. *Classic, Romantic and Modern.* Chicago: University of Chicago Press, 1961. p 2.

3. Beilharz, Peter. *Postmodern Socialism: Romanticism, City and State.* Melbourne: Melbourne University Press, 1994. p 29.

wards a common goal. Instead, Romanticism is a term applied to writers, philosophers and artists sharing similar themes, symbols and ideals originating in the Romantic era of early nineteenth century Europe.

This difficulty of defining Romanticism in a concise and coherent format leads to the question of how one can define Romanticism or usefully employ the term to describe characteristics of a diverse and fragmented movement like neo-Paganism. It appears to be, if not an all-purpose term of categorization, then at least a vague term with no precise systematic meaning or coherency. Its broad use in diverse academic disciplines to describe a variety of philosophical, aesthetic and cultural themes indicates that, like the term postmodernism, it is a broad term utilized to unite a range of divergent yet interconnected themes. For the purposes of interpreting neo-Paganism as a Romantic oriented movement, Romanticism is defined here as a particular combination of philosophical, aesthetic, literary and artistic ideals originally developed in the nineteenth century in response to the onset of industrialism, the Enlightenment and technocratic positivism. In this case, what is being described by the term "Romantic" is not so much a political, literary or social movement, but rather an aesthetic and cultural episteme within Western social and cultural formations.

The development of the Romantic episteme in Western culture is dominated by two central themes. Firstly, the theoretical basis of Romanticism is heavily oriented around the philosophy of the creative and transcendent imagination developed by Kant and appropriated by early German romanticists, most notably Schelling and Schlegel. Secondly, the development of Romanticism was heavily influenced by the social, cultural, economic and political issues of the time. Of particular importance was the rise of industrialism and the middle classes, combined with the fragmentation of traditional social, cultural and political structures. Additionally, the development of Romanticism was strongly influenced by issues of cultural autonomy and authenticity in a Europe dominated by emergent nationalism and radical cultural transformation.

The Philosophy of the Transcendent Imagination

Arguably, the most influential manifestation of the Romantic ideology in Western culture was the development and idealization of the philosophy of the transcendent or creative imagination. This is the philosophical perspective that reality and meaning, as we experience it, is not defined purely by empirical sensations, but is creatively defined and reconfigured through the process of the creative imagination. According to Kearney, one of the most critical stages of the philosophical development of the creative imagination, as an underpinning of Romantic theory, is the shift in Hume's empiricist model of human nature and reason from a model of enlightenment positivism towards radical skepticism. There are two aspects to this correlation. Firstly, there is the fact that Kant, whose theory of the transcendent imagination formed much of the core of German Romantic thought, was heavily influenced by Hume's writings. Secondly, Hume's difficulties are indicative of problems found by other empirical positivists of the era that were to be resolved via the application of this new philosophical perspective.

Like many other Enlightenment positivists, Hume proposed to eliminate superstition, imagination and metaphysics from human experience, leaving positivist rationalism and empirical data as the foundation of human experience and reason. As he wrote, with a certain dramatic flourish,

> If we take in our hand any volume; of divinity or school metaphysics, for instance; let us ask, Does it contain any abstract reasoning concerning quantity or number? No. Does it contain any experimental reasoning concerning matters of fact or existence? No. Commit it then to the flames for it can contain nothing but sophistry and illusion.[4]

Hume attempted, via extreme empirical positivism, to illustrate how knowledge, reason and science could dispense with all appeals to transcendent beings and deities; how it could establish its own foundations for the immanence of human reason and the possibilities of human experience. However, while Hume's initial postulate was to define human experience purely in terms of sense impression and systemic repetition of sensation, he became a radical skeptic. He found that once reason was divested of its structural, theoretical and metaphysical basis and reduced to empirical experience, the nature of rationality and human experience became an association of arbitrary sense impressions joined by an equally arbitrary fictionalism in the imagination of the perceiver.

Attempting to bypass metaphysics and transcendent ideals or deities as a foundation for knowledge, Hume postulated that all knowledge was born of an association between images and ideas, thereby giving meaning to sense impression. The cognitive and reasoning processes of human experience were not categorized by abstract metaphysical or logical laws, but were instead produced via psychological regularities in the experience of sense impressions.

---

4. Hume, David. *Enquiries Concerning Human Understanding and Concerning the Principles of Morals*. London: Methuen Press, 1977(1777). p 165.

The association of experience with reason and ideas is governed by perceptive functions of resemblance, contiguity and causation. Thus, via the association of sense experiences with resembling images in the mind, one can develop theories of causation and consequently a foundation for knowledge.[5]

In Hume's theory, the development of association with images derived from sense impression and sense impressions themselves, form the foundation and the limitations of what it is possible for the human subject to know and experience. Reason and science cease to be autonomous structures defining reality and are instead products of imaginatively created associations between sense impressions experienced as images in the mind. It is the principle of imagination that permits the association of cause and effect in sense impression and it is this same principle that defines the continued existence of external objects and experiential reality:

> The illusion of the identity and endurance of the self is based on the relations of contiguity and resemblance that we experience among our perceptions. Identity is nothing really belonging to these different perceptions and uniting them together, but is merely a quality we attribute to them, because of the union of their ideas in the imagination.[6]

From this perspective, both reason and reality are fictions created by the association of images in the imagination. However, Hume insists that while reality and reason may extend no further than the association of images derived from sense impressions in the human imagination, it is necessary that we act upon these fictions and arbitrary associations as if they possess an external universal meaning. For without these fictions, human experience would lack any sense of unity, contiguity and order. In short, human reason and experience would be impossible.[7]

This dilemma, which forms the crux of Hume's utilization of the creative imagination, is one of the central issues driving the development of Kantian transcendent idealism and its later appropriation in Romantic thought. If belief in the association of reason and experience is entirely fictional and a creation of the human imagination in the realm of ideas, then reason as a source

---

5. Hume, David. *A Treatise of Human Nature.* London: Penguin Books, 1984(1739). p 676.

6. Hume, David. *A Treatise of Human Nature.* p 307; Kearney, Richard. *The Wake of Imagination Towards a Postmodern Culture.* Minneapolis: University of Minnesota Press, 1988. p 164.

7. Kearney, R. *The Wake of Imagination Towards a Postmodern Culture.* pp 160-174.

of universal truth is impossible. One is thus left with a choice between a false and arbitrary reason, and philosophical anarchy. As Hume writes:

> Nothing is more dangerous to reason than flights of the imagination, and nothing has been the occasion of more mistakes of the philosophers ... If we embrace this principle and condemn all refined reasoning, we run into the most manifest absurdities. If we reject it in favor of these reasonings, we subvert entirely the human understanding. We have therefore no choice betwixt a false reason and none at all ... For my part I know not what to do in my present case.[8]

Whilst Hume was trapped in a dilemma of extreme relativism in his quest to define a universal basis for reason and science, Enlightenment and scientific rationalism continued unabated in the philosophical community, due in no small part to its effectiveness in developing industry, material wealth and state power. However, in Germany, Kant took up the issues raised by Hume's radical empiricism and attempted to define a new basis of human reason and the preservation of harmonious social order.

As opposed to locating the essence of human experience and morality in sense impressions associated by an arbitrary imaginative function, Kant sought to locate the foundation of human reason in what he termed the transcendent imagination. For Kant, the transcendent imagination is that which grounds the objectivity of sense experience with the subjectivity of the perceiver. Rather than trying to locate this basis for joining reason and experience via metaphysics, Kant defined the human imagination as the precondition of human experience. For Kant, nothing could be known about the world unless it was first transformed by the synthetic power of the human imagination. In essence, imagination links the perceptive structure of the cognitive subject with the empirical data of sense impression. Thus for Kant, transcendental refers to the presuppositions required for the possibility of experience in the human subject, as opposed to any metaphysical or otherworldly body of universal forms and ideas.

Claiming that Hume awoke him from his "dogmatic slumbers", Kant sought to rehabilitate the possibility of objective knowledge by establishing the validity of the subjective imagination as a transcendent synthesis of sensory and intelligible experience. Imagination thus ceases to be defined as an arbitrary or relativising function, but instead becomes the source and structure of pos-

---

8. Hume, D. *A Treatise of Human Nature*. pp 314–316; Kearney, R. *The Wake of Imagination*. p 167.

sible knowledge. Imagination also links patterns of thought and the structure of experiential interpretation with the sensory input of empirical data. Thus imagination becomes an original production of human consciousness. Consequently experience, images and symbols are not merely static empirical data, but are creatively defined and interpreted by the imaginative and interpretative functions of the human mind. As Kant writes,

> The affinity of appearances and with it their association, and through this, in turn, their reproduction according to laws, and so experience itself, should only be possible by this transcendental function of imagination ... For without this transcendental function no concepts of objects would themselves make up a unitary experience.[9]

This had important influences on the rise of Romantic thought. One was that it redefined the role of the imagination in the process of knowledge and human expression in a radically unique form, compared to the derogatory and awkward definition of the imagination posited by Enlightenment empiricism, particularly that of Locke and other British empiricists. Secondly, whereas art and beauty were perceived as negative and detrimental to the function of reason, Kant's transcendent idealism rehabilitated the role of art and imaginative expression as that which is beautiful to the senses and creatively original. Art is thus not judged by its ability to mimic experiential reality, but by its ability to transform objects of reality into new forms of beauty and expression. This understanding of the creative imagination was developed further into more extreme forms by several German philosophers, most notably Fichte, Schlegel and Schelling. For these writers imagination became defined as the creative energy that reconciles freedom and necessity, being and becoming, determinism with human will. According to Schelling, there was nothing that was not founded upon or made redeemable by imagination and the "productive and synthetic imagination is the pinnacle of all philosophy".[10] For Fichte, imagination became the quintessential component of being and the definition and experience of the self and thus fundamental to the possibility of human experience. As he writes,

> Every act of reflection is an act of self-determining, and the reflecting subject immediately intuits this act of self-determining. But it in-

---

9. Kant, Immanuel. *Critique of Pure Reason*. London: Everyman's Library Press, 1993(1781). pp 134–135; Kearney, Richard. *The Wake of Imagination Towards a Postmodern Culture*. p 171.

10. Schelling, Freidrich Wilhelm Joseph. *The System of Transcendent Idealism*. Richmond: Virginia University Press, 1978(1800). p 349.

tuits this act through the medium of the imagination, and accordingly, it intuits it as a sheer power of self-determination ... Consequently, in one and the same undivided act, pure thinking is made sensible by the imagination, and what is made sensible by the imagination is determined by pure thinking (reciprocal interaction of intuiting and thinking).[11]

Schelling described the development of the transcendent imagination in philosophy as the end of old metaphysical and positivist thought and symbolized the birth of the new "Romantic" as opposed to the "Classical" era. He also felt that this new era would finally be able to reconcile the progress of science with the mystical and ineffable in human experience and society. Schelling's desire to accomplish this process was manifested in the very style and form of his presentation. Whereas Enlightenment philosophers had proceeded by rigorous and painstaking logical argument, Schelling and his followers utilized incantatory formulations, enigmatic aphorisms and sententious repetitions. Logical syllogism gave way to visionary rumination. This formal approximation of philosophy into the realm of poetry was not accidental, but was a statement of a desire to change the very content of philosophical reasoning. Thus, according to Schelling, the objective world is only the original, still unconscious poetry of the human spirit. Art and philosophy should produce a conscious expression of reality which articulates the unconscious nature of being and human existence. Furthermore, this unconscious reality is one in which all people participate via the constant application of the creative imagination.[12]

Schelling promoted a new pantheistic interpretation of nature and humanity's role in the physical world. Rather than nature being chaotic or merely a clockwork mechanism it was, for Schelling, directed towards a higher goal expressed in the creative individualism of human imagination. It was moved by a spiritual force dormant in the natural world but fulfilled in the imagination of human beings. The unrestricted creative imagination of the autonomous human being was able to understand and become empathically linked with the workings of this spiritual force in nature. Consequently, it was the artist and poet that represented the ultimate expression of human existence rather than the scientist or philosopher. Art was the means of expressing the spiritual dimension of the world; clothing it in artistic forms that could

---

11. Fichte, Johann Gotlieb. *Foundations of Transcendental Philosophy*. Breazeale, Daniel (Trans). New York: Cornell University Publications, 1992(1796). pp 74–75.

12. Gouldner, Alvin. *For Sociology: Renewal and Critique in Sociology Today*. London: Allen Lane, 1973. pp 326–327.

inspire the creative imaginative function of the human mind. The artist was the person who stood between the external physical world and the transcendent function of the human imagination and could reconcile the two.[13]

The theoretical perspective of these early German Romantics bypassed the rigid limitations set by Kant as to what can and cannot be known and the essence of beauty and nature. It also actively sought to break apart the oppositions between nature, reason and art; forms long believed to exist as diametric opposites within Western epistemology. For Schelling, imagination creates both nature and art, both real objects of the world and the ideal objects of culture including the ideas of reason itself. It is imagination that creates both works of art and experiential reality. The development of transcendent idealism involved a radical transformation of the role of the human in nature and art. Human experience was placed in the center of the perceivable universe creating reality for the human subject, instead of the human subject being located within an objective Newtonian clockwork reality existing independently of the human subject. As he writes with regard to the possibility of understanding nature,

> Whoever is absorbed in research into Nature, and in the sheer enjoyment of her abundance, does not ask whether Nature and experience be possible. It is enough that she is there for him; he has made her real by this very *act*, and the question of what is possible is raised only by one who believes that he does not hold the reality in his *hand* … How a world outside us, how a Nature and with it experience, is possible—these are questions for which we have philosophers to thank; or rather with these questions philosophy came to be. Prior to them mankind had lived in a (philosophical) state of nature … At that time man was one with himself and the world about him … Many never lose it and would be happy in themselves, if the fateful example did not lead them astray; for Nature releases nobody willingly from her tutelage and there are no *native* sons of freedom.[14]

Developing in tandem with the development of the philosophy of the creative imagination in Romanticism was a broad socio-cultural, economic and political transformation in Europe. The appropriation of Kantian idealism by the

---

13. Gildea, Robert. *Barricades and Borders: Europe 1800–1914.* New York: Oxford University Press, 1987. pp 130–131; Gouldner, A. *For Sociology.* pp 326–327.

14. Schelling, Friedrich Wilhelm Joseph. *Ideas for a Philosophy of Nature as an Introduction to the Study of this Science.* Cambridge: Cambridge University Press, 1988(1797). pp 9–10.

early German Romantics and its development into a broad European trend of Romantic thought is heavily influenced by the fundamental changes occurring in Europe at the turn of the eighteenth century. Of particular importance in the contextual socio-cultural structure underpinning the development of Romantic thought are the French Revolution, the industrial revolution and the unique position of Germany during this period.

Romanticism: The Historical Dimension

The coining of the term "Romantic", and the appropriation and development of Kant's transcendental idealism by early German Romantic scholars, occurred at a particularly significant time in German history. Germany at the beginning of the nineteenth century was not a nation state, but an ideal of an emergent German identity and a sense of cultural and political unity and autonomy were beginning to form during this period. In addition, Germany during the Napoleonic era had a social and political interest in maintaining cultural and political autonomy from France. This was particularly important with regards to French modernization and industrialization.[15]

The industrialization and corresponding pattern of social and political upheavals did not occur evenly across Europe. In particular, Eastern and Central Europe experienced the industrial and political revolutions of the eighteenth and early nineteenth centuries significantly later than either England or France. This meant in practice that the German states had to deal with two simultaneous processes of social and cultural reform. On the one hand there were the problems inherent with German processes of industrialization, the rise of the middle class and the secularization of society, whilst on the other hand there was the problem of defining the German response to industrialization and modernization in France and, to a lesser extent, in England. This difficulty was further exacerbated by the widespread disillusionment with the destructive and violent aspects of the French revolution, once perceived as representing the ideals of freedom, liberty and equality.[16]

German intellectuals were thus faced with two central difficulties. Firstly, they had to define a means of modifying and reconfiguring German social and cultural identity to fit with the newly emerging social and political order, in line with the burgeoning perception of German social and cultural homo-

---

15. Gouldner, A. *For Sociology.* pp 326–327.

16. Gildea, R. *Barricades and Borders.* pp 130–131; Gouldner, A. *For Sociology.* pp 326–327.

geneity. Secondly, German intellectuals were generally disposed to reject the alternative presented by the French positivists and humanists, for reasons of disillusionment with the French revolution and the need to preserve the then fragile sense of German cultural autonomy. Consequently, Germany was placed in a quandary of being faced with an increasingly unworkable social and cultural order in the changing economic and political climate, yet were unable to accept the predominant French alternative. For this reason, German attitudes to modernization were fundamentally based in developing new strategies to overcome this quandary.

German intellectuals were unsure of their direction and approaches to modernization, yet were under increasing pressure to develop uniquely German approaches to the process of industrialization and political reform. Thus even though change was perceived as inevitable, many intellectuals felt that a simply political or economic solution to the issues raised by modernization was impossible. Instead, many Germans felt increasingly drawn towards the sphere of cultural development. The development of this "Romantic" episteme and cultural structure laid the foundations of Germany's approach to modernization and its concurring process of rapid social and cultural transformation.

Unwilling to accept the changing present, and conscious of a need to preserve German cultural autonomy from France, the early German Romantics sought to transcend the weaknesses of the old feudal order whilst remaining culturally autonomous and uncorrupted by bourgeois industrialism. As Gouldner writes,

> The Romantics lived in a world of transition between an unsatisfactory present and an unworkable past, between decaying feudal tradition and an emerging bourgeois reform. Living in a world in which the conventional social maps had lost their effectiveness, but in which acceptable new ones had not yet been formulated, it was to the individual self as the maker of meanings that they turned rather than to the traditional rules.[17]

It was in this context that a handful of German intellectuals, centered around Schelling and the brothers August and Friedrich Schlegel, gathered together in the late 1790s to publish the Journal *Athenaeum* that served as the base platform for the emerging German Romantic tradition. The German Romantics were ill at ease with the society in which they functioned, yet did not see political action of the French variety as appropriate or constructive. Instead,

---

17. Gouldner, A. *For Sociology*. p 130.

pulled by the conflicts between the changing present and unworkable past, they sought to reach out to the ineffable and sublime qualities in the natural world and embedded in human nature. This aesthetic reconfiguring of the philosophical project took two forms for the authors of *Athenaeum*. One was the aforementioned appropriation of Kantian transcendent idealism by Schelling, the other was an appropriation of images from history, nature, folklore and mythology that were deemed to represent that which was autonomous, creative and ineffable about the human spirit. As Gouldner writes,

> The German Romantics could now have the best of both possible worlds: linking the modern to the past, they could extol the achievements of German culture, while at the same time calling for its improvement. They could now reject the French alternative and still acknowledge that the German present needed to be transcended. They could pursue "development" without endorsing "progress". They could look forward to renewed greatness without neglecting the past or holding it in contempt.[18]

In Romantic thought, the past was perceived as a source of cultural authenticity. The past was continually appropriated and reconfigured to find images and symbols which could be defined in relation to the present social order as autonomous and creative within the structure of the creative imagination. Above all else, Romanticism involved a search for cultural authenticity and the revitalization of European culture, through an appropriated and reconstructed past, that was perceived to represent the essential character of Europe's cultural and spiritual heritage. In particular, the Romantics sought an authentic past uncorrupted by civilization and the artificiality of science and vulgar consumerism. The Romantics set themselves the task of collecting folklore, legends, fairy tales and artwork of their own national heritage or conversely that of colonial societies, searching for that which was autonomous and authentic. The Romantics particularly focused on indigenous traditions of cultural symbols and folklore.

In many nations, this appropriation of the past took on extremely nationalistic and localized expressions. In particular, German Romanticism was especially concerned with issues of cultural autonomy and a newly forming national identity. Jakob Grimm, in particular, was concerned with the concept of German folklore, stories and legends being a manifestation of the collective cultural identity of the German people. Consequently, many Romantics

---

18. Gouldner, A. *For Sociology.* p 326.

deliberately avoided and condemned historical representations perceived as hybrid or constructed, focusing instead on indigenous folk traditions perceived as representative of the collective "unconscious", as it were, of the German people. Peter Murphy describes this phenomenon as,

> Where the Augustans looked to a syncretic past, the Romantics looked for an authentic past. Romanticism destroyed the eighteenth century cosmopolis in favor of cultural nationalism. The Romantics looked inwards to indigenous (aboriginal) traditions often dubbed "Gothic". The Roman-Renaissance-Augustan propensity for cross-cultural borrowing was repulsive to the Romantics. They set themselves in different national contexts, to collect fairy tales, catalogue the legends and extant Gothic ruins, indeed anything indicative of the "aboriginal origins" of German, Scottish or English cultures. They reacted vehemently against roman cosmopolitanism and the practice of "cultural loans".[19]

However, even in this nationalist approach to cultural and historical appropriation there was a strong transcendentalist element. For it was within these indigenous traditions that the great myths, symbols and legends, perceived as common to all people, were expressed in a uniquely nationalist or colonial contexts. Jakob Grimm went so far as to claim that God had planted these myths and legends into the minds of all people as an expression of the universality of the creative imagination.[20]

As Romanticism developed and gained popularity in the artistic and intellectual realms, its allegiance to traditional forms of historiography and national boundaries became increasingly strained. In later generations, many Romantic scholars took an increasingly transcendentalist approach, seeking universal forms of cultural expression whilst rejecting traditional historiography and cultural barriers. They deliberately blurred the lines between fiction and fact so as to prioritize the impact and cultural significance of their reconstructed representations of the past. As Gouldner writes,

> Perhaps the most general aspect of Romantic anti-traditionalism was its revolt against the conception that art should be governed by reason, i.e. by a disciplined conformity to certain received impersonal rules. Romanticism was thus free enterprise in art and literature. It

---

19. Murphy, Peter. "Romantic Modernism and the Greek Polis." *Thesis Eleven*, Vol 34, 1993. pp 44–45.

20. Gildea, R. *Barricades and Borders.* p 132.

was the artistic equivalent of the bourgeois doctrine of *Laissez Faire* ...
The Romantics rebelled on every front against the once honored con-
ventions of the artistic community and its classical tradition: they welcomed a *mélange* of times, tones, moods and places in one artistic
product, counterposing it to the classical doctrine of the unities ... [21]

Some Romantics were also heavily influenced by the experience of colonialism utilizing symbols, legends and images from other cultures, predominantly
from the east but also from Polynesia and Africa. This was particularly prevalent in French expressions of Romanticism where representations of the primitive, as less corrupted by civilization and thus more pure and closer to nature, became strong influences on cultural representation of modernity and
the colonial experience. As Andrew Ross states of the influence of Polynesian
colonialism on nineteenth century Romanticism,

> Most of this mythology, which was not only the material evidence for
> the theories of Rousseau and Diderot, but also the ecological myth of
> subsistence harmony, was based on Louis de Bougainville's goggle
> eyed descriptions of the carefree sexual behavior of the women of
> Tahiti during the twelve day stay of his crew on that island. In fact, if
> you wanted to chart an exact time and place of the invention of the
> idea of free love and the invention of the idea of communism—these
> very specific economies of Romantic nature—then you could do
> worse than cite the sensational response on the part of Bougainville
> and Cook. Although the Romantic fashion of natural innocence
> among European intellectuals did not last long, the Polynesian story
> about carefree peoples living in a state of nature is still a powerful
> compensatory element of Western skepticism about the ultimate so-
> cial value of limitless growth and development.[22]

Whilst the different methodologies utilized in appropriating symbols from the
past may appear irreconcilable, there is a common element between them.
What links these ideas together is a common search for cultural authenticity
and a sense that the past or the primitive, conceived as more authentic and
natural than the industrialized present, offers unique insights into the essence
of human cultural identity and its place in the physical world. Where En-

---

21. Gouldner, A. *For Sociology.* p 327.

22. Ross, Andrew. "Cultural Preservation in the Polynesia of Latter-day Saints." In Bennet, David. *Cultural Studies: Pluralism and theory.* Melbourne: Melbourne University Press.
1993. pp 4–5.

lightenment thought rejected images associated with the primitive, the feminine and nature in an attempt to free humanity from the bonds of superstition and natural catastrophe, romanticists reified these images and reconfigured them as authentic, sublime and liberating from the tyranny of industrialism and scientific rationality.

The Romantics progressively broke with the Enlightenment conception of a static nature about which one could find objective truth and control as a means of progressing human nature. Romantic thought transformed the conception of nature from a static mechanism "radiant with order and value", to nature existing as a "dynamic, diverse cosmos in a constant state of becoming".[23] Pauline Johnson defines the central spirit of Romanticism as a revolution in the human mind against thinking in terms of static mechanism, and its reconfiguration in terms of conceptualizing the world as dynamic organism. In other words, she defines the Romantic episteme as entailing a shift from Newtonian scientific rationality to that of mutually transforming structures of organic process. She defines the values associated with this perspective and manifested in the work of Romantic scholars as diversity, growth, the unconscious and the creative imagination. As she writes,

> The Romantics looked upon the enlightener's belief in a natural order of interlocking purposes as a repressive dogma which could no longer capture the turbulent and fragmentary experience of modern individuals. And, according to many of the interpreters, the lasting significance of the Romantics lies in the early and still distinctive formulation they gave to that epochal question which has been the ongoing legacy of the collapse of this Enlightenment anthropology: what, the Romantics asked, with ever growing confidence, is the ground of value?[24]

The Romantics responded to this question not through the laws of science or behavior, but through the application of the creative imagination and the search for cultural authenticity in the human subject. Where Enlightenment scholars saw in the power of science a way for humans to redefine the world in accordance with their ideals, Romantics saw science as a repressive dogma that limited human creative autonomy. For the Romantics, nature was not the perceived limiting factor restricting the potential for human autonomy and

---

23. Johnson, Pauline. "The Quest for the Self: Feminism's appropriation of Romanticism." *Thesis Eleven.* Vol 41. 1995. p 78.

24. Johnson, P. "The Quest for the Self." p 78.

creativity as in Enlightenment thought. Instead, it was through one's experience of the sublime and spiritual aspects of the natural world that the essential creative impulse behind human rationality could be expressed. One of Romanticism's most severe criticisms of industrialization and science is that it distanced the human subject from nature and alienated them from their natural environment. Not only was nature important for its ability to inspire the creative imagination, it also represented a more authentic way of living free of the structure, rigors and control of conservatism, positivism and objectifying science.

Romantics, like Enlighteners, were seeking a unifying sense of order and meaning in a rapidly changing world. However, for the Romantics, a wider range of interpretive and perceptive structures was required to create an *authentic* basis of understanding than that provided by the sciences. Imagination and feeling were integral parts of human expression and ultimately were perceived as being equal with, if not supplanting, sense and reason in order to create a deeper and more holistic understanding of the world and the human experience. The struggle for human autonomy and freedom should be manifested in a search for archetypal forms and essences of experiences and objects, rather than the process of scientific categorization and observation. Goethe, for example, attempted to find the essences of plants by integrating his observations with the creative perceptions of his own imagination. As Schelling stated, "To philosophize about nature means to create nature for nature's true meaning can be produced only from within man's intellectual imagination".[25] In this way, human experience was relegated to the center of possible knowledge, governed by the influence of humanity's unique capacity of creative imagination. It enhanced the objects of human experience and recreated them as symbols and images laden with meaning and creative expression.[26]

Romanticism sought to endow the ordinary with the pathos of the extraordinary, the *sublime*. By creating new sources of meaning and expression derived from emancipation of the creative and transcendent human imagination in history and nature, the Romantics sought to act as an antidote to the radical objectification of human existence. It was a movement for the revitalization of European culture in the industrial era to parallel the equivalent transformation of European society in the realms of economics, technology and politics. It transformed and revitalized the perception of art and nature

---

25. Cited in Tamas, Richard. *The Passion of the Western Mind.* London: Pinicuto, 1996. p 369.

26. Tamas, R. *The Passion of the Western Mind.* pp 369–370.

in society, and created a new basis for understanding European culture and history for a society in which both were increasingly under threat from the new social order of bourgeois industrialism and secularization.[27]

Romanticism is thus much more than simply an "emotional moment in the nineteenth century".[28] It has become a central part of the cultural formation and social structure of modern society and contemporary society's response and understanding to the development of modernity. As Peter Beilharz writes,

> Romanticism, as Peter Murphy suggests becomes a major part of the modern. Indeed, it could be identified as the cultural dominant in the modern. Evidence of this is conspicuous in everyday institutional life, as for example in the extraordinary influence of Rousseau's *Emile* on contemporary educational and schooling practices. Other cultural critics like Christopher Lasch and Richard Sennett connect this to the overwhelming narcissism which pervades modern and post-modern culture. Romanticism is always vulnerable to the cult of the individual, and after the collapse of communism ours is especially the age of the individual.[29]

What then are the ideals that link Romanticism together as an episteme within Western modernity? The most fundamental of these ideals is the, previously discussed, reification of the creative imagination, which forms much of Romantic theoretical configuration. Another aspect of Romanticism is a strong reliance on the appropriation of symbols from the past, nature and pre-industrial societies as means of defining socio-cultural identity. Romanticism is also characterized by a vilification of the objectifying and corrupting aspects of science and industrialization. Finally, "Romanticism" has a rather ambiguous relationship with Western modernity, or at least caricatures of Western modernity defined as universalist reason.[30]

Romanticism and Modernity

For the Romantics, the modern was not marked by the eruption of science and rationalism, but was defined by innovations in the arts, philosophy and

---

27. Gouldner, A. *For Sociology.* pp 327–328.

28. Beilharz, P. *Postmodern Socialism.* p 31.

29. Beilharz, P. *Postmodern Socialism.* p 31.

30. Hansen, Thomas. "Inside the Romanticist Episteme." *Thesis Eleven.* No 48. SAGE: London. February 1997. p 23.

literary culture. The distinction between the Romantic and the Classical promoted by Schelling, with a focus on artistic and religious components, had the effect of redefining the place of science in contemporary society. Specifically, it diminished the significance attributed to science as the characterizing innovation of the new historical epoch. Nineteenth century Romanticism thus attempted to displace the Enlightenment conception of the modern as centered on reason/science/technology, in favor of social and cultural revitalization based on appropriating symbols from the past and the philosophy of the transcendent imagination.

Romanticism is much more complex than simply an expression of latent traditionalism acting in response to modernization as technological progress and social transformation. In many aspects, Romanticism contained many strong anti-traditionalist emphases. One of the central aspects of Romanticism is a revolt of artistic and intellectual elites against the social and cultural establishment, and against standards that govern social and cultural activity and representations. As Gouldner writes,

> If the Enlightenment was the intellectual's critique of society, of religion and of politics, Romanticism was the revolt of an intellectual and artistic elite against its own internal subculture. In this degree then Romanticism was the substitution of aesthetics for politics, of cultural criticism for social criticism; and it was a demand for artistic freedom in place of political freedom.[31]

To this extent, the relationship between the Enlightenment and Romanticism is not Janus faced with one side looking to the future and the other into the past. Both Enlightenment and Romantic thought are fundamentally concerned with transforming the present to change the future. They are both concerned with the past as a mechanism to justify social and cultural transformation, but the lessons they draw from the past, and the symbols they appropriate, are radically different. However, both the Enlightenment and Romantic epistemes are concerned with reshaping the human subject in accordance with abstract ideals of autonomy and authenticity. For these modernist epistemes, an eternal process of self-reform and self-cultivation are essential components of the never ending process of cultural and social transformation. As Gouldner writes,

> The modern only begins to manifest itself when in answer to the question "What is distinctively human?" Romanticism replies not by

---

31. Gouldner, A. *For Sociology.* p 327.

referring to man's eternal capacity for reason and universal rationality, but, instead, to his creative originality, to his individuated capacity to feel and to dream uniquely. The modern begins to emerge when man is seen not merely as a creature that can discover the world, but also as one who can *create* new meanings and values, and thus change himself and fundamentally transform his world, rather than unearth, recover or mirror an essentially unchanging world order.[32]

Far from being simply latent traditionalism acting in knee jerk response to technological, social and cultural transformation, Romanticism is quintessentially a modernist movement. It is centrally concerned with the transformation, development and progress of the human subject. Western modernity is marked by the concepts of the new; progress, science, industrialism and the transformation of the human subject in the social and physical environment. However, this force for social, economic, and political development and transformation is also marked by an integrated episteme of cultural and aesthetic transformation through which the new social formations, technological developments and humanity's changing relationship with nature can be understood and interpreted. As Thomas Hansen writes,

> The Romantic episteme marks in a certain way the final breakthrough of modernity as a cultural system, as it for the first time posits *originality* and notions of *autonomy* and *self grounding* of human beings, cultures and social forms as marks of the highest cultural and political value. If modernity as a cultural system of secularized thought is fundamentally characterized by its anthropocentricism and celebration of a break with the past, the Romantic celebration of human will autonomy, of an emerging human spirit, the mystique of the artistic self creation and individual genius, etc., marks the consummation of that cultural system. [33]

Since its development in the late eighteenth century, the Romantic episteme has formed a constant critical companion to the positivist, technocratic, industrialist and teleological interpretations of human experience that form an integral part of Western modernity. As modernity, conceived as universalist reason and technocratic industrialism, has developed and transformed over time, so too has its countervailing Romantic episteme. One of the most in-

---

32. Gouldner, A. *For Sociology.* p 327–328.
33. Hansen, T. "Inside the Romanticist Episteme." p 23.

teresting aspects of the development of these "mutually reproducing discursive fields"[34] is the tendency of Romantic interpretations of the modern to be based in caricatures of modernity existing as universalist reason, unrestrained industrialism and, ironically enough, cultural and moral conservatism. What makes this particular representation of modernity interesting is that the conflict between Romanticism and modernity, whilst represented as a conflict between progress and science versus tradition and cultural expression, is located in an argument about which tradition is truly modern. In other words, it concerns whether Enlightenment or Romantic approaches to modernization are better able to encapsulate the human condition and thus further the development of human autonomy, freedom and creativity.[35]

Romanticism and the Construction of Paganism in Nineteenth Century England

According to research conducted by historian Ronald Hutton, 19th century England interpretations of the diverse conglomeration of religious, magical and cultural practices associated with Paganism and Witchcraft are dominated by four main ideological trends. Firstly, there was the colonial imagery of the religion of savages dominated by images of human and animal sacrifice, superstition and idolatry. This perspective was largely projected onto the traditions of colonial societies and many religions and cultures of the Orient such as the "Thugee" cults in colonial India. Typically, this approach was extremely reliant upon a theoretical basis developed from social Darwinist interpretations of history. This interpretation of pre-Christian religions as being representative of a backward or undeveloped form of civilization, was considerably strengthened by the strongly ideologically driven and often biased reports of missionaries and explorers.[36] It was also driven by social interpretations of evolutionary theory perceiving the development of religion as a movement from primitive and fearful superstition, to that of ordered and enlightened monotheism as represented by Christianity.

The second discourse of Paganism focused on the achievements of Pagan Greece and Rome as the prime example of the highest form of culture and so-

---

34. Hansen, T. "Inside the Romanticist Episteme." p 23.
35. Gouldner, A. *For Sociology.* pp 327–328.
36. Hutton, R. *Triumph of the Moon.* p 113.

ciety that Paganism could aspire to. In this light, the Paganism of ancient Greece and Rome was perceived as being second only to Christianity in glory, morality and grandeur. The traditional admiration for the achievements of Greece and Rome and its scholars, combined with the perception of the Greece and Rome of antiquity as a Golden Age of Western civilization, was a central theme in European history and culture since the Renaissance era. The achievements of classical Greece and Rome also served as a source of inspiration for the Enlightenment, art and science. These two factors made it difficult to characterize the deities, festivals, art and culture of the classical world with the same contempt reserved for that of the orient and colonial societies. Essentially, it was believed that the Paganism of Greece and Rome represented the highest order of civilization, with the exception of modern Protestant Christianity, and was consequently a source of virtues and ideals that should be incorporated into modern European Christianity.[37]

These two perspectives dominated interpretations of Paganism and pre-Christian religion in the eighteenth and nineteenth centuries. However, these perspectives increasingly came under pressure from two counter discourses inspired by the development of Romantic thought. The first of these was the Theosophical Society. Theosophy was based on the concept that behind the more sophisticated and complicated manifestations of contemporary religion lay an original, pure and authentic body of common wisdom. In this light, it was believed that all forms of religious expression were different manifestations of the same source of religious wisdom. Consequently, the differences between religious beliefs were perceived to be the product of the corruption of the original pure form of spiritual Enlightenment by social, cultural and political influences. The Theosophical Society argued that by a comparative study of all religions, rituals and beliefs, the primal source of the numinous and of pure spiritual knowledge could be recovered, leading to an enlightened utopian age.[38]

The other counter discourse of Paganism was hostile to both Christianity and Western modernity when conceived as universalist reason and industrialism. It described the religions of Greece and Rome, and indigenous expressions of Pagan belief by Celtic, Gallic and Germanic people, as inherently superior to Christianity. The religions of antiquity and prehistory were believed to be more joyous, liberating and harmonious with both human na-

37. Hutton, Ronald. "The Background to Pagan Witchcraft." In Ankarloo, Bengt and Clark, Stuart. *Witchcraft and Magic in Europe: The Twentieth Century.* The Athlone history of Witchcraft. Vol 6. London: Athlone Press, 1999. pp 18–19.

38. Hutton, R. *Triumph of the Moon.* pp 20–21, 73–74 & 158.

ture and the natural world. It was also believed that the religions of antiquity and prehistory could pose a viable alternative to the corrupting, objectifying, limiting and destructive aspects of Christianity and Enlightenment industrialism.

The German Romantics in particular were centrally involved in developing the association of pre-Christian Paganism with ideals and associations of Romantic culture. At the end of the eighteenth century, the Enlightenment idealization of ancient Greece and Rome became fused with the Romantic nostalgia for an authentic and culturally autonomous past, integrally linked with nature. Johann von Schiller's Poem "The Gods of Greece" was a powerful lament for a lost Pagan wonderland of beauty and freedom in which the natural world was infused with divinity and the sublime, creating a sense of joy and wonder and a sense of unity with life and nature. Holderlin, Schlegel and Schelling, and other members of the German Romanticist movement, such as it was, also took up this theme. However, as previously discussed, this appropriation of classical motifs was very quickly subsumed into a search for uniquely German folklore and customs in a particularly nationalist context.

This orientation from images of Paganism derived from Greece and Rome to that of German *Volk* folklore and customs came to the fore in Wilhelm Mannhardt's systemic study of German folklore and customs, as a means of defining the unique and authentic German cultural identity. In the newly formed German state, the development of a German folkloric and homogenous cultural identity took on immense significance and strongly influenced the interpretation of folklore and pre-Christian Paganism towards a specifically nationalist context. This pattern was generally repeated throughout Europe. In France in particular, the appropriation of Pagan motifs and the development of Christianity were heavily linked to representations of popularist anti-clericism and anti-establishment practices influenced by the unique context of post-revolutionary France. This is well illustrated by Michelet's interpretation of the Witchcult, as the remnants of a pre-Christian fertility cult, which was profoundly anti-aristocratic and anti-clerical in nature and flirted with Satanism and the Black Mass as a symbolic opposition to the abuse of power by Church and state.[39] In England however, the adoration of the Pagan past and its associations with the countryside took on immense significance when combined with social upheavals of the enclosure movement and industrialization. The image of Paganism linked with nature became synonymous

---

39. Michelet, Jules. *La Sorciere*. London: Oxford University, 1966(1862). pp 127–128 & 138.

with the growing cultural opposition to the destruction of the English countryside and traditional social organization of rural life. This also led to a common theme, heavily promoted by the Folklore Society, that the countryside represented a solid link with England's culturally authentic national past.[40]

According to Hutton, one of the most critical aspects of the phenomenon of the idealization of the English rural sector in the nineteenth century was the massive demographic shifts that were occurring in England at this time. At the beginning of the nineteenth century, approximately 80% of the English population lived in the countryside and by 1910 over 80% lived in the towns and industrial centers. The sheer speed and inevitability of this social change, wrought by the industrial revolution, promised to many English intellectuals a twentieth century England consisting of one gritty, dark smoky industrialized wasteland stretching from coast to coast.[41] From a Romantic perspective, this new development of the mass urban lifestyle was condemned, not just because of the sheer rate and scale of demographic transformation, but also because it was perceived as socially, culturally, physically and mentally unhealthy and devoid of beauty and meaning. A consequence of this was that the countryside became associated with the virtues that the city was perceived as lacking. It was not simply regarded as more beautiful and healthy, but as being stable, dependable, rooted and timeless. Its working people became credited with a superior wisdom founded upon generations of living in close contact with nature and inheriting a cumulative hidden knowledge. This organic, immemorial lore was viewed as both a comforting force of resistance to the dramatic and unsettling changes of the nineteenth century, and as a potential force for redemption.[42] These themes were strongly adopted by virtually all the English Romantic poets and artists. Wordsworth's "*The World is too much with us*" and Byron's "*Aristomes*" both drew heavily on Schiller's work of classical antiquity and interlinked with a love of the English countryside. A more radical group of scholars gathered in 1915–1916 around Leigh Hunt, Shelly and Keats, who felt that Christianity was inadequate to deal with the needs of the age and the depredations and objectification of Enlightenment

---

40. Bennet, Gillian. "Geologists and Folklorists: Cultural Evolution and the Science of Folklore." *Folklore.* Vol 105 (1994) pp 25–37; Hutton, R. *Triumph of the Moon.* pp 117–118; Marsh, Jan. *Back to the Land: The Pastoral Impulse in England from 1880 to 1914.* London: Quartet Publishing, 1982. p 35; Williams, Raymond. *The Country and the City.* London: Chatto and Windus, 1973. ch 21.

41. Bennet, Gillian. "Folklore Studies and the English Rural Myth." *Rural History.* Vol 4. 1993. pp 77–91; Hutton, R. *Triumph of the Moon.* pp 117–118.

42. Hutton, R. *Triumph of the Moon.* pp 117–118.

rationality and industrialism.[43] They proposed an alternative in the revival of Ancient Paganism and folklore that could be spread throughout the world to create a sublime and happier world, existing in harmony with the natural world and human nature.

This increasingly strident critique of industrialism and reification of the Pagan tradition had particular significance for the development of the nineteenth century spiritualist movement. Many occult and spiritualist movements integrated a love of English rural culture and the English countryside with Pagan motifs from classical antiquity as a central component of their cultural and ideological identity. Many of these occult oriented movements combined the ideal of a static countryside, whose folklore provided a continual link with an authentic England of Antiquity, with a love of the achievements and perceived greatness of the classical Pagan past of Greece and Rome.[44] Such cultural constructions attempted to integrate what was perceived as the best of Roman and Greek high culture with Romantic representations of the English countryside as a new source of authentic English cultural identity linked with a sense of communion with nature defined in terms of a search for spiritual fulfillment and cultural authenticity.

This conception of static, eternal and prehistoric origins for English rural folklore had several predominant characteristics. Firstly, it characterized the only significant rituals and folklore in England as rural and essentially different, in origins and observance, to the folklore and ritual of the town and city. Secondly, it regarded these rituals and beliefs as timeless and immemorial relics of a distant and Pagan past. Thirdly, the people who practiced these rituals and folklore were perceived as inarticulate, having lost any sense of the meaning and significance of their behavior, thus necessitating the research and interpretation of educated outsiders. Finally, this perception of the English countryside was infused with a sense that the countryside was a place of mystery and magic, resistant to the changes wrought by industrialism and modernity, and perceived to offer an antidote to the ills of the Enlightenment.[45]

There are several origins for this conception of the English countryside as a static and timeless source of prehistoric folklore. One of the most critical was the pressure on the newly formed academic discipline of folkloric studies to present itself as a science. According to Gillian Bennett, one of the most

---

43. Hutton, R. "The Background to Pagan Witchcraft." pp 18–19 & 26–29; Hutton, R. *Triumph of the Moon.* pp 112–118.

44. Hutton, R. "The Background to Pagan Witchcraft." pp 36–50.

45. Hutton, R. *Triumph of the Moon.* pp 112.

critical consequences of this pressure was an attempt to link the study of folk-lore with the newly formed disciplines of evolutionary theory and geology. The unique integration of geology, folkloric studies and evolution within the Folklore Society resulted in a perception of the past history of humankind being recorded as folkloric fossils buried in layer after layer of cultural strata. When applied to the study of culture and folklore the evolutionary and geo-logical model suggested that the human condition was essentially universal, but had developed at different rates according to racial, social, cultural and class factors in a social Darwinist fashion. Folklore and custom became rep-resented as cultural fossils left over from earlier stages of civilization, and a comparative study of these fossils could produce a general picture of the pre-historic past and a blue-print of human religious and cultural development. The Folklore Society leapt to promulgate this new theory and claim scientific justification for their discipline.[46]

One of the most significant consequences of this approach was the neces-sity to create the illusion of a static and unchanging countryside. There was already a strong basis for this perception in Romantic thought however, in the context of an academic discipline there needed to be a more systemic basis for this perception. Additionally, after the 1850s, the dominant trend of the Eng-lish economic, political and artistic elite was generally oriented, for a wide va-riety of reasons, against the influence of institutionalized religion. Finally, the development of English nationalism also sponsored the perception of a uni-versal existent English cultural identity, transcending the waves of invasion, conversion to Christianity, the Reformation and counter-Reformation. and the industrial revolution. A consequence of this was that the influence of major upheavals in English society were continually under emphasized, or ig-nored, in favor of a perception that such changes only influenced the intel-lectual elite and life in the cities and towns.[47]

This unique integration of Romantic interpretations of the countryside and the rural with the appropriation of Enlightenment discourse by the Folklore Society was to prove critical in the development of the ritual, folkloric and historiographical practices of the neo-Pagan movement. It would also serve as a tool for the unification of the magical and spiritual ideas of theosophy with the nationalist appropriation of folklore, folk customs and ritual magic. In particular, the integration of folklore with ritual magic and theosophy, and

---

46. Bennet, G. "Geologists and Folklorists". pp 25–37.

47. Bennett, Gillian. "Folklore Studies and the English Rural Myth". pp 77–91; Hut-ton, R. *Triumph of the Moon*. pp 116–117.

the theoretical basis for doing so provided by the Folklore Society's usage of evolutionary theory and comparative symbolic analysis, was to prove fundamental in the construction of Gerald Gardner's Wiccan movement, the wellspring of late twentieth century Pagan and Witchcraft revivalist movements.

Another prominent feature associating medieval Europe with Paganism was the strong impetus amongst Protestant Churches, governments and intellectuals, following the Reformation, to associate Catholicism with Paganism as a means of discrediting Roman Catholic ritual and modes of worship. The tactics involved in this procedure, originating in sixteenth century Germany, were largely focused on attempting to prove that most of the ceremonies of the medieval Church were based on an appropriation of Pagan practices and that Catholic Churches were based on the sacred sites of former Pagan temples. This tactic was extended in the seventeenth and eighteenth century to condemn popular forms of revelry and social gatherings deemed immoral, disorderly or subversive by the Church. This long association led to the perception amongst many European scholars that Europe remained largely Pagan in beliefs and practice, with Catholic based Christianity being solely in the purview of the ruling classes until the Reformation.[48]

By the end of the nineteenth century the term Pagan, and consequently the term Witch, had become laden with associations of English cultural identity and competing Romantic and Enlightenment interpretations of modernity and industrialization. The means by which the terms Witch and Pagan were configured, and the discourses associated with each representation, had become an ideological battleground for various sectors of English society. In particular, the images associated with Paganism and Witchcraft had become a point of contention between those who saw Romantic ideals of a Pagan past as an opposition to science, rationality and progress, those who idealized the Pagan past as an antidote to the ills faced by christo-centric industrialized society and those who felt that the moral and social fabric provided by Christianity was being eroded by idealizing the Pagan past over the Christian present. The basic structure of representations relating to the character and symbolic significance of the Pagan, the rural and the Witch were well established by the end of the nineteenth century. It was these discourses, and the interaction and integration between Enlightenment and Romantic constructions of Pagan belief, Witchcraft, industrialism, nature and the primitive, that were to set the stage for the development of the neo-Pagan movement in the late twentieth century.

---

48. Hutton, Ronald. "Finding a Folklore." *The Pomegranate: A Journal of Neo-Pagan Thought.* Issue 12. May 2000. pp 4–15.

4

GERALD GARDNER AND THE
ORIGINS OF WICCA

Now I am an Anthropologist and it is agreed that an anthropologist's job is to investigate what other people do and believe, and not what other people say they should do and believe. It is also part of his task to read as many writings as possible on the matter he is investigating, though not accepting such writings uncritically, especially when in conflict with the evidence as he finds it. Anthropologists may draw their own conclusions and advance any theories of their own, but they must make it clear that these are their own conclusions and their own theories and not proven facts; and that this is the method I propose to adopt. In dealing with native races one records their folklore, stories and religious rites on which they base their beliefs and actions. So why not do the same with Witchcraft.[1]

Gerald Gardner and the Wiccan Movement

Gerald Gardner is perhaps the most significant figure in the development of neo-Paganism. Operating out of the context of nineteenth century Romanticism and, in particular, nineteenth century Romantic discourses of Paganism, Gardner integrated the ideas surrounding Pagan beliefs and practices into a coherent, structured and practical format. In creating his vision of a Pagan revival he drew upon a wide variety of source material from folkloric, esoteric and historical sources. Of particular significance was the theory of Pagan survivals, the methodology and historical analytical practices of the Folklore Society and the rich English folkloric tradition. Similarly, in creating the rituals, symbols and practices of his Wiccan belief system, Gardner drew

---

1. Gardner, Gerald. *Witchcraft Today*. London: Rider Press. 1954. pp 18–19.

upon a broad range of established lore and ritual from the occultist and ritual magic traditions of English society. Gardner integrated these strains of English culture within the ideological and cultural matrix of English Romanticism and created a body of religious and magical practise that celebrated the Romantic idealization of the countryside, opposition to Enlightenment industrialism and the ideal of an authentic and eternal English national culture. Critical to this analysis is the pioneering work of historian Ronald Hutton, whose detailed empirical research is arguably the most detailed and well researched analysis of the historical circumstances surrounding the development of Gardner's Wiccan movement.

Who Was Gerald Gardner (1884–1964)?

The foundation myth of the Wiccan movement, the origin of the twentieth century neo-Pagan revival, was first publicly expounded in Gardner's 1960 biography written by the well-respected writer on Sufi mysticism, Idries Shah. However, actual authorship of the biography was credited to the work of Jack Bracelin who was a prominent spokesperson for Gardner's Wiccan movement.[2] Furthermore, due to the fact that most of the information contained within the biography was dictated or supplied by Gardner himself, the work was essentially autobiographical in character. This had a profound impact on the representation of Gardner, in his biography, as it oriented the biographical work towards promoting Gardner's desire to construct his own history, and that of the Wiccan movement, in a specific format suitable to the promotion of the Pagan/Wiccan revival movement.[3]

The text tells the story of a relatively uneventful working life as a plantation manager in the British colonies of Malaya, Borneo and Sri Lanka, followed by a period of employment as a customs officer in Malaya. The setting and description of Gardner's working life draws heavily on the British colonial myth. The cover photo from his biography, for example, is of Gardner as a muscular, moustachioed man on a riverboat in the jungle, revolver placed

---

2. Baker, James. "White Witches: Historic Fact or Romantic Fantasy." In Lewis, James (Ed.) *Magical Religion and Modern Witchcraft*. New York: State University of New York Press. 1996. p 188; Hutton, R. *Triumph of the Moon*. pp 204–205.

3. Adler, M. *Drawing Down the Moon*. pp 60–62; Baker, J. "White Witches: Historic Fact or Romantic Fantasy." p 186; Hutton, Ronald. *Triumph of the Moon*. pp 204–205; Hutton, Ronald. "The History of Pagan Witchcraft." pp 43–44.

prominently at his side.[4] However, despite this drawing upon the colonial adventurer mystique in his visual representations, Gardner's escapades, as described in the biography, do not feature the action and heroism usually ascribed to the British colonial entrepreneur. The one event featuring violence, Gardner's response to an anticipated attack by head-hunters in Borneo, turns out to be a false alarm leaving an image of Gardner's posturing with firearms as a caricature of self deprecating humour rather than an example of heroics.[5] The text describes a life typical of many English public servants and entrepreneurs in England's pre Second World War colonial territories. He manages plantations, resolves conflicts between natives, writes a dissertation on Malay weaponry and retires to England in 1936 where he settles in New Forest, so as to better protect his large collection of native artefacts in the advent of war.[6]

In two respects however, Gardner's life, according to his biography, differs from the commonplace life history of the colonial English public servant. Firstly, Gardner possessed a keen interest in the supernatural and the occult, and a desire to share his experiences and studies with like-minded people in the widespread English spiritualist movement. To this end, he shared a great deal of time with theosophists, Freemasons, Rosicrucians and other members of the English occult and spiritualist community. Most notable of these were the members of the Golden Dawn, a prominent English occult organization, and Aleister Crowley, noted magician and occultist and notorious head of the Ordo Templi Orientlis.[7]

Secondly, Gardner was an extremely active antiquarian, amateur anthropologist and archaeologist. These interests led him to pioneer research in certain areas of Malayan Archaeology, numismatics (the historical/archaeological study of coins, tokens and medals), folkloric studies and maritime history, and to write several academically credited monographs in these fields. Upon his arrival in England in 1936, he immediately became involved in local archaeology, folkloric studies and antiquarian research. He also maintained close contact with the Folklore Society, joining in the late sixties, and first published

---

4. Bracelin, Jack. *Gerald Gardner: Witch*. London: Octagon Press, 1960. Cover photo and Plate 10 pp 98; Hutton, R. *Triumph of the Moon*. p 205.

5. Bracelin, J. *Gerald Gardner: Witch*. pp 37–56.

6. Bracelin, J. *Gerald Gardner: Witch*. pp 56–102 & 168–183; Hutton, R. *Triumph of the Moon*. p 205.

7. Adler, M. *Drawing Down the Moon*. p 60; Bracelin, J. *Gerald Gardner: Witch*. pp 26, 168, 170 & 178–181; Hutton, R. *Triumph of the Moon*. pp 205–206 & 216–222; Hutton, R. "The History of Pagan Witchcraft." pp 50–51; Valiente, Doreen. *An ABC of Witchcraft Past and Present*. New York: St Martin's Press, 1973. p 30.

his study of the supposed Witches coven in New Forest, upon which he was to base his Wiccan movement, in the Folklore Society's journal. Additionally, Gardner maintained a close friendship with Margaret Murray, the noted English folklorist and Egyptian archaeologist, whose work "The Witch Cult of Western Europe" was to become the historical basis of Gardner's claims concerning the surviving Neolithic Witch cult in New Forest. Similarly, Murray was an enthusiastic supporter of Gardner's claims, writing the preface of Gardner's text on the New Forest coven, "*Witchcraft Today*". Murray and Gardner also collaborated in writing a paper on Witchcraft relics and folklore in 1939.[8]

The New Forest Coven

According to Gardner's biography, in 1936 he came across the Rosicrucian Theatre in Christchurch Hampshire whilst on a bicycle ride in the country. He joined this company in order to develop associations with people who shared his interest in antiquarianism and the occult.[9] Some members of this organization introduced him to a wealthy local lady, nicknamed "Old Dorothy", who was a hereditary Witch of the kind described in Margaret Murray's "*Witch Cult in Western Europe*". Dorothy's group claimed to represent the remnants of the old religion, surviving as a Witch cult that traced its ancestry back through the medieval era to antiquity. Gardner described the group as composed of partly hereditary Witches and partly Rosicrucians, under the leadership of a wealthy local lady he later identified as Dorothy Clutterbuck. He was initiated into this Witch coven in 1939 and participated in its rituals until the late sixties. He then proceeded to involve himself in the occult world at large so as to find further information on Witchcraft practices. However, Gardner remained dedicated for the rest of his life to the task of reviving the "Old Religion" of Pagan Witchcraft and informing the world of its presence.[10]

Gardner claimed that in 1946 he obtained the permission of the coven to publish their rituals in fictional form, leading him to write the novel "*High Magic's Aid*". He also claimed that he was given access to an ancient text de-

---

8. Hutton, R. *Triumph of the Moon.* pp 224–225; Hutton, R. "The Background to Pagan Witchcraft." pp 34–35.

9. Bracelin, J. *Gerald Gardner: Witch.* p 159.

10. Adler, M. *Drawing Down the Moon.* pp 61–62; Bracelin, J. *Gerald Gardner: Witch.* pp 164–167; Gardner, G. *Witchcraft Today.* Hutton, R. "The History of Pagan Witchcraft." pp 45–46. Hutton, R. *Triumph of the Moon.* pp 205–206; Purkiss, D. *The Witch in History.* pp 37–38.

scribed as "*The Book of Shadows*", that contained the folklore tradition of the coven and all its magical rites, rituals and philosophical perspectives that gave him a wider body of material to publish in his writings. According to Gardner, the repeal of the English anti-Witchcraft laws in 1951 allowed the coven to cease its fear of prosecution and harassment, thereby permitting them to promote their continued existence and publish material from their secret "*Book of Shadows*" without fear of legal reprisal or police harassment. Consequently, Gardner began in the mid 1950s to give a series of press interviews on behalf of the coven and to ultimately write the book "*Witchcraft Today*" which was to become the textual foundation of the early Wiccan movement.[11]

Gardner invariably presented himself as the epitome of Enlightenment rationality in his writings, as illustrated by the quotation at the outset of this chapter. His work on Witchcraft was integrally linked with the ideal of reviving an authentic English religion, and claims of historical and cultural legitimacy were consistently justified and explained in Enlightenment styled narratives of facts, analysis and a loosely empirical historiography. He also sought the support of the academic establishment, most notably Margaret Murray of the Folklore Society, who was more than happy to co-operate due to the support Gardner's contention gave her thesis and to the fact that Gardner's description of Witchcraft history was critically based on her research.[12] According to Gardner, the rituals of the New Forest coven consisted of dances to promote fertility, in line with Murray's theory of Witchcraft being the surviving remnant of pre-Christian agrarian Witch cult, feasts of consecrated food and drink, and ceremonies designed to link the mind, soul and body with the spirit world and nature, however, the darker aspects of Murray's interpretation of the Witch cult were eschewed in favour of less confrontational images of pagan folklore.[13]

The Witches were described as venerating a god and goddess, with secret names only revealed to initiates. These divinities were believed to represent masculine and feminine essences in nature and humanity: the god image was held predominant in winter, whilst the goddess was held predominant in summer. The coven worked magic within a circle drawn with a consecrated sword or knife, believed to contain the spiritual energy the coven raised in ritual. They divided this circle into four cardinal points, each marked with a penta-

---

11. Adler, M. *Drawing Down the Moon.* pp 62; Bracelin, J. *Gerald Gardner: Witch.* p 192; Hutton, R. *Triumph of the Moon.* p 206. Purkiss, D. *The Witch in History.* pp 37–38.

12. Hutton, Ronald. *Triumph of the Moon.* pp 224–225.

13. Bracelin, J. *Gerald Gardner: Witch.* p 168–169; Gardner, G. *Witchcraft Today.* pp 17–32 & 51–62.

gram corresponding to the four elements. North, the element of earth, was believed to be the most sacred. The coven believed in reincarnation, practised nudity as a means of enhancing magical power and attempted to develop psychic and spiritual powers amongst their membership.[14] They were led by a high priestess, with a supporting priest, and the coven was divided into couples for ritual purposes. Training and initiation were always conducted between people of alternate gender. They divided the year into eight ritual cycles and used eight ritual tools, of which the most crucial was the knife, the censer and the rope. Trance and ecstasy through ritual, dance and song were critical components of their practise and they attempted to know their deities not as external manifestations of divinity, but personal expressions of the divinity within themselves.[15]

Gardner presented his description of the New Forest coven as an anthropological study of the surviving remnants of a Neolithic Witch cult. He also attempted to base his historical, cultural and social background for the coven on the Romantic Witchcraft histories of Charles Leland, Jules Michelet and Margaret Murray. He vigorously promoted his depiction of Witchcraft, which he named Wica from an Anglo Saxon term for a male magical practitioner. (After his death the term was changed to the more accurate Old English term "Wicca" but retained Gardner's pronunciation of the hard "c" instead of the Anglo-Saxon pronunciation of "ch.")[16]

After Gardner's announcement in the early 1950s of a surviving Witch cult and his subsequent attempts to revive the "Old Religion", many other occult practitioners also claimed to have had either hereditary lineage or to have found a surviving Witch cult and formed their own competing tradition. Most notable of these was Alex Sander's "Alexandrian" Witchcraft movement, named after both the ancient Egyptian seat of learning and as a pun of its

---

14. Gardner, G. *Witchcraft Today.* pp 20–22, 28–29 & 31–32.

15. Gardner, G. *Witchcraft Today.*

16. According to research by James Baker, while "Wicca" is the correct masculine term for the Anglo-Saxon "witch" Gardner's usage of the term is somewhat suspect and its historical significance is somewhat problematic. In particular, Gardner's original spelling of "Wica" was changed to support the contention that it referred to the craft of the wise instead of its pejorative description of illegitimate or evil magic. Furthermore, when the spelling was corrected to "Wicca" Gardner's pronunciation was used to ensure it would remain distinct from its negative historical connotations. While the original translation of "Craft of the Wise" has largely been abandoned by contemporary Wiccans, the new interpretation "to bend or shape" is also etymologically problematic. Baker, J. "White Witches: Historic Fact or Romantic Fantasy." p 177–178; Hutton, R. "The History of Pagan Witchcraft." pp 45–46.

founder's name. It was from here that the neo-Pagan movement spread across England and into America. Invariably, as these revivalist Witchcraft movements moved into new areas, people would claim hereditary ascendency of their own and come into conflict with the traditionalists of Gardnerian and, later on, Alexandrian Witchcraft.[17] Consequently, the newly emerging neo-Pagan movement was plagued by conflict, an often hostile press and vigorous opposition from multiple Christian and religious conservative organizations. However, despite these difficulties the concept of a surviving nature religion linked with the Witch crazes of the early modern period and the "Old Religion" of the neolithic, based on Murray's thesis, spread throughout much of the Anglophone world.[18]

The Critique of Wiccan History

There have been numerous critiques of Gardner's claim to have discovered and revived an authentic and empirically verifiable pagan witch-cult in England. Some of the most notable are Aiden Kelly's *Crafting the Art of Magic*, Ronald Hutton's *Triumph of the Moon* and Doreen Valiente's *The Rebirth of Witchcraft*. Whilst a full and detailed study of the veracity of Gardner's claims is beyond the scope of this book, it is necessary to examine the basis by which Gardner's model of a surviving Pagan Witch cult has been largely rejected by historians. At the most basic level, the similarities to Margaret Murray's now largely discredited thesis are such that the claims concerning the group's rituals being genealogically descendent remnants of a neolithic Pagan religion are dubious at best. Similarly, the extent to which Gardner rather blatantly inserted his own ideological, cultural and spiritualist ideals into his description of the New Forest coven, whilst claiming that his information was merely descriptive anthropological data, also lends support to a dismissal of his claims.[19] According to research by James Baker, even at the time of publication, the Folklore Society were extremely sceptical of Gardner's claims, having had no previous contact with any rituals, traditions or legends even remotely resembling Gardner's model of a surviving pagan Witch cult in their extensive collection of data. Furthermore, despite Gard-

---

17. Hutton, R. *The Triumph of the Moon*. pp 289–308.

18. Hutton, R. *The Triumph of the Moon*. pp 241–251.

19. Baker, J. "White Witches: Historic Fact and Romantic Fantasy." pp 184–185; Hutton, R. "The History of Pagan Witchcraft." pp 45–46 & 51–52.

ner's claims that the movement existed in secrecy, it is extremely dubious that any hereditary traditions of Witchcraft in the community would fail to leave traces in the broader community and in historical records. As Baker comments,

> If religious was as old and widespread as would be necessary for even a minority of the English and American claimants to have been connected with families with such initiatory practices, then it is inconceivable that their beliefs and symbols would have no echo in the historical record which contains so many other Pagan and magical practices and symbols. On the other hand, if traditional or "hereditary" Wicca was so small and secret as to escape *any* detections (and any professional historian will recognize how ephemeral, insignificant and localised a sect would have to be to escape all notice), then it is hardly possible that it could have been of any importance before Gardner and his successors blithely laid the whole thing open to the world.[20]

However, according to sources close to Gardner such as initiates Doreen Valiente and Ray Buckland, Gardner admitted that the rituals and belief systems he found in the New Forest coven were extremely fragmentary, thus requiring that he fill the gaps with the best historical, cultural and anthropological data that was available at the time in order to create a fully integrated religious movement. Occult writer Francis King claimed that Gardner had contacted a coven consisting of a hybridised mix of surviving folk tradition and middle class occultist and spiritualist traditions in New Forest, but he quickly grew bored with their rituals and decided to create a more romanticised, elaborate and mythologized version of his own.[21] Gardner also stated to confidants that the group's members were old and that he was afraid of the last remnants of the Old Religion dying out.[22] This belief that the movement was going to die out without drastic interference certainly appears to be an overriding concern on the part of Gardner. As he wrote in *Witchcraft Today*,

> I think we must say good-bye to the witch. The cult is doomed, I am afraid, partly because of modern conditions, housing shortage, the

---

20. Baker, J. "White Witches: Historic Fact or Romantic Fantasy." p 185.
21. King, Francis. *Ritual Magic in England*. London: Neville Spearman, 1970. pp 179.
22. Adler, M. *Drawing Down the Moon*. pp 65–66 & 83–85; Purkiss, D. *The Witch in History*. pp 9–40.

smallness of families, and chiefly by education. The modern child is not interested. He knows Witches are all bunk.[23]

Unlike much of the literature of the period, and the dominant historical interpretation of early modern Witchcraft in the Folklore Society, Gardner described his coven of Witches as being led by half hereditary Witches and half former Rosicrucians led by a prominent wealthy, well educated and highly regarded local lady. As such, it is supported by the description of the group put forward by noted occultist Francis King in his own description of surviving magical practices in rural England.[24] The fact that Gardner did not describe the Witch cult as a group of rural working class English under the leadership of a traditional cunning man or woman lends a certain degree of weight to his contention, by virtue of the fact that his description was not in accordance with dominant cultural trends of the time, nor was his claim in line with existing historical research on the nature of European Witches and Witchcraft.[25] This uncharacteristic distancing from the cultural stereotype of the cunning woman leading a cult of nature worshippers stands in sharp contrast to Gardner's more dubious and self aggrandising claims in his biography of two degrees and a PhD, amongst other bogus qualifications which were later revealed to be false by Doreen Valiente in the early 1980's.[26]

Further information relating to Gardner's claim of having contacted a group of practising Witches in the New England forest coven emerged in research conducted by Doreen Valiente in the1980's. After an exhaustive effort Valiente's research indicated that the Dorothy Clutterbuck described by Gardner was in fact a woman who lived under her married name of Dorothy Fordham. Furthermore, Valiente's research indicated that both Dorothy and Gardner were living in Highcliffe during the 1930's and that there was a functioning Rosicrucian theatre operating at New Forest at that time.[27] This material is supported by extensive research by historian Ronald Hutton; Dorothy Fordham/Clutterbuck lived at Highcliffe from the 1930's to the 1940's and died in 1951 at the age of seventy. From her family documents at Sommerset House, the family graves at Highcliffe Churchyard and local newspapers from the pe-

23. Gardner, G. *Witchcraft Today.* p 217.

24. King, F. *Ritual Magic in England.* p 179.

25. Hutton, R. *Triumph of the Moon.* p 207.

26. Valiente, Doreen. *The Rebirth of Witchcraft.* Washington: Valkyrie Press, 1989. pp 41–42.

27. Valiente, Doreen. "The Search for Old Dorothy." In Farrar, Janet & Stuart. *A Witch's Bible: The Complete Witch's Handbook.* Washington: Pheonix Publishing, 1996. pp 283–293.

riod in question, Hutton's research indicated that Fordham/Clutterbuck was a conservative Anglican and Tory party member, a devout Christian, and close friend and consultant to the local vicar. She spent a great deal of her time voluntary community organizations such as the Girl Guides, the British Legion and the Seamen's Mission. She was an enthusiastic proselytiser for the Conservative Party and was married to a Tory affiliated Justice of the Peace. She died in May of 1951 with her diaries and personal effects surfacing in the 1980's, primarily through Valiente's research. However, in these papers there was no overt mention of either Witchcraft or Gardner, though there is some reference to a divine presence in nature and images of fairies. [28] The predominance of these images in popular literature and English folklore suggest that, whilst significant, these representations of the English countryside are scarcely conclusive evidence for membership in a surviving hereditary Witchcult.[29]

The results of Hutton's detailed and extensive research suggested that "Either Dorothy Fordham/Clutterbuck lived one of the most amazing double lives in history, or else Gardner has played a cruelly funny trick on posterity by making it imagine the local epitome of respectability standing stark naked in

---

28. Hutton, R. "The History of Pagan Witchcraft." p 46; Hutton, R. *Triumph of the Moon*. pp 207–208.

29. Philip Heselton presents a counter argument that Dorothy's diaries in fact contained numerous but concealed references to witchcraft beliefs and practices. An example was that references to nature without obvious orthodox Anglican references implied a "strong and deeply felt pagan expression", likewise reference to a wicked fairy is taken to be a coded reference to a witch. Similarly, he argues that lines in verse referring to a numinous powerful being aligned with nature and goodness imply belief in a great nature Goddess. Heselton postulates that Dorothy Clutterbuck was in fact the founder of the New Forest Coven and that Gardner and his Rosicrucian contacts, such as Dafo, joined after they had already met at the Rosicrucian theatre. However, much of this material is extremely subjective and can be found in many non-occult writings of the period. The idealization of the natural world was also common current in the approach to nature presented in Romantic literature, which, even if many poets did have Pagan revivalist leanings, was certainly not based in any surviving neo-lithic Witchcult. Similarly, what evidence is presented by Heselton to argue that the movement was in fact composed of hereditary Witches, is largely based in hearsay and anecdotal evidence after Gardner had already established his movement in the 1950's and was in the process of publishing his claims to the general public. As a consequence, while Heselton's material develops a further level of complexity in attempts to determine the origins of Gardner's Wiccan movement, there is little evidence presented to undermine Hutton's major contentions. Despite his strongly pro-Wiccan stance Heselton is forced to admit that what evidence exists for the New Forest coven is circumstantial and is unproven. For more information see Heselton, Philip. *Wiccan Roots: Gerald Gardner and the Modern Pagan Revival*. Berkshire: Cheively, 2001. pp 110–115, 164–166 & 200–215.

the New Forest and summoning up covens".[30] An alternative figure for Gardner's informant was presented by Hutton in the name of Dafo, a known associate of Gardner who was both a practising Rosicrucian and a prominent member of the local spiritualist movement.[31] He claimed that Dafo, a leader in the local Rosicrucian theatre company, had a long history of associations with English occultists and was a long-term associate of Gardner. Hutton claimed that in all probability the actual source of Gardner's claims about the New Forest coven originated with his experiences with Dafo and was elaborated with Gardner's own knowledge of folklore, occultism and Dafo's own ideas concerning ritual and magical practice. However, the argument that the movement was a surviving remnant of a neo-lithic pagan Witch cult is extremely doubtful. Not only are there problems with the lineage presented by Gardner, the fact that the Witch cult presented by Gardner differs markedly from virtually any surviving historical data concerning English Paganism, the targets of Witch persecution, or the practices of traditional Cunning men and women, further undermines Gardner's contention.[32]

There have been many hypotheses put forward with regards to the probable nature of the group that Gardner may have come in contact with, if in fact he was in touch with a group identifying itself as a Witch cult at all. Hutton suggests that he may have also been in contact with the Pagan branch of the, nominally Christian, Woodcraft Chivalry movement. The movement was active in the area at the time and Gardner was friendly with some of its members. However, there is also evidence to suggest that the Pagans had left the movement by the early 1930s and there is little evidence of the group's continued existence in New Forest after 1935. Additionally, the kind of Paganism described by the Pagan branch of the Woodcraft Chivalry society is very different to the kind of Paganism described in the Wiccan movement.[33] Another model is Francis King's aforementioned argument that the movement described by Gardner was a hybridised mixture of English Folklore and ritual

30. Hutton, Ronald. "The History of Pagan Witchcraft." p 47.

31. Hutton, Ronald. *Triumph of the Moon*. pp 212.

32. There is extensive information available regarding English Witchcraft beliefs, folklore and trials, some of which has already been detailed in earlier chapters. For an overall synopsis see Baker, James. "White Witches: Historic Fact or Romantic Fantasy." pp 180–181. For more detailed information see, Thomas, K. *Religion and the Decline of Magic*; MacFarlane, A. *Witchcraft Prosecutions in Essex, 1560–1680;* Sharpe, J.A. *Instruments of Darkness: Witchcraft in Early Modern England.*

33. Hutton, R. "The History of Pagan Witchcraft." p 47; Hutton, R. *Triumph of the Moon.* pp 162–167.

occult practices of the local Rosicrucian and spiritualist community is another plausible model. Francis King, in his history of ritual magic, describes a conversation in 1953 with the occultist Louis Wilkinson who claimed that in the late 1930s or early 1940s he was in contact with members of the New Forest Coven.[34] He also confirmed Gardner's story of a united ritual by English Wiccans to ward off German invasion.[35] He also gave details of the ritual, stating that the Witches rubbed bear fat on their bodies, to ward off the cold, and that they used narcotic mushrooms to experience visions.[36] However, Hutton disputes this claim on the basis that it is dependent on 20 year old second-hand information, that bear fat is not readily available in England and that the information provided on the activities and members of the New Forest coven appears extremely vague and unconvincing.[37]

It seems that the only thing that can be stated with any certainty is that Gardner possibly could have been involved with an existing coven in New Forest, and that this coven may have been involved with a wide range of possible movements and individuals about which there is little information. In other words, without major new sources coming to light, little can be said about the actual veracity of Gardner's claims, except that it may be possible to interpret the history and rituals Gardner ascribed to the Wiccan movement as a means of searching for influences and origins for the material Gardner utilised in the construction of Wicca. This difficulty in verifying Gardner's claims, or indeed many of the historical claims made by modern Pagans based on Gardner's hypothesis, has led to a certain degree of anxiousness in the neo-Pagan community. While Gardner spoke to his associates about the fragmented nature of the rituals and his need to borrow from his anthropological and ritual magic background, there has been a certain degree of questioning as to whether Gardner had in fact been in contact with any hereditary Witches at all.[38] Certainly, Gardner's attempt to credit himself with a PhD, and his portrayal of Witchcraft as an authentic existing system based on anthropological empirical research, was a rather shameless way of gaining credibility for his newly formed Wiccan movement. It could be argued that from its very inception the neo-Pagan movement was grounded in a post-modernist deliberate blurring of the lines between fiction and reality, but here Gardner's attempt to gain credibility is intentionally set within Enlightenment discourses of his-

---

34. King, F. *Ritual Magic in England*. pp 179–185.
35. Bracelin, J. *Gerald Gardner: Witch*. p 167.
36. King, F. *Ritual Magic in England*. pp 176–181.
37. Hutton, R. *Triumph of the Moon*. pp 214–215.
38. Purkiss, D. *The Witch in History*. p 40; Valiente, D. *An ABC of Witchcraft*. p 157.

torical legitimacy and his claim to authenticity is intentionally oriented towards the language of mainstream interpretations of empirical research, as the quote opening this chapter illustrates.

None the less, despite the apparent unsupportable basis of Gardner's thesis and the various neo-Pagan responses to the issues raised by this, Wicca does appear to have a traceable history in English history and culture. This history and the origins of the myths, rituals and historical claims of the Wiccan movement are extremely important in understanding contemporary Wicca's socio-cultural and ideological construction. The first aspect of this is the appropriation of the Witchcraft history of Margaret Murray and its context within the integration of Romantic and Enlightenment narratives by the Folklore Society. The second is tied to England's long history of occultism and ritual magic.

The Folklore Society and Wiccan History

Gardner's historical claims and the rituals and symbols with which he characterised his Wiccan movement were, to a large extent, products of the Folklore Society. Of particular importance in the construction of the Wiccan movement was the extent to which the theory of Pagan survivals had come to dominate perceptions of folkloric origins and ritual. This was especially important in the conclusions reached via the comparative methodology developed by Sir James Frazer and utilised by the Folklore Society membership in the study of Witchcraft and Paganism. There were several reasons for this fixation on the concept of Pagan survival in the Folklore Society. Firstly, there was the overarching structure of the English Romantic aesthetic and its threefold shift, from a perception of the past located in Pagan Greece and Rome, to that of a Christian Merry England and then finally to a focus on indigenous Celtic and Anglo-Saxon Paganism. The adoption of the evolutionary method by the Folklore Society, in which the folklore of England's rural sector was perceived to offer an insight into England's primordial past, led to a perception of a static and timeless English countryside which contained cultural fossils of a England's Pagan origins. This perception of a timeless and eternal countryside existing as a window in England's cultural evolution, was central to the construction of the English rural sector's beliefs and folklore existing as cultural fossils from a prehistoric Pagan past.

It was within this context of a perception of a static and eternal countryside perceived to contain the cultural fossils of a primordial Pagan past that the Folklore Society operated and developed its unique comparative approach to the study of folklore and ritual. Of particular importance in the development of this methodology was the attempt by many members of the Folklore Society, in particular Sir James Frazer and Sir Edward Tylor, to elevate the study of folklore to that of a science.[39] It was felt by several prominent individuals in the Folklore Society, in particular the aforementioned Tylor and Frazer as well as George Stocking, George Gomme, Andrew Lang and Edwin Hartland, that by adopting the language of natural sciences and cultural evolution combined with a systemic basis of comparative analysis, the study of folklore would be able to achieve credibility as an academic discipline. If, as Tylor and Frazer argued, there is an evolutionary or teleological development from magic to religion and then to a deist scientific rationality, then, by studying the world views, religious beliefs and folklore of history and societies deemed to be representative of Western civilizations past, a scientific basis for understanding human cultural and philosophical evolution could be found. Thus, through the adoption of the language of science, the study of folklore could move from a hermeneutic discipline to a predictive science that could determine universal truths about human nature, its cultural evolution and the role of belief and folklore in history.[40]

In the long term, this attempt to transform the study of folklore into the premiere science of culture failed to gain credence within the academic community. By the 1920s, the study of folklore as a science was increasingly absorbed into the more scientifically respectable disciplines of anthropology and archaeology that had, by that stage, abandoned the notion of cultural fossils. However, at the turn of the century, the idea of comparative studies of folklore had a great deal of popular support and the work of Frazer, in particular, had an immense impact on the perception of folklore and the role of mythology in popular culture.[41] The methodology used by the Folklore Society was essentially a process by which the folklore, ritual and beliefs of the English rural sector were collected, interpreted and assigned meaning as cultural fossils from which contemporary urban England was descended. Whilst this process did involve a broad ranging systemic and empirical collection of folklore, dances, festivals, rituals and legends, there were continual metholog-

---

39. Bennett, G. "Geologists and Folklorists." pp 25–26; Hutton, R. *Triumph of the Moon.* pp 112–113.

40. Bennett, G. *Geologists and Folklorists.* pp 25–28; Greenwood, Susan. "The British Occult Sub-culture" in Lewis, James (Ed.) *Magical Religion and Modern Witchcraft.* New York: State University of New York Press, 1996. p 178.

41. Bennet, G. *Geologists and Folklorists.* p 34; Hutton, R. *Triumph of the Moon.* p 113; Hutton, R. "The Background to Pagan Witchcraft." p 27.

ical criticisms raised by the academic community. The primary criticism of the Folklore Society related to the charge that within its methodological approach there was little room for the individuals under scrutiny to speak for themselves.[42] It was assumed that the people were simple and ignorant of the true significance and origins of their rituals, folklore and beliefs. From this perspective, it was only the interpretive skill of the folklorist that could actually attribute significance to festival, ritual and legend, and thus bring to light its true meaning and origins.[43] The problems inherent in any interpretive, cross cultural comparison, and the disregard of the rural population's beliefs and histories of their own socio-cultural activity, led to many of the rituals, festivals and legends being interpreted out of context from the role they played in the societies from which they originated. This difficulty was compounded by the problem that if the rituals, folklore and symbolism used by communities were cultural fossils in a perceived static countryside, there was little room for the contemporary development of ritual and folklore. Similarly, the approach of the folklore society did not account for the massive role played by events like the Reformation, the Enclosure Movement or the Industrial Revolution in the shaping of folklore and community events and festivals. Nor did this Romantic assumption allow room in the Folklore Society's research for the continual process of change, and socio-cultural and economic transformation of communities residing in the English countryside. Similarly, this methodological approach allowed little possibility for expressions of the will, understanding, or self-determination of the rural English population to express their own interpretations of folklore, ritual and legends.[44]

The second criticism of the Folklore Society's methodology and practice related to the extent to which some practitioners would falsify data and take it out of its context in order to conform to the theoretical basis of comparative analysis. Margaret Murray, for example, was savagely criticised for her use of material from England and parts of France to account for Witchcraft across the European continent.[45] Frazer was also criticized for his routine rewriting

42. Hutton, R. *Triumph of the Moon.* pp 112, 116–117, 119 & 127–131.

43. Hutton, R. *Triumph of the Moon.* pp 117 & 127–131.

44. Bennett, G. "Folklore Studies and the English Rural Myth." pp 77–90; Hutton, R. *Triumph of the Moon.* pp 120 & 127–131.

45. Cohn, N. *Europe's Inner Demons.* pp 105–106 & 126–130; Henningsen, G. "Ladies from Outside." In Ankarloo, B. & Henningsen, G. *Early Modern European Witchcraft.* Oxford: Clarendon Press, 1990, pp 191; Hutton, R. *Triumph of the Moon.* pp 198–200; Hutton, Ronald. *Pagan Religions of the British Isles: Their Nature and Legacy.* Blackwell: Oxford University Press, 1991. pp 308–316.

of source material for use in his conclusions.[46] However, despite these criticisms, Frazer and Murray's work was to prove influential in the early part of the twentieth century and were central in influencing public thought relating to the nature of Witches, Paganism and Witchcraft. In this light, Gardner's membership within the Folklore Society is especially significant, as it was not only the source of his construction of Witchcraft as a surviving fertility/nature cult, but it also gave rise to his methodology of interpretation in which material was taken, reinterpreted and altered to suit specific theoretical conclusions.

Frazer's work integrated both Romantic and Enlightenment interpretations of culture, society and history in Western culture. From one perspective Frazer, was centrally focused on the concept of cultural authenticity and he drew heavily on the Romantic fixation on the countryside in creating his landscape of English folklore as fossils of the past. According to Mary Beard, Frazer's *Golden Bough* represented a "Journey through the underworld of belief in which the familiar rituals of the English countryside were integrally linked with savage and foreign rites in an exciting and unsettling way".[47] This perception was typical of the Romantic approach to culture, where the everyday was enhanced and linked with the sublime, the anti-rational, the natural world and was centrally fixated on the idea of cultural authenticity and autonomy as a source of national and cultural identity.

Alternatively, Frazer's work could be perceived as an Enlightenment narrative; deriving reason, order and meaning from the primeval chaos of superstition and folklore. Frazer's strong secularist and anti-religious orientation as well as his vocal support of Tylor's attempts to discredit religion and create a more rational basis for the social and cultural order of English society, also supported this perspective.[48] One of the central arguments of the *Golden Bough* was the claim that ancient peoples shared the belief in a dying and reviving God, who represented the animating spirit of fertility and growth, and was manifested in the ritual sacrifice of kings and tribal leaders when their powers failed.[49] This was a prominent theme in Margaret Murray's work, *The*

---

46. Leach, Edmund. "Golden Bough or Gilded Twig." *Daedalus.* Spring 1961. pp 374–376.

47. Beard, Mary. "Frazer, Leach and Virgil : The Popularity (and Unpopularity) of 'The Golden Bough.'" *Comparative Sudies in Society and History.* 34, 1992. pp 203–204.

48. Ackerman, Robert. *J.G.Frazer : His Life and Work.* Cambridge: Cambridge University Press, 1987. pp 1–32, 97 & 213; Hutton, Ronald. *Triumph of the Moon.* p 112.

49. Frazer, J.G. *The Golden Bough: A Study in Magic and Religion.* London: Macmillan Press, 1974(1922). pp 397, 508, 515 & 705. The theme of a dying and revived God forms one of the central claims of the book regarding the symbolic significance of peasant ritu-

Witch Cult of Western Europe. Frazer's attempts here to link Christianity with what he held to be a superstitious and erroneous belief system was in many ways an Enlightenment attack against Christianity.[50] From this perspective, Frazer's continued support of Enlightenment ideals of rationalism, his support of attempts to move the study of folklore into a science, his confirmed atheism and his attacks, along with Tylor and Lang, against what he believed to be the superstitious and unsubstantiated aspects of Christianity, suggest that Frazer was firmly oriented towards Enlightenment ideals of rationalism and science. However, at the same time Frazer's work was centrally located within Romantic discourse. His focus upon cultural authenticity, the centrality of the countryside as an antidote to the ills of industrialism and his continued search through the past for authentic cultural origins and self knowledge, all serve to locate him within the context of Romantic conceptions of culture.[51]

What this integration of Romantic and Enlightenment narratives suggests is that, for Frazer, they were integrally entwined together in his exploration of folklore, symbolism and ritual. Frazer, in particular, is a prime example of the means by which the Folklore Society and Romantic histories of paganism illustrate the ambiguities of Romanticism and its often complex yet integrated relationship with versions of Enlightenment thought. Furthermore, this integrated structure of Romantic and Enlightenment themes was an integral part of the Witchcraft histories developed by Margaret Murray and appropriated by Gerald Gardner. It was in this context that Margaret Murray attempted to use the Frazerian comparative method of folklore studies in her research into Witchcraft history.

Margaret Murray's Witch Cult

Murray's approach was to re-examine the trial records and other surviving literature and folklore of medieval and early modern Europe relating to Witch-

---

als in rural Italy and forms the basis for the claim that there are universal symbolic themes behind mythology and folklore that was to become so important in the work of Jung. The numbered pages refer to specific instances of reference to rituals of dying and revived Gods, a theme which is also prominent in Murray's thesis.

50. Hutton, R. *Triumph of the Moon.* pp 113–117.

51. It is worth noting that some Christians interpreted the central mythology of a dying and resurrected God as evidence that Christianity was the highest and most complete expression of a theme through which God had expressed himself throughout history.

craft beliefs and practices. She then attempted to compare these beliefs, historical records and folklore in order to find patterns of beliefs and rituals, and interpreted her findings via Frazer's theory of pre-Christian society being dominated by sacrificial fertility cults. Her central argument was that what early modern Witchcraft literature represented was in fact a misinterpretation of a pre-Christian fertility cult of the kind described by Frazer in *The Golden Bough*.[52] Her work followed two basic assumptions. Firstly, she believed that Witchcraft beliefs could not be studied in isolation from their cultural, social and historical context. Secondly, she felt that the writings and folklore regarding Witchcraft could neither be interpreted literally nor dismissed as superstitious nonsense or propaganda.[53]

Murray's first findings ascertained that belief in Witchcraft and magic were an integral part of medieval and early modern European society. She also found that the general populace openly feared magic and Witchcraft, and that people often freely admitted to Witchcraft and magical practices without forced confession or torture. In this light, Murray concluded that there really were people practicing Witchcraft in early modern European society. However, as opposed to representations of Witchcraft as devil worship, which was the dominant perception of Witchcraft by the established religious and secular authorities of the early modern period, Murray postulated that the people described as Witches were in fact participants in a highly organized and clandestine Pagan fertility cult.[54]

Operating from the assumption of an existing pre-Christian organized Pagan cult surviving into the early modern period, Murray applied a number of theoretical principles developed by Frazer in *The Golden Bough* as a means of ascertaining the nature and characteristics of the symbolism, religious principles and socio-cultural structure of its belief systems and practices. Murray's analysis emphasized the importance of fertility and sexuality in rituals, as well as a close connection with nature and the prominence of agrarian based rituals and beliefs. The focus of the religion was based around a fertility God/Goddess of birth and renewal whose ritualistic life cycle was a metaphor for the cycle of life and passage of the seasons.[55]

---

52. Adler, M. *Drawing Down the Moon*. p 47; Hutton, R *Triumph of the Moon*. p 195; MacFarlane, A. *Witchcraft Prosecutions in Essex, 1560–1680: A Sociological Analysis*. London: Harper and Row, 1970. pp 16–18; Murray, Margaret. *The Witch Cult in Western Europe*. Oxford: Clarendon Press, 1962(1921). pp 12, 233 & 236.

53. Ginzberg, Carlo. *Ecstasies: Deciphering the Witch's Sabbath*. London: Penguin Books, 1992. pp 20–25. Murray, M. *The Witch Cult in Western Europe*. pp 1–20.

54. Adler, M. *Drawing Down the Moon*. pp 46–49; Murray, M. *The Witch Cult in Western Europe*. pp 12, 233 & 236.

55. Adler, M. *Drawing Down the Moon*. p 47.

This polytheistic god image was manifested in the two faced horned god known as Janus, Mithras or Dianus in equal masculine and feminine aspects that served as the spiritual focus of Pagan cults across Europe. According to Murray, Witches practiced a joyous religion based upon regular festivals of feasting, singing, dancing and shamanic visions. Witchcraft was closely linked with herbalism and magical ritual, and played a strong role in bonding together localized communities. Murray also perceived the Witch cult as multi-classed, incorporating all sectors of society, from the nobility to the rural peasantry.[56]

In Murray's construct, she saw Christian inquisitors and secular authorities engaged in a massive campaign of propaganda and persecution, designed to demonize these Pagan beliefs and represent them as an evil onslaught against the established social and moral order. The Pagan god became represented as the Christian devil, fairies became demons, festivals became orgies and dark Sabbaths, and the Witches were represented as evil people who sacrificed their soul for the sake of transitory wealth and power.[57] Murray states little about the nature or necessity of this representation of early modern Witchcraft by Church and secular authorities. Similarly, the political implications of her analysis in terms of racial, gender and class conflicts in the context of early modern and medieval society are also largely ignored. Operating within the confines of a Frazerian comparative analysis, Murray's work was almost exclusively focused on the representation of symbols relating to fertility and nature as an expression of the ritual and folklore pertaining to agrarian life within the context of the English rural experience.[58]

Whilst a groundbreaking and original work, much of Murray's thesis had already been postulated by earlier Romantic scholars and it is certain that Murray drew upon this earlier material in creating her thesis. Central amongst these Romanticist inspired historical approaches is the work of Jules Michelet, writing in the mid nineteenth century. Michelet's analysis of early modern Witchcraft was based extensively on his perceptions of the oppression of the peasantry by a corrupt and oppressive nobility and Church hierarchy, combined with an idealism relating to the moral supremacy and authenticity of an agrarian lifestyle. Michelet's book, "*La Sorciere*", portrays Witchcraft as a symbolic protest by a dis-empowered peasantry against an oppressive social order. He describes the Sabbaths as festivals where peasants would gather to-

56. Murray, M. *The Witch Cult in Western Europe.* pp 12, 140, 233, 236.

57. Murray, M. *The Witch Cult in Western Europe.* pp 140–144.

58. Kephart. M J. "Rationalists vs Romantics among Scholars of Witchcraft." In Marwick, Max (Ed.) *Witchcraft & Sorcery.* London: Penguin Books, 1970. pp 327–328.

gether to perform ancient Pagan rituals and blend satirical farces directed against the clergy with songs and festivities. He claims that by the fifteenth century this increasingly open defiance of the existing social order became epitomized by a "Black Mass" worshiping the ancient Pagan gods against the work of the Church. At the centre of this ritual he placed the image of a priestess described as having "A face like Medea, a beauty born of suffering, a tragic, feverish gaze, with a torrent of black untamable hair falling as chance takes it, like waves of serpents. Perhaps on top crowns of vervain, like ivy from tombs, like violets of death".[59] At this festival, a statue of a horned fertility god with a large erect penis was constructed to represent a combination of the Pagan god Pan and the Christian Satan as an image of the servant in revolt against an oppressive Church and nobility.

This image of a horned god, combined with the prominent role of the priestess, was believed, by Michelet, to represent a metaphor of the peasantry's deep concern with nature, fertility and germination in their daily lives, and was also a site of protest against the absence of a connection with nature by the dominant social and religious order of early modern Europe. For Michelet, like many other French Romantic scholars, the key to understanding the significance of Witch gatherings was political resistance against an oppressive social, religious and political system, and the servicing of spiritual and social issues not met by the established social and religious order of the time.[60] While Murray did not particularly focus on political issues directly in her theory of early modern European Witchcraft, there were strong political themes against the evils of industrialization, alienation from nature and Christian conservatism implicit in her work. These Romantic themes were to become critical in the cultural configuration of Gardner's Wiccan movement and its many offshoots in the post war era.

Another major influence on the work of both Murray and Gardner was that of Charles Leland. Writing at the turn of the century, just prior to Murray's embarkation into English folklore, Leland was an amateur folklorist and a member of the Folklore Society who argued for the survival of ancient Paganism and associated Paganism with the accusation of Witchcraft in early modern Europe. In Leland's *Aradia, Or the Gospel of the Witches*, he claimed to have discovered a member of a surviving neolithic Witch cult called Madalena. He also claimed that she could "Astonish even the learned by her

59. Michelet, J. *La Sorciere*. pp 127–128 & 138.
60. Hutton, R. *Triumph of the Moon*. pp 138–140; Purkiss, D. *The Witch in History*. 34–36.

knowledge of Latin Gods".[61] Leland represented the figure of Madalena as a repository of eternal Pagan wisdom and magical knowledge. Furthermore, he claimed that through her assistance he gained access to a secret text called "*The Gospel of the Witches*". The "*Gospel*" tells of a cult worshiping a figure called Diana the Queen of Witches and of her union with Lucifer the Sun from which a daughter named Aradia is born. Following the path laid out by Michelet, Leland describes Witches as being a source of rebellion against the corrupt Church and state by the rural peasantry and disenfranchised.[62]

There is a remarkable similarity between Gardner and Leland's work. Not only does Gardner utilize Leland's mythical informant as a source of legitimacy for his claims about Witchcraft, he also associates this figure as a repository of timeless wisdom and ancient magical knowledge. Both Leland and Gardner have their informant give them a sacred book containing the secrets of Witchcraft and magic buried for centuries and both authors claim the mythical informant secretly initiated them into a coven of hereditary Witches whose line stretches into antiquity.[63] Gardner and Leland also shared a fundamental representation of the Witchcraft persecutions and corresponding mythology of Early Modern Witchcraft, being the result of a Christian persecution against surviving Pagans. For both writers, the figure of revelation, nature and wisdom is a woman who must be brought to light via the academic discipline and research of the male investigator.[64]

In relation to the work of Murray, Leland represented a long held Romantic tradition of belief in the timeless wisdom of Pagan antiquity, a reconnection of humanity with nature and Witches as a source of social dissidence against the forces of modernity. Murray drew upon these themes in her research into early modern European Witchcraft, but unlike Leland or Michelet's approach' Murray systemically utilized empirical evidence to support her claims and operated from what was, at the time, an academically credible methodology of folklore research. Essentially, Murray's research was an application of Frazerian method upon the Romantic representation of Paganism and Witchcraft as an antidote to the ills of modernity, a reconnection with nature and rebellion against a culturally repressive Church, with her research

---

61. Purkiss, D. *The Witch in History.* pp 36–37; Hutton, R. *Triumph of the Moon.* pp 141–148.

62. Hutton, R. *Triumph of the Moon.* pp 141–148; Leland. Charles. *Aradia Or the Gospel of the Witches.* London: Pheonix Publishing, 1990. p 111; Purkiss, D. *The Witch in History.* p 36.

63. Purkiss, D. *The Witch in History.* pp 37–38.

64. Purkiss, D. *The Witch in History.* pp 38; Leland. Charles. *Aradia.* pp 111–112.

being empirically based on the comparatively small amount of evidence available at the time.[65]

Murray's hypothesis represented a major change in the way in which Witchcraft has been perceived, in both academic research and popular culture. Prior to Murray's work, the history of Witchcraft in academic circles had been dominated by Enlightenment interpretations that promoted the strength of reason and science against superstition and religion. As stated in the second chapter, Elliot Rose rather flippantly describes these discourses of Witchcraft beliefs as the "Bluff" school, which perceived Witchcraft beliefs to be purely ignorant superstition, and the "anti-sadducee" school, which described Witchcraft as a threat manifested in real existent satanic cults engaging in vicious anti-human practices.[66] Alongside these two perspectives were the Romantic interpretations of Romantic folklorists and historians, such as Jules Michelet and Jakob Grimm who perceived Witchcraft as the surviving remnants of pre-Christian Paganism. Murray's work reinvigorated this interpretation through its legitimization of these Romantic interpretations of Witchcraft history, by applying their claims in the context of Enlightenment narratives of empirical validity.[67]

Murray's work also brought to light the work of related historians, like Jules Michelet, whose more politically orientated and anti-modernist representation of medieval Witchcraft brought new depth to interpretations of early modern Witchcraft from both feminist and agrarian Romantic perspectives.[68] Most of the feminist interpretations of the Witch persecutions during the early modern period owe at least an indirect debt to Michelet and Murray's representation of Witchcraft as a marginalized sector of society linked to femininity and nature, in opposition to a patriarchal and oppressive Christianity and secular government.[69] Of particular significance is the work of Barbara Ehrenreich and Deidre English in their examination of Witchcraft accusations. In their analysis, they argued that the wellspring of Witchcraft accusations was the attempt by the male medical profession to discredit feminine natural med-

---

65. Ginzberg, C. *Ecstasies : Deciphering the Witch's Sabbath.* p 9; Hutton, Ronald. *Triumph of the Moon.* p 195.

66. Rose, E. *A Razor for a Goat.* pp 7–10.

67. Hutton, R. *Triumph of the Moon.* pp 199–201; Hutton, R. "The Background to Pagan Witchcraft." p 33.

68. There is an ongoing debate throughout feminist circles relating to the legitimacy and veracity of these Witchcraft histories and their relevance to contemporary gender based issues. This is discussed in detail in chapter 5.

69. Adler, M. *Drawing Down the Moon.* pp 56–59; Purkiss, D. *The Witch in History.* pp 38–39.

icines and midwifery through claims the practice of midwifery was linked to Paganism and Diabolism, an hypothesis which relies almost exclusively on the work of Murray and Michelet.[70]

The means by which the ambiguous term "Witch" was constructed as a surviving fertility cult, the association of Paganism with devil worship as Christian propaganda against surviving Paganism, the association between Paganism and nature and even details like the dual God/Goddess and the role of the priests and priestesses, were drawn directly from Murray's work. Murray's work was also widely influential through its adoption by sectors of the English Romantic literary movement in England and by many English occultists, particularly with successor orders of the Golden Dawn. Here her work was interpreted as an alternate narrative of the rise of modernity, a cultural manifestation of a sense of eternal English national identity and the decline of Medieval Catholicism. These trends in English culture were to prove central in the formation of Gardner's Wiccan movement. They integrated the long tradition of English ritual magic and secret societies within the context of Romantic culture and also pertained closely to a revival of English nationalism. The histories produced by the Folklore Society, particularly the work of Margaret Murray, served to legitimate the interpretation of English culture and English national identity as rooted deep within the folklore and beliefs of the English countryside. They gave the network of symbols and images of Romantic culture and ideology a basis in Enlightenment interpretations of historical legitimacy. Furthermore, these Romantic folkloric histories united two predominant epistemological themes in English society of the Enlightenment and Romanticism in the one historical representation. This ambiguity was to become an integral part of the Wiccan movement's location as a right wing nationalist movement based in Romantic cultural motifs and an ambiguous relationship to scientific rationality and knowledge. However, there is another aspect to the development of Gardner's Wiccan movement that had an immense impact on the structure of Wiccan rituals and beliefs, as well as the ambiguous relationship with science and social conservatism in the early Wiccan movement. This was the relationship between Romanticism, the Enlightenment and the long tradition of English ritual magic and secret societies.

---

70. Kephart, M. J. "Rationalists vs. Romantics." p 327; Purkiss, D. *The Witch in History,* 1996. pp 19–20 & 34–36.

5

WITCHCRAFT AND THE
EUROPEAN OCCULT MILIEU

One of the most critical cultural trends in the formation of twentieth century neo-Paganism is the European tradition of learned ceremonial magic. There is an extremely long and obscure history of occultism in Western Europe. The very secretiveness of its practice and the penchant for grandiose historical claims amongst its practitioners makes historical study extremely difficult. However, despite large gaps in historical evidence there are certain elements of occult history that can be stated with a degree of certainty. There is also a definite traceable link between the broad occultist revival in nineteenth century Europe and Gardner's appropriation of Masonic, Rosicrucian and Theosophist ritual and symbolism in the Wiccan movement.

The origins of eighteenth and nineteenth century ritual magic in Europe can be traced back to the appropriation of Cabbalist and ancient Greek philosophy by sectors of the Christian Church and the burgeoning scientific movement in the twelfth and thirteenth century. In particular, elements of the Church on the Iberian Peninsula led by Ramon Lull, attempted to use the Jewish ritual of Cabbala, combined with Aristotelian and Pythagorean thought, as a means to better understand the will of God and the nature of the natural and supernatural world.[1] Spain in the thirteenth and fourteenth centuries was dominated by three main philosophical and religious traditions. Catholic Christianity was predominant over most of Spain but much was still dominated by Islam. At this time, Spain also contained the largest and most influential population of Judaism outside of Palestine. The religious and philosophical context Lull operated within, whilst being dominated by Christian thought, was heavily influenced by the rich and sophisticated philosophy, art and science of the Spanish Moslems. Similarly, the Spanish Jews had spent a

---

1. Skinner, Stephen. Divination by Geomancy. London: Routledge, 1980. pp 103–106; Yates, Frances. *The Occult Philosophy in the Elizabethan Age.* London: Routledge, 1999(1979). p 9.

great deal of energy developing Judaic philosophy and ritual and, in the late thirteenth century, had increasingly become involved in mystical practices, particularly the Cabbala.[2]

Cabbala means literally "Tradition". Its practitioners believe that its rituals and practices originated from the time when God gave "The Law" to Moses. The underlying basis behind the esoteric tradition was that a second revelation, given by God to Moses, contained the secret meaning of "The Law" which could only be interpreted via the mastering of a secret language of codes and calculations. This second revelation, and the means to interpret it, was passed down orally through initiates in various Judaic mystical traditions. The text of scripture was interpreted as containing a holy language through which God could speak directly to humanity and this language was the language of creation itself. In the Judaic tradition, the application of Cabbala was perceived as a meditative exercise designed to create a more in-depth knowledge and interpretation of the scriptures. However, it could also be interpreted as a form of mystical sorcery, but such practise was specifically forbidden within the Torah. In this sense, the practice of Cabbala was to some extent frowned upon by the mainstream Judaic tradition. However, it was also understood to be a mystical cult based extensively in the Torah and the Hebrew language which was believed to represent the holy language through which God had communicated to the Jewish people. This led to a rather ambiguous perception of Cabbalist studies by both Jews and Christians. Some felt it represented a degradation or corruption of scripture, whilst for others it was interpreted as a theosophical tradition that could find hidden and universal truths in the study of scripture.[3]

Lull, like many other Christian philosophers of Spain during the thirteenth and fourteenth centuries, utilized an almost theosophical interpretation of the Jewish Cabbala. He perceived it to be a kind of mysticism in which hidden meanings could be drawn from religious texts via elaborate manipulation of the Hebrew alphabet, mathematics and geometry, thus linking aspects of science, as a source of truth in nature, with the truth of divine revelation.[4] It was in this context that Lull conceived the rather tolerant, for the era, theosophi-

---

2. Hillgarth, J.N. *Ramon Lull and Lullism in Fourteenth Century France*. London: Oxford University Press, 1972. p 244; Yates, Francis. *The Occult Philosophy in the Elizabethan Age*. London: Routledge. 1979. pp 9–10.

3. Bernal, Martin. *Black Athena*. London: Vintage Books, 1987. pp 148–150; Hutton, R. *The Triumph of the Moon*. p 82; MacKenzie, Norman. *Secret Societies*. London: Aldis Books, 1997. pp 134–135; Singer, C. *The Legacy of Israel*. Oxford: Oxford University Press, 1927. p 274; Yates, F. *The Occult Philosophy*. pp 2–3.

4. Yates, F. *The Occult Philosophy*. p 9.

cal concept that by integrating the philosophy and mathematics of the Greeks via the Arabs with Cabbalist methodology, in the context of Christian faith and mysticism, hidden meanings about God, scripture, faith and the natural world could be discovered for the benefit of Christendom. The central driving concepts behind Lull's theoretical approach were the theory of the four elements, the doctrine of emanations and the magical/spiritual significance attached to divine or true names by which the spirits, demons and angels could be commanded. Lull also attempted to integrate his mystical occultism with astrology, interpreting the signs of the Zodiac and the positions of the planets in accordance with the doctrine of the elements and their perceived relationship with the physical world.[5] Interestingly enough, Lull was against the use of astrology for the creation of horoscopes or fortune telling, as he believed that this represented a form of determinism that challenged the will of God. Instead, Lull utilised astrology as a means of perceiving correspondences between the physical world and the heavens from which one could draw meaning from events. Lull believed that this was an expression of Greek Platonic thought in which the events, meanings and actions of the physical world were expressions of the pure ideas generated in the heavens, the realm of ideas in Platonic thought.[6]

The Cabbala, as interpreted by Lull and his associates in thirteenth and fourteenth century Spain, was centrally dependent upon the concept of "Sephiroth" or emanations of the divine. It was believed that all beings were emanations of the divine source, God. This theory was in itself an outgrowth of Gnostic influences on Christian theology in medieval Europe. The angels were believed to exist close to the will and nature of God. Subsidiary emanations were less close to God and more corrupted by the material world. As the remoteness from God increased so did the memory and knowledge of God become less immediate and more vague. The philosophy of emanations spread over Europe amongst the intelligentsia during the fourteenth and fifteenth centuries, often combined with variations of the Cabbalist method, as appropriated by Lull and others, as a mystical practice. This expansion was necessarily closely linked with the growing popularity of Greek philosophy in its many forms, especially the doctrine of neo-Platonism.[7]

In 1495 a prominent expert in Christian Cabbalist ritual, Pico Della Mirandolla, followed in the footsteps of Lull and integrated Cabbalist technique with Christian and Greek philosophy in order to prove the existence of Christ

---

5. Yates, F. *The Occult Philosophy.* p 10–11.

6. Yates, F. *The Occult Philosophy.* pp 9–15 & 17–19.

7. Wallis, R. *Neo-Platonism.* Charles Scribner: New York, 1972. pp 61–69, 144–149; Yates, F. *The Occult Philosophy.* pp 2–6, 11–14.

as the Son of God via magical ritual and meditation on scripture. In the process he, like Lull before him, developed an integrated mystical system of Pythagorean geometry combined with Jewish Cabbala and created a system of hermetic occult magic in which one was believed to be able to control the natural and supernatural world via the manipulation of numbers, geometric forms and mystical symbols derived from the Hebrew alphabet. Mirandolla integrated the neo-Platonic mythos of Renaissance Christianity with the cult of angels and emanations to make a complex integrated magical system for the control of nature and the spirit world. Into this matrix he integrated elements of popular folk magic and figures from folklore, but interpreted them in terms of the Christian mythos. He also believed in the universal significance of the four elements, with a fifth element of spirit manifested in the symbol of the Pentacle that also represented the human body with its five limbs and was used to represent the five wounds of Christ in early Christian mythology.[8]

It was at this point that many of the fundamental characteristics of European occultism formed; the circle divided into four elements with each marked by a pentacle or holy symbol; the belief in a controllable supernatural world of angels, demons and spirits which corresponded to essential aspects of existence; a love of magical ritual combined with complicated manipulation of scriptures, mathematical formulae and alchemy. Over the next few centuries, other writers integrated into this mystical milieu the Zodiac, elements of the burgeoning scientific movement and magical practices. Nevertheless, the overall ritual, philosophical and epistemological basis of European occultism was established in the fifteenth Century.[9]

Due to the limitations of space, a thorough study of European occultism until the nineteenth century is impossible here. However, there are several critical issues raised by the development of occult practices in medieval Europe that have an immediate bearing on this study. Firstly, the mutual experience of sharing practices and beliefs deemed inimical to the interests of the Church began a pattern whereby Renaissance occultists, scientists and business leaders would segregate themselves into organizations where they could discuss issues of mutual interest free from the confessional power of the Church.[10] Often these

---

8. Bernal, M. *Black Athena.* pp 153–155; MacKenzie, N. *Secret Societies.* p 135; Wallis, R. *Neo-Platonism.* pp. 171–172; Yates, F. *The Occult Philosophy.* pp 17–27.

9. Skinner, S. *Divination by Geomancy.* pp 88–140; Hutton, R. *Triumph of the Moon.* pp 67–69.

10. Hobsbawm, E. *Primitive Rebels: A Study of Archaic Social Movements.* London: Manchester Press, 1959. pp 150–153; Hutton, R. "The Background to Pagan Witchcraft." p 4; Hutton, R. *Triumph of the Moon.* p 53.

groups would be extremely secretive and require the performance of ritual, code words and gestures to gain admittance. Typically, these gestures and rituals would be extremely anti-clerical in nature, representing dissatisfaction with the influence of the Church over government and the established socio-cultural order. They also represented an alienation of the intellectual elite from Church practices and the restrictions of Church dogma amongst the European intelligentsia.[11] Secondly, the occult practices of Renaissance Europe were fundamentally integrated with the burgeoning scientific movement. A mutual love of alchemy and mathematics, a dislike of Church dogmatism and control of the intelligentsia combined with a genuine fascination with the functioning of the natural world, led occultism and science to be close allies until the rise of secularism in the Enlightenment era.[12] Many of the major historical figures associated with Renaissance science such as Paracelsus, Galileo and Copernicus were also fundamentally involved in the study and practice of occultism and hermetic studies, particularly the practices of alchemy, the Cabbala and the magical significance of geometry and astronomy as part of a wider appropriation of Greek and Semitic thought. Even later scientists, such as Sir Isaac Newton, were involved in this association between occultism and hermeticism with the burgeoning scientific movement.[13]

Whilst initially allied with the burgeoning sciences in the Renaissance era, the hermetic/cabbalist tradition fell between the gaps created by the conflict between Protestant and Catholic Churches and between religion and secularist thought during the Early Modern period.[14] This was exacerbated by the fact that the bulk of scientists and scholars chose to side with the Protestant movement and its more secular anti-mystical approach to the natural and social sciences.[15] Increasingly, occultists found themselves dismissed by the scientific

11. Hutton, R. *Triumph of the Moon.* p 62; Hutton, R. "The Background to Pagan Witchcraft." pp 3–4 & 8.

12. Skinner, S. *Divination by Geomancy.* pp 88–140. Thorndike, Lynn. *A History of Magic and Experimental Science.* Vol ii. Columbia: Columbia University Press, 1934. pp 800–870; Wallis, R. *Neo-Platonism.* pp 131, 160, 170 & 172–173; Yates, F. *The Occult Philosophy in the Elizabethan Age.* pp 61 & 81–85.

13. Bernal, M. *Black Athena.* pp 28–34 & pp 162–172; Skinner, S. *Divination.* pp 88–140; Thorndike, L. *A History of Magic.* pp 800–870; Wallis, R. *Neo-Platonism.* pp 131, 160, 170 & 172–173; Yates, F. *The Occult Philosophy.* pp 61 & 81–85.

14. Hutton, R. *Triumph of the Moon.* pp 68–69; Yates, F. *The Occult Philosophy in the Elizabethan Age.* pp 61–71 & 88–93.

15. Outram, Dorinda. *The Enlightenment.* New York: Cambridge University Press, 1995. pp 32–33, 39, 44–46, 49 & 50; Weber, Max. *The Protestant Ethic and the Spirit of Capitalism.* London: Allen & Unwin, 1976. pp 168 & 249.

community, from the late seventeenth century onwards, as superstitious whilst being simultaneously attacked by Church authorities for secretly being sorcerers and devil worshipers. Additionally, the belief by many occultists that they could achieve divine revelation via their own research was perceived by the Catholic Church, during the sixteenth and seventeenth century, to be a direct threat to the authority of the Church hierarchy, leading many occultists and alchemists to be executed, tortured or otherwise harassed.[16]

The occult and secret society tradition was fundamentally characterised by this divide between occultists and the two prominent discourses of science and religion in Early Modern Europe. In England in particular, the membership of secret societies and occultists were uniformly drawn from the economic and political elite, and desired to be associated with the values of the aristocracy and socio-political status quo.[17] However, English occultists were continually placed in a position of conflict with the Church and the scientific and political establishments. One of the most important aspects of the English occult tradition was the continual adoption and appropriation of scientific language and the claim to be a science, whilst simultaneously criticising the effects of rationalism, industrialism and scientific rationality on society. Similarly, this ambiguity was also reflected in the behaviour of many occultists who perceived themselves as Christians and operated their ritual within a Christian mythos, yet routinely criticised the beliefs and practices of the Christian Church.[18]

Freemasonry and Nineteenth Century Secret Societies

In the late eighteenth century and early nineteenth century, there was a tremendous increase in the number of secret societies and organizations amongst the European intelligentsia. The centrepiece of these organizations was Freemasonry.[19] According to historian David Stevenson, the origins of Freemasonry and its many breakaway elements were in Scotland at the end of

---

16. Gijswift-Hoffa, M. "Controversy c.1680–1800." pp 225–236 & 242–245; Yates, F. *The Occult Philosophy.* pp 61–71.

17. Hobsbawm, E. *Primitive Rebels.* pp 153, 161, 163 & 165; Hutton, R. *The Triumph of the Moon.* pp 58–60.

18. Hutton, Ronald. *The Triumph of the Moon.* 66–83 & 157–170; Hutton, Ronald. "The Background to Pagan Witchcraft." pp 3–7 & 11–13.

19. Godwin, J. *The Theosophical Enlightenment.* New York: State Library of New York Press, 1994. pp 216–222; Hobsbawm, E. *Primitive Rebels.* pp 162–163; Hutton, R. "The Background to Pagan Witchcraft." p 4.

the sixteenth century. William Schaw, the Royal Master of Works, either devised or supervised the development of the craft of Masonry into a national and, later, international network of guilds and lodges under the title of the Mason's Word. The term "The Mason's Word" referred to the use of a password used to identify an individual as a member. The organization was open to those who were not necessarily masons by trade and followed the prescribed goal of developing the medieval association of masonry and architecture in conjunction with the alchemical, occult and Cabbalist associations in the sciences of geometry and mathematics.[20] The ultimate result of this organization was the creation of secure and well protected spaces in which ethics, magic, science, religion and philosophy could be discussed freely by the European economic, political and social elite, and practical skills and scientific knowledge could be imparted and shared amongst its members and the craft guilds.[21]

At the end of the seventeenth century the Masonic system had spread to England, where it adopted the title of Freemasonry and was then exported to France, Germany and Spain. In England, unlike France where Freemasonry and occultism became associated with anti-establishment and anti-clerical politics, the Freemason movement was predominantly used as a place where the intelligentsia could share a free and open intellectual life in conjunction with the established social and political order. As the movement progressed the rituals became more elaborate and the degrees of initiation multiplied. Furthermore, the component of occult practice and the claims of access to ancient, secret and esoteric knowledge grew increasingly grandiose.[22] In this context, many sub-branches of Freemasonry broke away from the central movement to form new organizations with different claims to arcane sources of knowledge. Most of these new organizations attempted to compete directly with the parent body and claimed to have preserved the same esoteric knowledge in a more pure and uncorrupted form. Organizations like the Illuminati, the Ancient and Accepted Rite, the Knights Templar and the Rosicrucians originated from this period with each claiming access to a more authentic body of ancient wisdom, supposedly transcending their Masonic origins.[23]

---

20. Hutton, R. *Triumph of the Moon*. pp 52–54; Stevenson, David. *The First Freemasons*. Aberdeen: Aberdeen University Press, 1988; Stevenson, David. *The Origins of Freemasonry*. Cambridge: Cambridge University Press, 1990.

21. Hobsbawm, E. *Primitive Rebels*. pp 155–160; Hutton, R. "The Background to Pagan Witchcraft." pp 3, 5–6 & 9; Hutton, R. *Triumph of the Moon*. pp 53–54.

22. Hutton, R. "The Background to Pagan Witchcraft." pp 3–10.

23. Hutton, R. "The Background to Pagan Witchcraft." pp 3–4; Hutton, R. *Triumph of the Moon*. pp. 57–58.

Another source of breakaway movements occurring at this time was the English Freemason's association with the political elite. These alternative secret societies offered to politicians, business leaders, scientists and others a major opportunity for economic and political networking, and the protection of industry from competition and industrialization.[24] Many of the craft guilds, industries and trades of the eighteenth century adopted Masonic styled motifs, ritual, methodology and a penchant for grandiose claims to ancient and esoteric knowledge, as a means to protect industry from the side effects of the industrial revolution, competition from overseas and non guild members, and to lobby politicians and business leaders.[25] The Miller's Word, for example, was an organization of grain workers and farmers designed to protect their industry from the enclosure movement and industrialization of the grain mills, whilst the Horseman's Word fulfilled a similar function with regards to the training and care of horses. These industry oriented secret societies also appropriated a broad body of magical folklore and ritual surrounding trades, particularly with regards to farming, carpentry, smithing and animal husbandry, thereby promoting the idea of secret knowledge passed down from master to apprentice in the performance of various crafts.[26]

The English conglomeration of occult oriented secret societies with the political and economic establishment in England was in stark contrast to the French experience. In France, the occult tradition and its corresponding network of secret societies became transformed into a network of French political and social dissidents who often incited activism against the Church and state. Particularly significant in this light was the rather prominent role played by the Freemasons and other related organizations in the providing of safe havens and networks of communication (on behalf of the revolutionary movement during the 1790s), and in the support and concealment of republican rebels in the 1830s.[27] Similar parallels can be drawn with the role of the American Freemason movement and the Irish Republican Brotherhood, also known as the Fenians, in the respective causes of American and Irish inde-

---

24. Hobsbawm, E. *Primitive Rebels.* p 163; Hutton, R. "The Background to Pagan Witchcraft." pp 6–8; Hutton, R. *Triumph of the Moon.* 58–61.

25. Hobsbawm, E. *Primitive Rebels.* pp. 157–158; Hutton, R. *Triumph of the Moon.* pp. 55–64; Hutton, R. "The Background to Pagan Witchcraft." pp 5–8.

26. Hamill, John. *The Craft: A history of English Freemasonry.* London: Aquarian Press, 1986. pp 18–26; Hobsbawm, E. *Primitive Rebels.* pp. 155–158; Hutton, Ronald. *Triumph of the Moon.* pp. 54–55, 59–64; Hutton, Ronald. "The Background to Pagan Witchcraft." pp 4 & 7–8.

27. Doyle, William. *The Oxford History of the French Revolution.* Oxford: Oxford University Press, 1989. pp 218–219; Hobsbawm, E. *Primitive Rebels.* p 163.

pendence.[28] What is particularly important here is that the move towards political activism was not so much a direct development of the nature of the organizations themselves but rather a case of social organizations becoming involved in the political ideals and aspirations of the broader community. In this light it is quite significant that the shift towards politicisation in French, Irish and American secret occult societies was accompanied by a reduction in the use of ritual, and a corresponding increase in secrecy and level of networking.[29] The shift towards politicisation was also accompanied by a growing secularisation of the movement's goals and ideals. Another major shift that came with politicisation was a change in membership orientation from the ruling economic and intellectual elite to the proletariat and dissident intellectuals.[30] As one French policing official noted,

> The French brotherhoods only become genuinely secret when their membership becomes proletarian, that is anonymous and in the back rooms of pubs and private houses instead of in elaborate lodge chambers whose equipment is, in any case, too cumbersome and elaborate to be in reach of the poor.[31]

One question that arises from this proliferation of secret societies, each with their own claims to ancient wisdom, folklore and the arcane, is why people felt it was necessary to seek ancient and esoteric origins for knowledge. This association of knowledge with an esoteric past stands in stark contrast to the association of knowledge and science with the new and the modern that was to become the hallmark of modernity and industrialism from the late eighteenth century onwards. These organizations, whilst associating themselves with the sciences and with secular knowledge, relied extensively on the reclaiming of arcane lore and ancient wisdom perceived as originating from a golden age in the distant past. Hutton argues that this association of the past with wisdom is representative of three major issues in human society. Firstly, all societies turn to the past as a means of authenticating ideas in the present. Secondly, Hutton claims that the value of these organizations as a sense of a safe area of intellectual freedom is enhanced by the belief that these spaces have remained unbroken and protected from time immemorial. Hutton's final rationale is that the process of initiation and transition through

---

28. Hobsbawm, E. *Primitive Rebels.* p 163–164; MacKenzie, Norman. *Secret Societies.* pp 160–180.
29. Hobsbawm, E. *Primitive Rebels.* pp. 166, 169–170 & 172–174.
30. Hobsbawm, E. *Primitive Rebels.* pp 166 & 171–172.
31. Hobsbawm, E. *Primitive Rebels.* pp 166.

levels of knowledge begets a sense of continuity accompanied by a curiosity concerning origins. This process also functions as the basis of legitimation for that secret knowledge, which provides a fertile ground for the creation of foundation myths. Another possible perspective is that these organizations provided a form of cultural structure in which one's identity, as a member of a secret society, was dependent on a sense of continuity with that identity as an eternal verity as opposed to a contemporary construct, and thus gave a sense of permanency to one's role in society. During the era of the industrial revolution, traditional forms of cultural and social identity were being dramatically eroded. Within this environment, these secret societies provided a sense of continuity with the past which, when combined with the security such organizations provided, served to offer a significant sense of stability. The development of foundation myths, combined with a sense of continuity of ritual and a basis in the cultural heritage of a social movement or ethnic community, forms a prominent role in creating a sense of common identity and solidarity towards a movement's ideals and goals via a ritually and symbolically inspired link with the past, artificially constructed as it may be.[32]

The influence of Freemasonry is difficult to overestimate in British culture. It was patronized by royalty, boasted over four million members and was omnipresent throughout town, countryside and city.[33] Its influence can also be measured by the fact that so many organizations instituted Masonic style rituals and methods in their practice. Many sectors of the trade union movement adopted the lodges, regalia and ceremonies of initiation found in Freemasonry.[34] In all these derivative splinter groups there were several characteristics that remained the same. They provided a safe place for members to network, discuss ideas and share skills and ideas. They claimed access to ancient and esoteric lore, to trade skills, science or magical knowledge and they engaged in elaborate rituals based upon an appropriation of Renaissance ritual magic and occultism.[35]

---

32. A full analysis of the role of claims to antiquity and its manifestation in ritual and symbolism is dicussed at the end of this chapter in relation to Hobsbawm's theory of "Invented Traditions." The material utilised here is, in part, derived from the arguments presented in Hobsbawm, E. *The Invention of Tradition*. New York: Cambridge University Press, 1983. pp 1–5; Hutton, R. *Triumph of the Moon*. pp 64–65; Hutton, R. "The Background to Pagan Witchcraft." p 10; MacKenzie, N. *Secret Societies*. p 152.

33. Hutton, R. "The Background to Pagan Witchcraft." pp 5–6.

34. Hutton, R. *Triumph of the Moon*. pp 58–59.

35. Hobsbawm, E. *Primitive Rebels*. pp 151–162; Hutton, R. "The Background to Pagan Witchcraft." pp 6–8.

The civilizations from which this ancient and esoteric knowledge was perceived to originate are extremely significant. Initially the source of ancient knowledge was attributed to biblical characters, in particular Solomon. By the end of the eighteenth century the focus was upon the figures of classical Greece and Rome such as Plato, Aristotle and Pythagoras. In the nineteenth century it became focused on the indigenous magical/religious practices of Europe with a controversial branch examining the beliefs of Asia and the near east.[36] However, this interest in the magical and religious beliefs of Egypt, India and China was vigorously attacked throughout the nineteenth century, leading to a number of further splits and conflicts within the occult movement.[37] In a very real sense, the civilization perceived as the source of the hidden and esoteric body of learning behind the occult tradition closely followed the cultural preoccupation of English society; allocentrically oriented on Palestine or Hellenic Greece and later egocentrically oriented on white Europeans as the ultimate source of wisdom and learning.

The whole body of learning was covered under the term "The Craft"; a term Gardner borrowed along with initiation rituals, the pentagram, the use of the four elements, the quartered circle, the claimed link with ancient wisdom and arcane law, and many key phrases and rituals.[38] Out of this widespread body of British occultism and mythos of ancient bodies of esoteric learning there arose two prominent Masonic splinter groups that were to prove critical in the formation of Gardner's Wiccan movement. These were the Theosophical Society of Helena Blavatsky, and the Order of the Golden Dawn and its successor movements such as the Ordo Templi Orientalis.

Madam Blavatsky and the Theosophical Society

A Russian noblewoman named Helena Blavatsky, after an abortive attempt to develop an occult society devoted to the study of hermeticism in Egypt in 1872, founded the Theosophical Society in New York in 1875 in close cooperation with long time associate and high ranking Freemason Charles Sotheran. From its outset, it was closely linked to Sotheran's attempt to pro-

---

36. Hutton, R. *Triumph of the Moon.* pp. 57, 71, 75, 77 & 80; Hutton, R. "The Background to Pagan Witchcraft." pp 6, 10 & 12.

37. Bernal, M. *Black Athena.* pp 191–211; Hutton, R. "The Background to Pagan Witchcraft." p 11.

38. Hutton, R. "The Background to Pagan Witchcraft." p 4; Hutton, R. *Triumph of the Moon.* p 54.

mote the study of Egyptian mystery religions, particularly the work of Cagliostro and the mythical Hermes Trismegistus, in the context of the already well developed repopularisation of the Hermetic tradition in 19th century Europe. Like Freemasonry and its various splinter groups, the Theosophical Society was organized into lodges and provided for intellectuals and occultists a safe working and networking space for ethical and religious discussion, and esoteric learning. To a large extent, this close approximation of the organizational structure of Freemasonry was a conscious effort on the part of Sotheran and fellow Freemason George Felt, who argued that the movement should be based on the Masonic model of secret societies so as to prevent the dilution of knowledge amongst the general and uneducated public. Sotheran and Felt, with the blessing of Blavatsky, argued that like the various Freemason splinter groups, the Theosophical Society should claim ancient esoteric origins and mystical origins for its knowledge base as a means of obtaining skilled members of other occult secret societies. Blavatsky went to the extent of claiming that she had received ancient universal wisdom from supposed immortal sages in Tibet such as the Mahatma Moya, while Felt presented the movement as a continuation of Egyptian mystery religions.[39]

Unlike Freemasonry however, the Theosophical Society was public and offered open lectures, publications and newspaper interviews, though debates about the value of this high public profile continued throughout the movement's history.[40] The essential belief promulgated by the Theosophical Society was the notion that behind the world's religions and magical practices, its folklore and philosophies, lay a single authentic, arcane and ancient body of universal wisdom. This wisdom could be obtained and developed for the good of humanity via a systemic, detailed and comparative study of the world's religions, folklore and beliefs.[41] To Blavatsky and her closest associates the most crucial sources of this knowledge were the religious beliefs and practises of the Far East, in particular Hinduism and Buddhism. One major side effect of this perception was that the teachings of oriental religions became widely available to the general populace in the west. Similarly, a consequence of this was the popularisation of the notion of reincarnation. Another major effect of the theosophical orientation towards the east was to add prestige, in occult circles at least, to those with experiences of the religions and practices of the Euro-

---

39. Godwin, J. *The Theosophical Enlightenment*. pp 277–290; Hutton, R. *The Triumph of the Moon*. pp 19 & 73–74.

40. Godwin, J. *The Theosophical Enlightenment*. pp 289–291.

41. Godwin, J. *The Theosophical Enlightenment*. pp 282–283. Hutton, R. "The Background to Pagan Witchcraft." pp 10–11.

pean colonies in Asia and the Indian sub-continent.[42] This orientation towards the east was also a source of some controversy, with some members claiming that the east was being granted importance at the expense of indigenous and classical sources of tlineknowledge.[43]

The Hermetic Order of the Golden Dawn

The Hermetic Order of the Golden Dawn, which formed concurrently with the Theosophical Society, also played a prominent role in the development of Gerald Gardner's Wiccan movement. To some extent, the Golden Dawn was a product of the dissatisfaction of some English occultists with the colonial and eastern orientation of the Theosophical Society, and its refusal to examine magic and occult ritual from a practical rather than a comparative theoretical methodology.[44] In contrast to the Theosophical Society or the Freemasons, the Golden Dawn was specifically formed for the practice and understanding of ritual magic. It also contained many members who broke from the Theosophical Society due to a dislike of the emphasis placed upon the east as a source of knowledge. Unlike the oriental orientation of the Theosophical Society, the practitioners from the order of the Golden Dawn preferred to focus on retrieving the "Ancient Wisdom" of classical Greece, Rome and Renaissance Europe, as well as the indigenous British traditions of folklore, magic and alchemy. For many members of the European occult community, the spiritual orientation towards the East by members of the Theosophical Society had become increasingly uncomfortable. Subsequently, the Hermetic Order of the Golden Dawn provided a suitably nationalist and Euro-centric approach to spiritualism and occult practices, and its development marked the growing division between occultists who allocentrically followed the Eastern mystical traditions and those who desired to follow the indigenous traditions of Western Europe.[45]

William Wescott and Samuel Mathers, two former leaders of the English Societas Rosicruciana and Kingsford Hermetic Society, initiated the creation

42. Cranston, Sylvia. *Helene Blavatsky Unveiled.* London: G.P. Putnam, 1993. pp 183–242; Godwin, J. *The Thesophical Enlightenment.* pp 307–331.

43. Hutton, R. "The Background to Pagan Witchcraft." pp 12; Hutton, R. *Triumph of the Moon.* pp 18–20 & 74; MacKenzie, N. *Secret Societies.* p 146.

44. Godwin, J. *The Theosophical Enlightenment.* p 223. Hutton, R. *Triumph of the Moon.* pp 74–76; Hutton, R. "The Background to Pagan Witchcraft." p 11.

45. Godwin, J. *The Theosophical Enlightenment.* pp 362–375; Hutton, R. *Triumph of the Moon.* pp 74–78; Hutton, R. "The Background to Pagan Witchcraft." pp 10–11.

of the Hermetic Order of the Golden Dawn and were responsible for its historical claims and practice of ritual. Like the Societas Rosicruciana, the Freemasons and the Theosophical Society, the Golden Dawn was organised into a system of lodges with degrees of initiation and was rooted in an appropriation of esoteric traditions.[46] Unlike the Freemasons or the Rosicrucians, it had no biases against gender or religion but nevertheless retained restrictions against certain races. It also took the rather radical step of being specifically orientated towards the practice of magic. Most other organizations professed to study magical practice and ritual as a means of greater understanding of spiritual matters, for ritual or for additional skills in the craft, but the Golden Dawn was unusual in the sense that the learning and *practice* of magic, demonology and alchemy was the central platform of its activities and underlying philosophy.[47]

Initially, the Golden Dawn utilised the long practised claim of ancient origins, but continued pressure from members and other organizations led to a change in its form of legitimisation. Instead of the typical claims of genealogical linkages with great philosophers or civilizations of the past, the Golden Dawn began to legitimate themselves via claims of an association with the German branch of the Societas Rosicruciana. Additionally, Wescott and Mathers copied Blavatsky's claim to have been given an ancient body of wisdom from semi-immortal sages living in remote isolation.[48] In the formation of the organization, Wescott was responsible for the theoretical and historical basis of the order and its claims to legitimacy and authenticity, whilst Mathers constructed the rituals, symbols and training program of its mystical and magical practices.[49] To do this, both individuals drew upon the same conglomeration of symbols, histories and rituals as most of the other occult groups. Mathers in particular utilised a mixture of Greek, Roman, Celtic, Nordic and Cabbalist sources, and integrated them with the Christian/Cabbalist ritual and magical practice of Renaissance Europe.[50]

Significantly, the Golden Dawn integrated Masonic ritual and forms with the practices of ritual magic and English folklore to create a uniquely English

---

46. Godwin, J. *The Theosophical Enlightenment.* p 362. Hutton, R. "The Background to Pagan Witchcraft." pp 10–11; Hutton, R. *Triumph of the Moon.* pp 76. Singer, A. & Singer, L. *Divine Magic.* p 73.

47. Hutton, R. *Triumph of the Moon.* pp 76–77. Godwin, J. *The Theosophical Enlightenment.* p 362.

48. Hutton, R. "The Background to Pagan Witchcraft." pp 10–11.

49. Hutton, R. *Triumph of the Moon.* pp 76.

50. Godwin, J. *The Theosophical Enlightenment.* p 362.

body of occult learning. It was this unique combination that was to become the ritual and philosophical basis of Gardner's Wiccan movement. It combined a particularly nationalistic focus with a theoretical basis derived from the Theosophical concept of a universal source of wisdom existing behind the world's religions. Of particular interest in the philosophical basis of the Golden Dawn was its conglomeration of Enlightenment and Romantic narratives. The Golden Dawn and other occult groups drew upon Romantic literature, art and philosophy in its construction of ritual. Like Romanticism, it was centrally focused on reclaiming the past and creating cultural authenticity. However, at the same time these occult organizations saw the practice of magic and ritual as a science and believed that only the obtaining of knowledge could enlighten humanity and achieve human autonomy from the natural world.[51] Additionally, whilst the members of occult organizations were frequently at odds with the Church and social norms of morality, they were also predominantly right wing organizations supporting the ideas of social Darwinism, and the class hierarchy of the wealthy over the disenfranchised and the European over the colonial and oriental.[52] Another interesting aspect of the Golden Dawn was the fact that its members, like the bulk of pre-twentieth century English occultists, perceived themselves as, at least nominally, Christians.[53] This is a common theme throughout the occult tradition. From its earliest origins, the occult movement in England was heavily oriented towards Christian traditions of mysticism, albeit conditioned by influences from Arabic, Greek and Jewish traditions of mysticism, magic and science.[54]

One of the most critical developments in the history of English occultism, and one critical to the development of the neo-Pagan movement, was the move from a Christocentric basis of spirituality to an appropriation of Pagan motifs and symbols in the nineteenth century. Under the influence of the Romantic trend in English nineteenth century culture many of the rituals, symbols and magical practices of the Golden Dawn came to utilise images initially from the classical Pagan past of Greece and Rome, and later from indigenous Celtic and Anglo-Saxon sources.[55] To Wescott and Mathers this was not a

---

51. Hobsbawm, E. *Primitive Rebels.* pp 163 & 165; Hutton, R. *Triumph of the Moon.* pp 20, 67–68, 174–175; Yates, F. *The Occult Philosophy.* pp 9–12 & 81–82.

52. Hutton, R. *Triumph of the Moon.* pp 360–361.

53. Hutton, R. *Triumph of the Moon.* pp 66–83. Godwin, J. *The Theosophical Enlightenment.* p 368.

54. Yates, F. *The Occult Philosophy.* pp 9–29, 79–85 & 95–127.

55. Hutton, R. *Triumph of the Moon.* pp 17–31, 79–81, 112–120; Hutton, R. "The Background to Pagan Witchcraft." pp 11–13 & 17–20.

major problem, as, from their theosophical perspective, they believed that these images were part of the same body of religious lore as Christianity and all the other world's religions.[56] However, in 1896 Mathers claimed to have been given a vision from the Goddess Isis who asked him to restore her worship to the people.[57] This reorientation towards the east disturbed many members of the Golden Dawn who were already becoming divided into two camps. A.E Waite, a close associate of the poet W.B. Yeats, led the Pagan branch that attempted to revitalise Celtic deities and images and establish a nationalist basis of cultural authenticity in ritual. The other faction was orientated towards an improved understanding of Christianity and they were increasingly disturbed by the increasingly Pagan direction the Golden Dawn was taking. The primary consequence of this was the fragmentation of the Golden Dawn in 1899 and 1900 into a myriad of smaller organizations such as the Ordo Templi Orientalis.[58]

Crowley and the Ordo Templi Orientalis

The Ordo Templi Orientalis of Aleister Crowley was to have an immense impact on the formation of the Wiccan movement and on the English occult movement in general. The passages in Gardner's Wiccan liturgy, particularly the "Charge of the Goddess", are known to be derived from Crowley's work, similarly, the use of the Chalice and Athame in Wiccan ritual is derived from Crowley's Sixth Degree ritual in the Golden Dawn.[59]

Crowley was a remarkable and ambiguous figure, both idealised and despised within his own lifetime. Caricatured as the great Satan, he openly enjoyed challenging the social mores and ideals of the social conservatives of his generation, whilst he privately maintained a more ambiguous position towards organized Christianity and commonly made derogatory comments in relation to its Romantic critics.[60] He demonstrated both a desire to shock and appear radical and controversial whilst at the same time craving respect from his

56. Hutton, R. *Triumph of the Moon.* pp 76–77.

57. Hutton, R. "The Background to Pagan Witchcraft." p 12; Hutton, R. *Triumph of the Moon.* pp 79–80.

58. Hutton, R. "The Background to Pagan Witchcraft." pp 12; Hutton, R. *Triumph of the Moon.* pp 79, 80–81 & 155–158; MacKenzie, N. *Secret Societies.* pp 146–147.

59. Bishop, Cat. "Embarrassed by our Origins." *The Pomegranate.* Issue 12. May 2000. pp 48–49.

60. Hutton, R. *Triumph of the Moon.* pp 175–176; Symonds, John. *The Great Beast.* London: MacDonald Press, 1971. p 239.

peers, and a desire to be taken seriously in the occult and later the academic community. Partly this related to his own contradictory goals of challenging social norms and religious complacency, whilst simultaneously positing an extensive study of magical practice he wished to be taken seriously as an academic and esoteric study of magic. However, Crowley's striving for notoriety and credibility was influenced by his financial shift in fortunes, from a wealthy gentleman, financially cushioned against the consequences of notoriety, to that of a man relying on the charity of his students and followers to survive, desperately attempting to gain credibility in the wider community.[61]

In the wake of the collapse of the Golden Dawn, Crowley continued in his own exhaustive study of magical and ritual magical practice. Central to his quest were the goals of elevating humanity beyond the herd and the confines of the physical world and the task of bringing oriental wisdom to Europe and of restoring Paganism to what he saw as its purest form. He never actually defined what he meant by "Paganism's purest form" however in his research into magic he used rituals from Egypt, Gnosticism, Renaissance hermeticism, Freemasonry, Indian beliefs and Christianity and integrated them together into a body of ritual practices and philosophical ideas reminiscent of theosophy. Critical to his concept of magic was the influence of the human will on the physical and supernatural world. In constructing this philosophy he borrowed extensively from the works of Nietzsche in both style and the use of Nietzsche's concept of the will to power.[62] He defined magic as the "Art or science of causing change in conformity with the will." Through this methodology he wrote extensively on magical practice and ritual from around the world searching for the role of human will in shaping reality. He felt that through a comparative and practical study of magical ritual, a science could be discovered which would enable the elevation of humans capable of asserting their will over reality and society into a higher form of existence.[63]

It is clear from Gardner's own comments and from the identical nature of many of the rituals, chants and magical practices that Gardner borrowed heavily from the work of Crowley in the creation of Wicca.[64] However, it is not clear how much of these borrowings reflect an appropriation of Crowley's actual work and how much is simply the result of Crowley's influence on the oc-

61. Hutton, R. *Triumph of the Moon.* pp 172.

62. Crowley, A. *Magick Without Tears.* Phoenix: Falcon Press, 1991. pp 131, 133 & 137; Hutton, R. *Triumph of the Moon.* pp 171 & 174.

63. Crowley, A. *Magick Without Tears.* p 32; Crowley, A. *The Confessions of Aleister Crowley: An Autohagiography.* London: Routledge, 1979. p 839.

64. Bishop, C. "Embarrassed by our Origins." p 48.

cult community. Additionally, considering the extent to which Gardner borrowed alternative source materials the utilization of Crowley's rituals, amongst other Masonic, Rosicrucian and hermetic materials, combined with the major philosophical differences between the work of Crowley and Gardner, indicates that this may simply be an example of the neo-Pagan practice of "Quoting out of context so as to recast the meaning."[65]

Despite the obvious debt to Crowley in the construction of Wiccan rituals and magical practices, Gardner's Wiccan tradition is in many ways quite distinct from the work of Crowley and other occultists. This is to a large extent symptomatic with the strong influence of Romantic cultural themes and the Witchcraft histories of the Folklore Society on Gardner's work. However, Crowley expressed ambivalence towards Paganism and Witchcraft as a source of magical power and this is illustrated by the fact that Crowley actively sought inspiration from the hermetic studies of eastern religions rather than focusing on national indigenous folklore. Similarly, his central goal of elevating the spirit of the ambitious and dedicated individual, beyond the reach of the natural world stood in contrast to the neo-Pagan and Romantic ideal of divinity being located within the natural world. This contrasts strongly with Gardner's Wiccan movement being centrally based in the ideal of a revival of Paganism and Witchcraft from antiquity, his nationalist focus on indigenous folklore and magical practices deemed to be representative of English culture and his desire to ground English culture back into the earth and nature through a revival of ancient Pagan spirits and deities. Similarly, Gardner's Wiccan movement eschewed many of the more extremely misogynist overtones of Crowley's work whilst still retaining a strong focus on sexually oriented ritual and symbolism in the tradition of Murray's model of Neolithic paganism.[66]

Gardner derived his rituals, symbols and philosophical/magical beliefs in the context of an already rich and multi-faceted cultural milieu. As a result the development of Wicca is fundamentally entwined in the rich tradition of English occultism and the works of its most prominent protagonists. Gardner's Wicca is very different in outlook and philosophical/cultural construction to many of the aforementioned occult movements yet it is heavily indebted to the rich symbols, rituals, beliefs and ideas that they gave to the occult tradition from which Wicca was formed. Wicca is, in a sense, the progeny spawned from the coming together of these occult traditions in the con-

---

65. Bishop, C. "Embarrassed by our Origins." p 48.
66. Bishop, C. "Embarrassed by our Origins." pp 48–52.

text of Romantic history and the socio-cultural context of post pax-Britannia England.

Wicca and the English Occult Milieu

The history of English occultism had an immense influence on the development of the Wiccan movement. Ultimately, the fragmentation of the Golden Dawn and the proliferation of smaller occult organizations led to a proliferation and fragmentation of occult images and themes throughout English culture. This fragmentation was also influenced by the strength of Pagan imagery and Romantic themes and symbols, such as the Goddess, the primal Pagan past and a sense of English national identity. Many of these themes were taken up by other organizations such as the Pagan break away branch of the Woodcraft Chivalry Association, a movement developed alongside Baden Powel's scouting movement. This organization adopted many Romanticist themes such as the idealization of the countryside and the England of antiquity and the Middle Ages.[67] Similarly, many popular and influential writers drew on this wide spread body of folklore, ritual and occult practice for their themes in art, literature and music. Many older surviving movements like the Rosicrucians and the Illuminati also began to be heavily influenced by both Romantic based Pagan symbols and the occult practices of the Golden Dawn.[68]

As previously stated, Gardner was heavily influenced by the long tradition of English occultism. He was a Rosicrucian and a co-mason, an associate of Blavatsky and familiar with the work of the Golden Dawn.[69] He also consulted with the work of Aleister Crowley and met him on at least one occasion in the construction of his Wiccan movement and its body of ritual practices and initiations.[70] Wicca directly utilised symbols like the pentagram and hexagram in addition to the sacred space of a quartered circle, the primacy of the four elements, the ritual of the "Guardians of the watch towers", the ritual process of initiation and many other rituals from the traditions of Freemasonry, the Golden Dawn, the Rosicrucians the Ordo Templi Orientalis.[71] Gardner also

---

67. Hutton, R. *Triumph of the Moon.* pp 163–164; Evans, I. *Woodcraft and World Service.* London: Douglas Press, 1930. pp 160–173.

68. Hutton, R. *Triumph of the Moon.* pp 75–83, 155, 157, 171, 177 & 236.

69. The term co-mason refers to a lay person attached to the Masonic movement.

70. Hutton, R. "The Background to Pagan Witchcraft." pp 44, 48–49; Hutton, R. *Triumph of the Moon.* pp 216–247.

71. Hutton, R. *Triumph of the Moon.* pp 55–58; Bishop, C. "Embarrassed by our origins." pp 48–50.

drew upon the work of other prominent Occultists like John Dee, advisor to Queen Elizabeth I, the notorious Aleister Crowley and Wescott from the Golden Dawn.[72] In this light, when Gardner created his Wiccan movement he was following in the footsteps of a long line of English secret societies originating out of the many branches of the early modern Freemason movement. As Hutton states, "Wicca is the last secret society to grow from the stalk of early modern free masonry."[73]

When Gerald Gardner formed his Wiccan movement he already had at his disposal a broad body of arcane lore, philosophy and folklore to utilise in the creation of a multi-faceted body of religious, spiritual and magical practise. He also had a well-developed historical basis upon which he could base his claims of access to esoteric wisdom, a basis that was broadly accepted in popular culture. Additionally, Gardner was operating in the context of a society in which the narratives of Romanticism, in particular the drive for an authentic national basis of cultural identity, were extremely strong. Similarly, in popular culture, literature and art the idealization of the countryside, the rustic and the rural were powerful images associated with the recreation of English national identity. For many English people, the loss of the countryside and the abandonment of the rural community for the factory left a nostalgic hunger for the idealized simplicity of rural life, for connection with the land.[74] Further, in an era where British colonial power and the era of Pax Britannia was on the wane, the appeal of an ancient, eternal and revitalised English national identity was particularly strong. Gardner drew these diverse threads together and created a new movement with the specific aim of creating an authentic, indigenous and, above all, national religion in which he hoped, in a truly Romantic sense, to create an English cultural revival.[75]

Furthermore, Gardner's Wiccan movement, prior to the sixties counter culture, shared many of the political affiliations of the English tradition of ritual magic and secret societies. Wicca at this point in time was not an activist, anarchist or left wing movement, despite its apparent opposition to the Church and many traditional social norms. Gardner was known as a strong Tory supporter and a political conservative. He was also a fervent nationalist and sup-

---

72. Hutton, R. *Triumph of the Moon.* pp 74–75; Bishop, C. "Embarrassed by our origins." pp 48–50.

73. Hutton, R. *The Triumph of the Moon.* p 65.

74. Bennet, G. "Folklore Studies." p 78–80; Hutton, R. *The Triumph of the Moon.* pp 117–119; Weiner, M. *English Culture and the Decline of the Industrial Spirit: 1850–1980.* London: Harmondsworth, 1985. p 51.

75. Rose, E. *A Razor for a Goat.* pp 200–2001.

ported British colonialism and Empire.[76] Similarly, Alex Sanders, prominent Wiccan and breakaway practitioner from Gardner, was a fervent supporter of the British Monarchy, class hierarchy and Empire. Even Aleister Crowley, notorious for his flirtations with Satanism, was a dedicated Tory supporter and was often very derogatory towards both feminism and socialism.[77] Several studies of the English occult and neo-Pagan movement prior to the late 1960s indicated that by far the majority of members were nationalists and social and political conservatives in political allegiance.[78] At this time the occult, spiritualist and neo-Pagan movements were the prerogative of the social and economic elite of England. Occult movements such as the Golden Dawn, the Ordo Templi Orientalis, the Freemasons and the Societas Rosicruciana were strongly oriented towards the social and political hierarchy, the monarchy, nationalism and the preservation of Empire. Very few individuals in the English occult scene were social or political radicals.[79] Wicca, and the notion of neo-Pagan identity are intrinsically based in representations of a pre-Christian Paganism and the Witchcraft beliefs of medieval Europe. As historian Eliot Rose rather flippantly writes of the Gardnerian Witchcraft revival and its relationship to Romantic literature and nationalism,

> The Witchcraft revival is a sort of literary production by a group of English men and women who were sorry to see England going to the dogs after World War II, and felt a return to Goddess worship would help prevent this. The Witch cult would happily combine the more aesthetically tolerable motifs of several former creeds and the least controversial ethical statements of all ages. Gods with Persian names and Greek bodies would prove, on examination to have thoroughly Bloomsbury minds.[80]

Despite their distancing from science, industrialism and rationalism, via the influence of the Romantic movement and its association with Paganism, English occultists uniformly utilised the language and methods of legitimation associated with the scientific community.[81] Similarly, many occultists, including Gerald Gardner, attempted to legitimate themselves with the creation of

---

76. Hutton, R. *The Triumph of the Moon.* pp 119 & 360.

77. Hutton, R. *The Triumph of the Moon.* pp 119, 360–361 & 364.

78. Smyth, Frank. *Modern Witchcraft.* MacDonald Press: London. 1970. pp 19–21.

79. Hutton, R. *The Triumph of the Moon.* pp 119, 360–361 & 364; Smyth, Frank. *Modern Witchcraft.* MacDonald Press: London. 1970. pp 19–21.

80. Rose, E. *A Razor for a Goat.* pp 200–201, 204, 206, 210, 217, 220 & 230.

81. Hutton, R. *Triumph of the Moon.* pp 20–21, 67–68 & 114–116, 219.

false degrees and other academic accreditation as a means of legitimating their points of view. It has been argued that this appropriation of the regalia of academic accreditation represented a means of receiving recognition from the wider society that occultists felt they deserved.[82] However, it also represented a desire to be recognized and accredited on the basis of traditional academic scholarship. This was further reflected in the practise of claiming ancient origins for their beliefs and rituals, based upon the language of empirical scholarship, even if it meant falsifying material to suit their historical claims. Gardner's approach in creating the Wiccan movement's history is representative of this. On the one hand he portrays himself as the paragon of objective rationality. On the other he created his neo-Pagan history in accordance with his desire for symbolic and psychological impact with scant regard for his own academic integrity.[83] Yet this model is not entirely out of character for Gardner. An elusive and flamboyant character, he was known for his sense of humour and ostentatious approach to research. According to an interview with former Folklore Society member Katherine Briggs by James Baker Gardner, at the time of the publication of *Witchcraft Today*, was perceived to be a flamboyant crank who enjoyed the shock value of bringing imposing knives to meetings and was a bad influence on young people, but at the same time possessing a wide but miscellaneous knowledge of anthropological and folkloric literature.[84]

Wicca and the Invention of Tradition

Like all religious, political, ethical and cultural dispositions and identities, the Wiccan movement depends upon symbols deeply rooted in a particular perspective of history and historical identity. Having a sense of identity and behaviour is, to a large extent, almost indistinguishable from perceived reference points and patterns of behaviour, that is to say historical narratives. When a particular formulation of cultural identity like Wiccan movement becomes dependent on a specific historical narrative, such as Gardner and Murray's representation of English Witchcraft as Paganism surviving Christian persecution, it becomes very clear that a sense of socio-cultural and historical

82. Hamill, John. *The Rosicrucian Seer.* Wellingborough: Aquarian Press, 1986. p 90; Hutton, R. *Triumph of the Moon.* pp 207; Richardson, Alan. *Priestess: The Life and Times of Dion Fortune.* Wellingborough: Aquarian Press, 1987. p 80.

83. Hutton, R. *Triumph of the Moon.* pp 219.

84. Baker, J. "White Witches: Historic Fact or Romantic Fantasy." p 185.

identity is dependent on maintaining the perception of legitimacy in that historical narrative. To some extent representations of the past play a role in creating symbols, rituals and ethical predispositions. However, historical narratives also play a normative role in creating a sense of commonality, community and shared identity within a movement. That is to say that historical narratives provide criteria, implicit or explicit, by which contemporary patterns of action, collective ritual and symbolic representations can be interpreted and given meaning by a community. Critical to this formation of cultural solidarity is the extent to which shared historical narratives are absorbed and replicated by the "collective memory" of a community via oral tradition, canonical literature and ritual. Of critical importance in this process is the means by which legitimacy is granted to historical narratives and how the community to which they hold meaning deals with challenges to these perspectives from outside sources.

As previously stated, when Gardner formulated his Wiccan movement he drew upon an already established literature, symbolic configuration, ritual structure and ideological base. As a result he had an already established network of narratives to draw upon in gaining acceptance of the validity of his Wiccan movement within certain circles of English society. Additionally, Gardner worked extensively to promote the legitimacy of his historical claims via the rhetoric and discourse of Enlightenment configurations of history. He presented his material as empirical facts and his underlying historical narrative as a factual account of medieval Witchcraft and the Paganism of antiquity. Consequently the means by which a sense of legitimacy was granted to the rituals, narratives and symbols pertaining to the formation of Wiccan identity was heavily based in empirical claims to truth given to the construction of historical Witchcraft and Paganism. In particular, the prominent role played by the Folklore Society and the Witchcraft history described by Margaret Murray had a strong formative role in the creation and legitimacy of Witchcraft identity within the Wiccan movement. This strong interconnection between history, ritual and cultural identity is particularly important within the Wiccan movement.

The early neo-Pagan movement's focus on creating the impression of an empirically verifiable past reaffirmed through ritual designed to create a sense of continuity with foundation myths in the movement's past bears considerable similarity with Hobsbawm's model of "Invented Traditions". In characteristically Romantic style, Gardner's Wicca was a movement designed to fulfil a perceived social and psychic need in an English nation he perceived to be faced with a loss of status, cultural history, industrialization, separation from the land and a loss of communal identity. It closely followed the ideological preoccupations of the Romantic episteme by focusing on issues of cultural authenticity, realignment with nature, idealization of femininity and an appropriation of a mythical past as a means to redefine the present.[85] In particular the attempt to utilise the English nationalist myth, along with the Folklore Society, to validate the perception of an eternal Pagan identity existing alongside eternal English identity shows considerable parallels with the "Invented Traditions" utilised by nation states to create a sense of national identity and history, instituted through government bodies such as schools, the military, public holidays and other public gatherings as defined by Hobsbawm. The actual terms Hobsbawm defines the term "Invented Traditions" as follows:

> "Invented tradition" is taken to mean a set of practices, normally governed by overtly or tacitly accepted rules and of a ritual or symbolic nature, which seeks to inculcate certain values or norms by repetition, which automatically implies continuity with the past.[86]

The attempt by Gardner and other prominent neo-Pagans of the sixties such as Alex Sanders, to posit themselves as the inheritors of a secret oral tradition of magical practice that pre-dated written history is a particularly pertinent example of Hobsbawm's concept of invented traditions. History is linked to formative events like the burning times, Celtic and Roman colonization and the industrial revolution and manifested via rituals inscribed in a secret "Book of Shadows" that serves to give a sense of continuity and timelessness to rituals designed to evoke a sense of connection with the primordial past. However, as will be discussed below, there are important differences between Hobsbawm's model of invented traditions as defined by the instituted rituals, symbols and histories promoted by nation states and that performed by religions and secret societies. In particular, the boundaries between instituted tradition and custom become far more ambiguous when practised by religious and social movements than nation states as religious models are far more empathically linked with the past as a source of identity and are continually in a process of evolution. Religious and social movements are also far more flexible in terms of interpretation of ritual, symbols and events than the more rigidly enforced models of instituted nationalist tradition.

Hobsbawm's model, focusing on the instituted traditions of nation states, perceives tradition to be significantly different to the rituals and symbols de-

---

85. Baker, J. "White Witches: Historic Fact or Romantic Fantasy." p 187.
86. Hobsbawm, E. *Inventing Traditions*. pp 1–2.

fined by custom, particularly with regards to customs as practised in pre-industrial societies. According to Hobsbawm, custom in pre-industrial societies acts as both a motor and a flywheel in the formation of cultural identity and patterns of behaviour. They do not preclude variation and change but they do require that change in the social, political and economic order must be compatible with established social norms and patterns of cultural interpretation. Consequently custom acts as a means of forcing discourse surrounding social, political and economic change to remain within the discourse of historical precedent and established power structures.[87] Hobsbawm also differentiates "Invented Traditions" from convention or routine which, while it may gain a symbolic significance, is dominated by practical considerations of efficiency and survival. From this perspective, any social practice that must be applied repeatedly will, in time, become formalised for the purposes of efficiency and the teaching of new practitioners. When turned into habit, routine behaviours and tasks gain a sense of invariance that can cause difficulties in dealing with unforeseen or unexpected events. These networks of routine and convention are not "Invented Traditions" as they are formed for technical rather than ideological developments although they may have ideological components or links to particular ideological or cultural constructions, for example the uniforms of soldiers or police officers[88]

The central features of Hobsbawm's model of "Invented Traditions" are the perception of invariance in ritual and symbolism and ideological or cultural affiliation the tradition implies. Inventing traditions is a process of ritualization and formalization characterised by reference to the past for the purposes of solidarity and cultural affinity.[89] Most commonly objects or events from antiquity that have a powerful psychological impact or cultural significance in a society are redefined and reconstructed as rituals and symbols for the purpose of creating cultural impact. Some prominent examples of this type are the creations of national mythologies and rituals linked to events perceived as formative in a nations history such as the 4th of July celebrations in the United States. Most religions also utilise invented traditions of this type. Easter, for example, draws upon a wide variety of symbols from Pagan, Jewish, Mithraic and Christian sources in order to form a permanent set of rituals and traditions of strong cultural impact associated with a formative event in the religion's history, thus serving to create a sense of affinity and community be-

---

87. Hobsbawm, E. *Inventing Traditions.* p 2.
88. Hobsbawm, E. *Inventing Traditions.* p 3.
89. Hobsbawm, E. *Inventing Traditions.* p 4.

tween Christians. It is important however to note that whilst religions and sub-cultures may be backed by political institutions or even be appropriated by them, they are not inherently defined by the necessity of institutions of political authority such as the nation state to serve social, political and cultural goals. There is a conceptual and functional difference between invented traditions as practised by religions and sub-cultures as opposed to those practised by nation states and political institutions, as the political, economic and cultural role they play in society is considerably different. To a large extent religious invented traditions are designed to create a sense of affinity with formative events in the religion's perceived past as a source of community, meaning and social values.[90] This application of history-defined rituals is somewhat different to the more overtly political objectives of nation states and political parties, although they may well draw upon religious sources for legitimacy.

It is worth noting that the Invented Traditions model if far from uncontested. The definition itself, differentiating between custom and invented traditions in extremely ambiguous and the definitions can become, in some cases, so blurry as to make an adequate distinction problematic. This is well illustrated by Dipesh Chakrabarty's critique of Hobsbawm where he argues that whilst the formula for defining "invented traditions" as distinct from custom, technical routine and "real" traditions may seem clear and unambiguous in practice its application is beset with difficulties. The differentiation between "real" traditions and "invented traditions" for example appears to be simply a case of empirical verifiability but if the traditions fulfil the same sociological role how are they to be distinguished in light of the inherent subjectivity of historical research? Similarly, if a created tradition does not stand for an invariant past then how are they to be differentiated from custom? Finally, Chakrabarty argues that the very basis of claiming an unchanging or static past is very much a post eighteenth century European phenomenon. It is not a claim that pre-industrial societies have made for themselves until very recently.[91] Similarly, as a constructed tradition gains longevity its meaning, construction and socio-cultural significance evolves and transforms it social meaning leading to a situation in which it becomes difficult to differentiate from custom or "real" tradition. Despite these problems in dealing with the ambiguities of defining an invented tradition, particularly dealing with the

---

90. Niebuhr, Richard H. *The Meaning of Revelation.* New York: Macmillan, 1941. pp 49–52.

91. Chakrabraty, Dipesh. "Revisiting the Tradition/Modernity Binary." In Vlastos, Stephen (Ed.) *Mirror of Modernity: Invented Traditions of Modern Japan.* Berkley: University of California Press, 1998. pp 286–287.

traditions and customs of indigenous societies, datable and formally instituted cultural practices and rituals or contemporary origins which can be clearly demonstrated to have risen to the status and perception of time honoured tradition are undeniably "invented traditions" of the Hobsbawmian model. This is particularly the case with regards to the Wiccan movement in that it is patently a created tradition of contemporary origin with a clearly identified inventor promoting an invariant past and ideology manifested through ritual and symbolism. Chakrabarty acknowledges power of the "invented traditions" model as a means of unmasking the ideological presuppositions and agendas of deliberately constructed and propagated traditions, rituals and social practices.[92] As Chakrabarty comments,

> Its [the "Invention of Traditions" model] more positive contribution may have been to raise a functionalist, but nevertheless interesting question about why "tradition" is called into being by the very demands of modernity itself: how do "traditionalising" claims function as "ideology" in times of rapid social change (such as the those produced by capitalist transformation or the genesis of a nation state)?"[93]

History and the application of culturally significant symbols form an essential component within the formation of religious belief and cultural identity. Psychoanalytical interpretations of symbols aside, historically oriented symbols and narratives like the Christian Cross, Pentacles or narratives of the Witch burnings play an intrinsic role in the construction of religio-cultural identity and aid in creating a sense of common heritage and solidarity within a movement or community. When a Christian celebrates Easter or the Eucharist or a Jew performs a memorial ritual to the Holocaust, they are attempting to create a psychological affinity with the original event as part of their contemporary cultural identity as a Jew or a Christian.[94] In this context it is arguable that a neo-Pagan, via ritual and symbolism, is at least in part, making a link to a shared past and construction of history that is believed to play a formative role in their cultural identity. The historical narrative, in the religious sense, is not a means of tracing causation but instead stands outside linear empirical history as a means of formulating cultural affinity and identity through a perception of a shared history defined in relation to the present. A symbol, in this sense, is timeless and acts as a means by which a com-

---

92. Chakrabarty, D. "Revisiting the Tradition/Modernity Binary." p 286.
93. Chakrabarty, D. "Revisiting the Tradition/Modernity Binary." p 287.
94. Lathrop, Gordon. *Holy Things: A Liturgical Theology.* Minneapolis: Ausburg Fortress, 1993. pp 136–137; Niebuhr, R. *The Meaning of Reveation.* pp 49–52.

munity or movement seeks solidarity through shared affinity with formative moments in their historical narrative.[95]

The actual relationship between empirical history and invented traditions is extremely ambiguous in the "Invented Traditions" model. Invented traditions are contemporary responses to novel social and cultural structures that refer to previous events with which the movement believes it shares an affinity and so the relationship to the empirically verifiable past is not purely indexical. In other words interpretations of the past are driven by contemporary social conflicts rather than an attempt to literally duplicate an empirical past irrespective of its contemporary social, cultural and political significance. One prime example of this type of enculturation of history is the divergence in the ways in which the Gospel narratives interpret the life of Jesus of Nazareth. The Gospels vary chronology, geography, formulaic sayings, even the persons involved in a given incident, as a vehicle for giving meaning to the particular socio-cultural context and ideological structure out of which each Gospel narrative is constructed. Parallels may be drawn with the way in which contemporary eco-feminist neo-Pagans respond to the challenge of patriarchy looking to the events of the "Burning times" as a model of male persecution of women. Alternatively a movement may create its own past through the creation of a fictitious history that creates a sense of continuity via long-term obligatory participation. In either case the models of invented tradition are constructed to create a sense of permanence and universality to the religious, social or cultural identity being promoted.

The affirmation of this mythological construction of history is based in prominent formative events and figures and is continuously reaffirmed via ritual and repetition.[96] However, it is worth noting that this process of response to social and cultural change is far from universal, particularly where the hegemonic influence of the nation state is only peripherally present in forming the invented tradition in question. With the nationalist model of invented traditions, the dominating feature is the impact of the apparatus of the nation state that can affirm cultural identity through invented traditions in a relatively uniform way. The central issue is the maintaining of a sense of universality to a particular worldview and a sense of homogeneity between a wide variety of cultural, political and economic divisions. The secrecy and sense of permanence in a movement which borders on the boundaries of a secret society, such as Wicca, intensifies the symbolic impact of a link with a

---

95. Niebuhr, R. *The Meaning of Revelation.* pp 49–52; Robinson, John. *Honest to God.* London: Billing and Sons, 1963. p 47.

96. Hobsbawm, E. *Inventing Traditions.* p 2.

past and reaffirms the sense of antiquity so important in maintaining the Wiccan sense of historico-cultural identity and the sense of authenticity attached to the movement.

In Hobsbawm's model of "Invented Traditions" the centrepiece of ensuring a tradition's longevity and legitimacy lies in the application of ritual and symbolism that serve to bond members of the movement together across both time and space and create an experiential or psychic link to the movement's construction of the past. This use of ritual to create social cohesion is particularly prominent in religious movements, traditional societies and secret societies. For religions, ritual is particularly important with regards to creating a legitimating link to the past as a vehicle for defining cultural identity and finding spiritual fulfilment. With religious rituals there is often a sense in which a ritual not only functions as a remembrance, a sense of solidarity with the initiating event, but also functions as a means of participation. For example, in the Christian Eucharist, the ritual is not only a remembrance; it also attempts to create a sense of identification with those first disciples sharing the bread and wine. There is also a sense in which the Christian participant is there, at table with Christ. The Minister may use such words as, "You are Christ's guests. You are here at his invitation." In a similar manner, the Jew participating in the Passover, in some sense is there in Egypt, with the formational community, eating the unleavened bread, preparing for the flight out of Egypt. The application of historical symbols serves as a means by which a common identity is experienced between people of a mythological past and people who have appropriated that identity in the present. An example of this model from a Pagan perspective is the following excerpt from *The Great Rite Invocation* from the traditionalist Alexandrian branch of neo-Paganism.

> *Assist me to erect the ancient altar,*
> *At which in days past all worshiped;*
> *The great altar of all things.*
> *For in times of old, woman was the altar.*
> *Thus was the altar made and placed,*
> *And the sacred place was the point*
> *Within the centre of the circle.*
> *As we have of old been taught that the point within the*
> *Centre is the origin of all things.*
> *Therefore should we adore it?*[97]

---

97. The Invocation of the Great Rite. http://whichwitchiswhich.tripod.com/id174.htm.

In this context, the belief that there is at least some indexical relationship between contemporary Pagan and Witchcraft movements and the Paganism and Witchcraft of antiquity is extremely important. If the sense of cultural identity and the psycho-cultural impact of its symbols and rituals are to be maintained there is a necessity for a movement's practitioners to believe that the history that is re-enacted and the connection with the primordial and mythic past that is perpetuated in ritual is representative of what actually occurred. That is to say that the historical claims of a religious movement must be perceived as accurate according to the generally accepted means of determining the veracity of truth claims of its practitioners. In the context of 1950s England the accepted means of determining the validity of an historical claim was that of empirically verifiable Enlightenment historiography. In this light maintaining the perception of neo-Pagan and Wiccan historical claims as representative of empirically verifiable facts was an extremely important part of maintaining the veracity of neo-Pagan socio-cultural identity and the impact of ritual.

Gardner's Wiccan movement represents an integration of Romantic and Enlightenment narratives in English society and culture. Its construction and ideological/cultural formation illuminate the extent to which Romantic and Enlightenment themes were interwoven together in the construction of social and cultural identity in nineteenth and early twentieth century English occultism and popular representations of the past and English cultural identity. The extent to which these themes are integrated in the construction of the Wiccan movement also illustrates the extent to which Romanticism and the Enlightenment are neither diametrically opposed nor inherently contradictory. Rather, Romanticism and the Enlightenment are fundamentally interconnected and interwoven throughout European social and cultural formations. In forming his Wiccan movement Gardner adopted the symbols, themes and ideological basis of Romanticism and integrated them with the discourse of scientific rationalism, nationalism and support of the socio-political status quo. If nothing else the sheer diversity, ambiguity and complexity of the Wiccan movement's socio-cultural formation is indicative of the extent to which these themes coalesce and interact with each other in Western society. Gardner's Wicca during the 1940's and 1950's was a movement intrinsically dependent on the creation of a sense of antiquity and identification with a specific representation of the past via ritual and symbolism and reaffirmed via the practice of ritual. The combination of a sense of identification with the past combined with the attempt to base the legitimacy of Wiccan beliefs and practices in the rhetoric of empirical historicity led to a situation where Wiccan identity was intrinsically tied to the maintenance of an "Invented Tradition" in the context of a unique melding of Enlightenment discourse combined with a fundamentally Romantic and nationalist ideological structure.

6

New Age Witches?
Neo-Paganism and the
Sixties Counter Culture

The Pagan movement is exploring social change in a way that I don't
see it done anywhere else. We are living with nudity, sexual freedom,
license for experimentation, freedom of thought and a loose, fun joy
that is unique. I don't see other "magickal" people developing a culture for boisterous joy. To find in expression, silliness, outrageous-
ness, pushing the limits—to find that in this there is spirit. If you
think about the dual meaning of the word "spirit" for a moment, I
think you have it … We're not following anybody. We're like explorers on a new planet in some ways. And we say as Discordians say,
"Don't make Plans."[1]

One of the most important developments of neo-Pagan tradition is its interaction with the New Age movement that came to prominence during the late
sixties. The influence of the New Age Movement is a significant watershed in
the development of the neo-Pagan movement as it fundamentally transformed
the character of neo-Paganism and Witchcraft as it was practised in the rigidly
hierarchical Gardnerian and English occult tradition. It led to the embracing
of an eclectic attitude to religion and culture that enabled the appropriation
of other cultural and religious traditions and laid the groundwork for the eco-
feminist neo-Pagan tradition that was to emerge during the 70s. The influence of the New Age Movement on the neo-Pagan tradition also fundamentally challenged the foundationalist or reconstructionist ideology that deemed
that authenticity in ritual, folklore and belief could only be supported by ver-

---

1. Letter by Discordian society member cited in Adler, Margot. *Drawing Down the
Moon.* p 336–337.

ification according to empirical interpretations of history. This embracing of eclecticism and rejection of the necessity for historical interpretations to be verified empirically led to a paradigm shift in the way neo-Pagan beliefs, rituals and philosophy were practised, evaluated and interpreted by its practitioners.

New Age Antecedents

At the time Gardner was formulating what would become the Wiccan movement in England, many Americans were engaged in their own variants of Pagan revival. The most prominent and influential aspect of the US Pagan revival was the manifestation of images of Hellenic antiquity in North American culture during the late nineteenth century. The Romantic Hellenist tradition of US neo-Paganism was predominantly followed by middle class cosmopolitan urbanites and was rather similar in structure to the revivalist traditions of pre-war England. Tracing the history of these movements is very difficult due to the lack of documentary evidence, the influence of subsequent neo-Pagan overlays and difficulties inherent in the verification of personal testimony. However, despite these problems it is certain that Hellenic based neo-Pagan religious and spiritualist organizations were beginning to rise to prominence in US cosmopolitan centres such as New York by the 1930s.[2]

According to Paul Heelas the antecedents of the New Age movement in the US preceded the sixties counter culture and the rise of Wicca and the English Pagan revival by almost a century. He argues that origins of the New Age movement are situated in the writings and movements of millenarian spiritualist movements in New York during the late nineteenth century. New York, during this era, saw a wide variety of new Spiritualist, Deist, Theosophical and Hellenist movements that drew heavily on Romantic constructions of pre-Christian Paganism and Eastern civilizations. Most notable of these is Madam Blavatsky's Theosophical Society that was also a prominent antecedent of Gerald Gardner's Wicca. These new religious movements rejected orthodox religion in favour of esoteric ritual and occult practices, the sacralizing of nature and a rejection of Western modernity.[3]

In this context, both the New Age and neo-Pagan movements were, to a large extent, products of the new spirituality movements that emerged out of a union between the European occult and spiritualist tradition with a reap-

---

2. Hutton, R. *Triumph of the Moon.* p 340.
3. Heelas, Paul. *The New Age Movement.* Oxford: Blackwell Publishers, 1996. pp 41–42.

propriation of early nineteenth century Romanticism. However, Michael York posits another source of the US New Age and neo-Pagan movements in America. He argues that despite very significant and prominent English influences the New Age and neo-Pagan movements have greater debts to the US transcendentalist and metaphysical tradition than to the English nationalist/esoteric revivals of Witchcraft in the sixties.[4] York argues that the ideological, symbolic and socio-cultural basis of the New Age and neo-Pagan movements were focused around a unique constellation of ideas that coalesced together in late nineteenth and early twentieth century America. He describes these influences as being a reappropriation of nineteenth century Romanticism, millenarian esoteric occult traditions, nineteenth century European spiritualism and an idealization of Hellenic civilization. These influences gave rise to a variety of deist, religious, occult and spiritualist movements that came to prominence in New York in the late nineteenth and early twentieth century. Some of the more prominent movements were the Theosophical Society, Astura, the New Thought Alliance and the Spiritual Frontiers Fellowship. These movements were given further impetus by the writings of the New England transcendentalist philosophers Emerson, Thoreau, Alcott and Fuller.[5]

These spiritualist movements rejected the authority of orthodox religion and encouraged an eclectic search for religious Enlightenment through spiritual experience based in the esoteric studies of various religious traditions and ritual practices. They embraced concepts like reincarnation, the supremacy of personal religious Enlightenment over obedience to doctrine and the need to dig deep into one's cultural and spiritual heritage to find Enlightenment in a personal journey of self-realization. They rejected the concept of sin and believed that evil was a manufactured construct for the purpose of social control.[6] In the early twentieth century however, many of these movements rejected eastern and Native American beliefs as a source of ritual and symbolic expression and instead began to focus on pre-Christian European, particularly Hellenic, traditions of religious belief and ritual practices.[7] It is out of these Hellenic neo-Pagan movements of the US that much of what we today call the New Age movement was to originate.

In the early twentieth century these new-religious movements continued to flourish and they were able to develop an increasing level of ideological

---

4. York, Michael. *The Emerging Network: A Sociology of the New Age and Neo-Pagan movements.* London: Rowman and Littlefield, 1995. p 33.
5. York, M. *The Emerging Network.* p 33.
6. York, M. *The Emerging Network.* pp 33–35.
7. Hutton, R. *Triumph of the Moon.* pp 75–76.

sophistication and public acceptance. A significant component of the solid-
ification of these Romantic spiritualist movements was public horror over
the destruction wrought by the First World War, the apparent collapse of the
world financial network in the aftermath of the 1929 stock exchange collapse
and public apprehension of coming war in the 1930s. Popular sentiment in
New York during this era of uncertainty gave increasing credibility to millenarian movements that fundamentally criticised the value of Western
modernity and technological progress. Another source of credibility came
through the appropriation of the psychoanalytical theories of Carl Jung. His
concept of a collective unconscious from which the prominent symbols of
Western civilization were given meaning helped to legitimise the Romantic
reconstruction of the past in terms of psychological value. The adoption of
Jungian analytical psychology also led to the belief that mythology played a
central role in interpreting the human psyche and society. This formed a
central theoretical component in the development of these new religious
movements.[8]

In this atmosphere occult, spiritualist and neo-Pagan movements flour-
ished. Like their counterparts in the UK, the movements in the US dropped
many of the oriental components to their symbolic and spiritualist practices
and instead focused intently on the reclaiming of what was believed to be
Western civilization's Hellenic Pagan origins. By the end of the 1930s several
neo-Pagan groups attempting to recreate Hellenic Paganism had come to
dominate the New York spiritualist and occult scene. These new movements
were heavily orientated around students of classical studies at New York uni-
versities as well as artists, architects and intellectuals of Hellenist orientation.[9]

Perhaps the most significant of these Hellenic Pagan revivalist movements
was the Church of Aphrodite established in Long Island, New York in 1938.[10]
Founded by Gleb Botkin, son of the court physician to the last Russian Tsar,
the Church of Aphrodite was focused intensively around the worship of a goddess whose beauty "tempted and allured" men to worship it as a symbol of the
divine feminine. This theme permeates his writings and several novels he
wrote on the Russian royal court such as *The woman who rose again*, *Immortal woman* and *Her Wanton Majesty*. In virtually all of his novels the male pro-
tagonist receives a vision of the Goddess Aphrodite who inspires him to create works of great beauty and overcome, in classic Romantic style, the

---

8. Heelas, P. *The New Age Movement*. pp 45–49.
9. Hutton, R. *Triumph of the Moon*. pp 75–80.
10. Adler, M. *Drawing Down the Moon*. p 233.

restrictions of Christianity and the objectification of nature by the forces of modernity.[11]

The stated goal of Botkin's movement was "to seek and develop love, beauty and harmony and to suppress ugliness and discord."[12] Whereas Christianity was perceived by Botkin to suppress desire in order to develop the spirit, he claimed that Paganism would develop the spirit through the embracing of nature and the divine feminine. As opposed to the unstructured systems of associations practised by many Pagans today, Botkin's system was constructed as a rigid hierarchical movement with an organized Church, clergy and liturgy. Botkin's movement was stridently anti-communist but was also against American style liberal democracy, arguing instead for a theocracy based on the worship of Aphrodite.[13] Botkin argued intensively against the idea that people should be free to live according to the whims of their own conscience. Instead, he felt that human nature should be driven by the dictates of a rightly informed perspective trained from childhood so that the properly conditioned soul could embrace the divine beauty and purity of the goddess Aphrodite. The goal was to further the capacity of the artistic and spiritual elite to greater heights of creativity rather than the promotion of the well being of the masses or human liberty.[14]

The organization began with only fifty members but increased rapidly over the next few decades and led to the formation of other neo-Pagan movements, despite Botkin's disproval of members interacting with other neo-Pagan organizations. Many prominent members left the organization to merge with other Romantic neo-Pagan movements or form new organizations such as the Church of All Worlds and Feraferia (a neo-Pagan organization based heavily on the writings of Robert Graves and his concept of a Pagan utopia called "New Crete"). The influence of the sixties counter culture also gave an outlet for disaffected members who joined a variety of new-spirituality movements in the late sixties. When Botkin died in 1969 the leadership of the Church of Aphrodite went to a former Baptist preacher by the name of W. Holman Keith who was converted to the faith in the early sixties. Keith is now regarded as one of the elder statesmen of the neo-Pagan movement but broke away over

11. Adler, M. *Drawing Down the Moon*. pp 233–236. Hutton, R. *Triumph of the Moon*. pp 340.

12. Seabrook, William. *Witchcraft: Its Power in the World Today*. New York: Harcourt & Brace, 1940. p 343–344.

13. Seabrook, William. *Witchcraft: Its Power in the World Today*. pp 342–345.

14. Keith, W. Holman. "Obituary for a Neo-Pagan Pioneer." *The Green Egg*. Vol IV. No 45 Feb. 1972. pp 33–34.

issues of dogmatism in the sixties and is now an elder in the Feraferia movement.[15]

Surviving Witchcraft Folklore in the United States

Another major source for the indigenous revival of magical/folkloric traditions in the US focused around various groups of European immigrants, particularly in the vicinity of the Ozarks in the rural mid Western highlands. Vance Randolph's survey of popular belief in the Ozark highlands in 1947 proved to be a major source of material for the US neo-Pagan movement. Randolph's survey found that that the Ozarks contained a very isolated population in which many traditions, folklore, ritual practices and folkloric beliefs about the supernatural had been imported from Europe and formed a significant part of daily life.[16]

Of particular importance in Randolph's research was the discovery of a serious belief in Witchcraft and magic that appeared to be very similar to the folkloric beliefs of Witchcraft and magic found in Early Modern Europe. Witches were not defined as cunning folk or healers but were regarded as people who practised negative or evil magic that could be only be countered by the actions of a cunning man or woman. One belief, which bore similarities to Early Modern European folklore, was that a Witch would be initiated into his or her power by a ceremony performed in a graveyard at midnight. This ceremony was believed to involve the renouncing of Christ and would be followed by sexual intercourse with an initiate in the presence of two witnesses, thus sealing a pact with the devil. Randolph interviewed two women who claimed to have undergone the experience, however he did not believe their testimony and stated that he thought they were mad or delusional.[17]

Other magical practices, beliefs and traditions also surfaced in Randolph's studies including hybridised variants of European and Native American beliefs. In many ways the supernatural beliefs, folklore and ritual practices of the Ozark rural population had undergone little change since the eighteenth and nineteenth centuries and thus gave a unique insight into the beliefs and practices of their rural European cultural heritage. This source of indigenous magical and folkloric material served as an excellent basis to legitimise claims

---

15. Adler, M. *Drawing Down the Moon.* pp 235–236.

16. Hutton, R. *Triumph of the Moon.* p 340.

17. Randolph, Vance. *Ozark Superstition.* New York: Columbia University Press, 1947. pp 265–266.

to authenticity in ritual, ancestry and beliefs by members of the neo-Pagan movement. In fact many neo-Pagan writers such as Margaret Murray, Gerald Gardner and Aiden Kelly claimed that the traditions uncovered by Randolph represented a true surviving Witch cult that vindicated their claims of direct lineage with pre-Christian Pagan Witchcraft religion.[18]

Randolph's findings and the development of the US Pagan and spiritualist movements were of immense significance to the English neo-Pagan traditions. This is particularly important with regards to the influence of Theosophy, the US Hellenic Pagan revival and the discovery of an apparent surviving Witch cult in the Ozarks at approximately the same time as Gardner went public with his "discovery" of the New Forest Coven. The development of these traditions served as a fertile bed of folklore and ritual practices, providing further support to the claims of the US based new spirituality movements and Gardner's Wicca. Similarly, the focus on Europe as the source of historical authenticity in folkloric and magical traditions gave a uniquely Euro-centric and, more specifically, an Anglo-centric orientation to the US Pagan revival.[19] This became particularly significant in the early sixties when several initiated Gardnerian Witches went to the US in order to establish covens and publicize Wicca.

In 1962 Raymond and Rosemary Buckland, third degree initiates of Gardner's Wiccan tradition, left England to begin a new coven in Long Island, New York. This has become one of the longest lasting and most prolific Wiccan organizations in the US.[20] The move to the US was part of a process that Bonewitz flippantly described as the "Witchcraft pyramid scheme". Gardner and his associates actively initiated as many people as possible and encouraged them to progress to the third degree of initiation where they could leave and establish a new coven under the auspices of Wicca and so continue the process. Raymond and Rosemary promoted their branch of Gerald Gardner's Wiccan movement as the only true source of the ancient Witchcraft tradition and attempted to direct growing interest in neo-Pagan and Witchcraft based religions towards Gerald Gardner's Wicca. The New York coven, and Raymond in particular, snubbed indigenous and eclectic Pagan traditions claiming that they were home made inauthentic copies of Gardner's Wicca and would be better served by becoming Gardnerian Witches. He wrote at the time,

---

18. Kelly, Aiden. *Crafting the Art of Magic.* pp 25–26; Hutton, R. *Triumph of the Moon.* pp 340–341.

19. Hutton, R. *Triumph of the Moon.* pp 340–341.

20. Bonewits, Isaac. *Witchcraft: A Concise History.* Pocket PC Press: New York. pp 93–95.

It says much for the success of Gerald Gardner in obtaining recognition for the craft as a religion, for its imitators are those who, unable to gain access to a coven, have decided to start their own. These do it yourself "Witches" would, on the face of it, seem harmless but on closer scrutiny are not so. They are causing considerable confusion to others who, seeking the true, get caught up in the false ... Why do people start such "covens"? Why not wait and search? For some it is just that they have no patience. They feel so strongly for the craft that they *must* participate in some way. By the time they eventually do come in contact with the true craft it is too late.[21]

However, when the marriage between Raymond and Rosemary collapsed in 1964, Rosemary was given custody of the coven and she immediately granted the position of high priestess to a close friend. This left Raymond unable to legitimately gain new converts under the Gardnerian system or form a new coven due to the rules of Wiccan initiation which required a recognized high priestess to officiate at all gatherings. In response Raymond retreated from his hostility to alternative or home made neo-Pagan religions and formed a new denomination of Wicca called Saex Wicca based on an appropriation of English Saxon mythology. Surprisingly Raymond made no attempt to claim that he represented an ancient tradition or had direct lineage with medieval Saxon Witches but instead openly acknowledged its contemporary origins.[22]

Raymond now encouraged and welcomed new versions of the "craft" as opposed to claiming homogeneity within the neo-Pagan tradition under Gardner. He articulates his new ideological perspective as follows,

That there are so many, and such varied, branches ("denominations" or "traditions") of Witchcraft is admirable ... We are all different. It is not surprising that there is no one religion that suits all people. In the same way then, there can be no one type of Witchcraft to suit all Witches. Some like a lot of ritual, while others are for simplicity. Some are from Celtic backgrounds, while others are Scots, Saxons, Irish, Italian or any number of others. Some favour a matriarchy; others a patriarchy and still others seek a balance. Some prefer to worship in a coven, while others are for solitary worship. With the large

---

21. Buckland, R. *Witchcraft from the Inside.* pp 79–80.
22. Bonewits, Isaac. *Witchcraft: A Concise History.* pp 95. Adler, Margot. *Drawing Down the Moon.* p 93.

number of different denominations, then, there is now more likeli-
hood of everyone finding a path they can travel in comfort.[23]

According to Bonewitz, Raymond's stamp of approval on self initiated, home
made or, at least, non-Gardnerian traditions significantly accelerated the development of self-made covens. The approval of such a prominent Wiccan
high priest allowed many Witchcraft groups to compete on relatively equal
footing with Gardnerian and Alexandrian covens, which subsequently led to
a population explosion of Wicca based movements across the US. Other initiates of Gardner followed suit leading to the spread of Wicca across most of
the Anglophone world. Raymond's embracing of eclecticism also left the way
open for the integration of the rigidly hierarchical and secretive Wiccan covens
with elements of the sixties counter culture and the US tradition of Hellenic
neo-Paganism. This was to have a substantial influence on the development
of American based neo-Pagan movements and the virtual absorption of the
US Wiccan tradition within the banner of the New Age movement.[24]

According to one of the founders of the Church of All Worlds, a prominent
New Age/neo-Pagan movement originating in the mid sixties, there was almost negligible contact between Wiccans and neo-Pagans of the Hellenic and
Theosophical tradition prior to their popularisation during the sixties counter
culture.[25] The neo-Pagan movement in the US, as it was prior to the sixties,
was closely tied to classical studies and tended to follow the mythology and
ideals presented in the books *Stranger in a Strange land* by Heinlein and *The
White Goddess* by Graves. The primary focus was on creating what was called
a Pagan consciousness rather than historical authenticity. This concept of a
Pagan consciousness represented a search for union with nature and an embracing of the divinity of the inner self.[26] Conversely, the early Wiccan tradition in the United States was focused on prominent figures in the Wiccan
movement located in England, such as Gerald Gardner, Doreen Valiente and
Alex Sanders and was oriented towards English mythology and Witchcraft history. The early Wiccan movement in the US also tended to utilise texts of folk-

---

23. Buckland, Raymond. *Buckland's Complete Book of Witchcraft.* Llewellyn Publishers:
Minneapolis. 1986. p 8.

24. Bonewitz, Isaac. *Witchcraft: A Concise History.* New York: Pocket PC Press, 2000. p
96.

25. Grimmasi, R. *Interview with Oberon.* Ravens Call. 3-23-2001. Copy received via e-
Mail from Oberon on 3-23-2001.

26. Adler, M. *Drawing Down the Moon.* pp 179, 233–282. Grimmasi, R. *Interview with
Oberon.* Ravens Call. Copy received via e-Mail from Oberon on 3-23-2001.

loric Witchcraft beliefs based in Europe such as Murray's *Witch Cult in Western Europe* and Gardner's *Witchcraft Today*.[27] The integration of these two Pagan themes, made possible by the exponential growth of Witchcraft and Wiccan based movements, was to lead to a major reconfiguration of what neo-Paganism meant to its practitioners. This integration also led to a large degree of cross-fertilization between the burgeoning New Age and neo-Pagan movements. In the context of the new spirituality, counter-cultural and political movements of the sixties, the structure of neo-Paganism was to be almost completely reconfigured by new variations of Pagan oriented beliefs, Witchcraft revivals and the New Age movement.

The Counter Culture and the "Age of Aquarius"

A full and detailed discussion of the sixties counter culture is far beyond the scope of this chapter. However certain prominent features are central to understanding the extent to which the counter culture formed an underlying context to the influence of the New Age movement on the neo-Pagan tradition. Of particular importance is the wide ranging popularisation of alternative religious practices, a context of youth oriented psycho-religious and cultural experimentation, the linking of spiritual/ritual/lifestyle practices with mass political action and social critique as well as the integration of new spirituality movements with established strains of critical thought such as feminism, environmentalism and libertarianism.

It is commonly assumed that the sixties counter culture originated in the predominantly white Free Speech Movement in Berkley during the early sixties.[28] However there are many dissenting opinions as to the origins of the sixties counter culture. Doug McAdams believes the sixties decade of rebellion, experimentation and socio-political critique originated within the Black civil rights protests of the sixties.[29] In contrast, Fredric Jameson argues that the origins of the sixties counter culture are located in the process of decolonisation of French and British Africa in the aftermath of World War II. He defines the sixties as a period where the marginalized of the Third World and their equivalents in the west asserted their rights and demands to be recognized by West-

---

27. Bonewits, I. *Witchcraft.* pp. 91–95. Hutton, R. *Triumph of the Moon.* p 91–92.

28. Stephens Julie. *Anti-disciplinary protest: Sixties radicalism and Post-modernism.* London: Cambridge University Press, 1998. p 11.

29. McAdam, Doug. *Freedom Summer.* London: Oxford University Press. 1988. p 117.

ern governments as human beings.[30] Conversely, Theodore Roszak argues that the wellspring of sixties radicalism was an aesthetic response to a sense of deep-seated alienation and disillusionment felt by many Americans with the process of secularisation and objectification of Western culture and society via the processes of modernity, industrialisation and commodification.[31]

What is certainly clear is that the experience of the sixties and the focus of sixties radicalism meant very different things to different sectors of society. It was a decade full of contradictions and conflicts, even between protest groups. The conflict between "politico's" and "yippies" stands out as a particularly apt example of this kind of conflict within and between counter cultures.[32] Despite the complexities of the era and the sheer diversity of counter cultural activities there are some clear influences on the New Age movement or "The Age of Aquarius" as it was called at the time. Of particular importance was the climate of experimentation with alternative life styles, religious experiences, cultural forms, radical politics and philosophies that served as fertile soil for the formation of a wide variety of new spirituality movements.[33]

Even within the context of these new spirituality movements there are a wide variety of interpretations over what the counter culture actually signified in spiritual, social and cultural terms. In a general sense the counter culture could be defined as a set of beliefs that radically rejected the validity of dominant social formations and cultural values of a society. Another interpretation focused on the people who prescribed alternatives to the dominant culture and accepted these beliefs and so tended to act in radical and non-conformist social patterns.[34] One prominent aspect of the counter culture was the use of symbols from marginalised religious practices and esoteric beliefs such as eastern religion, mysticism, magic, astrology and occultism. Another perspective is illustrated by Richard Neville in his book *Play Power* in which he describes a generation linked by common inspirations, dissatis-

---

30. Jameson, Fredrick. *Periodizing the sixties: The Sixties without Apology.* Minneapolis: University of Minnesota Press, 1984. pp 178–209.

31. Roszak, Theodore. *The making of a Counter-Culture.* New York: Doubleday Books, 1973. pp xiv–xxviii.

32. Stephens, J. *Anti-Disciplinary Protest.* pp 27–30. This conflict, as documented by Julie Stephens, focuses of the conflict between traditional forms of leftist protest, ideology and activism and those of movements which argued against conforming to traditional models and instead opted for a model of protest based in irony, symbolic disorder and "play power".

33. Heelas, P. *The New Age Movement.* p 50.

34. Newton, Janice. "Aborigines, Tribes and Counterculture." *Social Analysis.* No 23. August 1988. p 54. Musgrove, P. *Ecstasy and Holiness.* London: Methuen, 1974. p 9.

faction with mainstream society and a life style centred on drugs, sexual freedom, experimentation and alternative forms of social, political, cultural and
spiritual expression.[35] Theodore Roszak describes the counter-culture as a
youth reaction against the tradition of Western modernity, industrialism and
faith in the capacity of science and rationalism to solve humanity's problems.
According to Roszak the counter culture was not only based in Romantically
inspired themes, but consciously drew on the Western Romantic tradition for
inspiration as a means of embracing the sacred, the natural and the feminine
as a framework for the pursuit of mystical, spiritual and social alternatives.[36]

During the sixties a large number of new spirituality movements formed
within this wide spread search for new structures of social and cultural organization and spiritual expression. These movements drew extensively on the
spiritualist, occult and esoteric movements of the late nineteenth and early
twentieth century. Predominantly they focused on the pursuit of personal Enlightenment, the freeing of the "inner self", a rejection of mainstream religious
traditions, an embracing of eastern and pre-Christian religion and a strong
opposition to modernity and "straight" society in general. Sydney Ahstrom
describes these spiritual traditions as characterised by "Intense moral indig-
nation, a deep suspicion of established institutions, and a demand for more
exalted grounds of action than social success, business profits and the national
interest."[37]

This climate of social critique and life style experimentation was characterised by communes, dropouts and pilgrimages to the east and other perceived sites of pre-modernity. It gave a significant boost to the popularisation
of neo-Paganism. Of particular significance in this search was the appropriation of symbols of marginalisation from Western culture, such as the Witch,
traditional societies and eastern civilization. This continual process of appropriation was combined with an idealization of pre-Christian, pre-patriarchal
and pre-modern societies. The Romantic, female oriented and anti-orthodox
ideology of the neo-Pagan movement supported a coherent cultural basis for
the critique of the political, social and cultural establishment of sixties America. It also offered an alternative source of spiritual experience with which to
embrace the Romantic critique of Western civilization that was not subject to
the rigid orthodoxy, patriarchy and hierarchical constraints associated with
many eastern religions in the popular imagination.

---

35. Neville, Richard. *Playpower*. London: Granada Publishing, 1971. p 207.

36. Roszak, T. *Where the Wasteland Ends*. xiv–xxviii.

37. Ahlstrom, Sydney. *A Religious History of the American People*. London: Yale University Press, 1972. p 1085.

During this period a wide variety of anti-authoritarian, anti-orthodox, anti-establishment spiritual organizations that drew upon Romantic constructions of pre-Christian Paganism were formed. Some of the more prominent movements were the Discordian Society, the Church of All Worlds, the Dionysian Society, the Druids and the Hesparians. These groups opposed the traditional political activist approach of socialists and anarchists and the hierarchical religious traditions of eastern faiths in favour of a reconstructed Paganism that would offer an antidote to the ills of Western civilization and modernity. The ideology of these counter-cultural neo-Pagan groups is well illustrated by the perspective of Frederic Adams, founder of the Hesparian neo-Pagan tradition.

> It is only through the maiden way that the balance can be restored in a way that will elevate freedom, playfulness, sensuality and the imagination. The flaw of Christianity—and most of the Eastern religions—is that they were forced to do things through asceticism and the images of the pure castrated male. Such an image would only continue the "Age of Analysis". In contrast the maiden way would provide the spiritual cohesion to begin a shift in history that would end the "prison of hierarchy and garbage heap of industrialism.[38]

This perspective of Paganism acting as an antidote to the ills of modernity, a characteristically Romantic approach to modernism, served as a rallying point for a wide variety of counter cultural perspectives and gave a spiritual dimension to many political movements. Segments of the feminist movement, particularly after the writings of Zsussana Budapest, appropriated the mythology of a matriarchal pre-Christian Pagan utopia and utilised the symbol of Gardner's persecuted Pagan Witch as a symbol of female oppression by the patriarchy.[39] The Women's International Terrorist Conspiracy from Hell or WITCH movement set the scene for the development of eco feminist neo-Paganism in the sixties and sixties.[40] Many environmentalists also saw Paganism as a form of spirituality that sacralized nature that could serve as an ideological and aesthetic counter to the influence of Western modernity and industrialism. It was also argued that Paganism could serve a source of personal, spiritual and sexual freedom from the constraining and rigidly hierarchical structures of Christianity and straight society in general.

---

38. Adler, M. *Drawing Down the Moon.* pp 246–247.
39. Hutton, R. *Triumph of the Moon.* pp 344–360.
40. The relationship between feminism and Neo-Paganism is discussed in detail in the next chapter.

Defining Neo-Paganism and the New Age

The Wiccan movement in America had, by the end of the sixties become increasingly integrated within the traditions of eclectic neo-Paganism and had become heavily influenced by the sixties counter culture and the New Age movement. The influence of these traditions had left significant portions of the English Wiccan movement in America fundamentally inseparable from neo-Pagan oriented elements of the counter culture. Consequently, the very conception of what was meant by neo-Pagan and Wiccan had undergone a massive transformation in this period. To be a Witch or a Pagan no longer necessarily meant that a person claimed direct lineal descent from a surviving pre-Christian magical, esoteric or religious tradition but rather denoted an attitude to religion and spirituality in general that was placed in contrast to the hierarchical and conformist religions of mainstream Western society and the orthodox traditions of the east. Neo-Paganism in the US also moved past its roots in Romantic Hellenism, although it remained an important source of inspiration. The issue of Western origins, during the sixties, became solidly replaced by allegiance to religious systems that followed a particular ideological approach to nature, social diversity, polytheism and women.

Paganism, by this definition, applies to religious or spiritual traditions that see the world or nature itself as divine. Other religions may have elements that cherish or idealise nature as a divine gift or see aspects of the divine in the natural world but they are not nature religions, as they do not see the natural world itself as the source of the numinous. Accordingly, within the perspective of many neo-Pagan movements coming out of the sixties, the term neo-Pagan applied to religious practices as diverse as Australian Aboriginal beliefs, the religions of ancient Greece and Egypt, Native American beliefs, Wiccans, Goddess spirituality movements, Siberian shamanism and Voodoo.[41] These religions, amongst others, are perceived to share in a belief structure that locates the source of divinity in the natural world rather than in an abstracted God image.

The philosophical construction of the Pagan consciousness being rooted in a sense of divinity located in the natural world is contrasted, in neo-Pagan thought, with the monotheistic religions of Christianity, Islam, Judaism and in religions that see the locus of divinity in an external God or principle that remains separate or even hostile to the natural world. Prominent neo-Pagan writer Miriam Simos (Starhawk) describes this perspective as follows.

---

41. York, Michael. *Defining Paganism*. The Pomegranate. Issue 11. Feb 2000. pp 7–9.

Our relationship to the earth and the other species that share it has also been conditioned by our religious models. The image of God as outside of nature has given us a rationale for our own destruction of the natural order, and justified our plunder of the earth's resources. We have attempted to "conquer" nature as we have tried to conquer sin ... The model of the Goddess, who is immanent in nature, fosters a respect for all living things.[42]

A belief in the equal validity of different religious traditions and an acceptance of polytheism is also considered to be important from this perspective. Adler describes this as being an attitude or a perspective rather than a literal belief.[43] A New Age Dictionary describes the neo-Pagan concept of polytheism as "A theory that Divine reality is numerically multiple, that there are many gods."[44] From this perspective the concept of polytheism is inherently tolerant and promotes a diverse, evolving, dynamic and creative world. Calls for unity, homogeneity, integration and conformity in many societies and nation states are perceived to be representative of the influence of a long-standing belief in monotheistic religions that do not tolerate diversity of opinion.[45] Adler quotes a New York Wiccan priestess who articulates this perspective;

A monotheistic religion still seems analogous to the "one disease—one treatment" system still prevalent in modern medicine. When worshipers view deity in a single way this tends to feed back a homogenous image. The worshipers begin (1) to see homogeneity as good and (2) to become homogenous themselves. Eccentricity becomes "evil" and "wrong." Decentralization is seen as a wrong because what is wrong for "A" cannot possibly be right for "B." A polytheistic worldview allows a wider range of choices. A person can identify with different deities at different times. Differences become acceptable, even respectable."[46]

From a neo-Pagan perspective polytheism is not the belief in a world of separate distinct Gods but is rather an acceptance of the principle that reality and the divine is multiple, fragmented and diverse. All nature is diverse and manifests itself in a myriad of forms and belief and cultural structures. According

---

42. Starhawk. *The Spiral Dance*. p 25.

43. Adler, M. *Drawing Down the Moon*. p 24.

44. Runes, Dagobert. *Dictionary of Philosophy*. New York: Philosophical Library, 1942. p 242.

45. Adler, M. *Drawing Down the Moon*. pp 24–25.

46. Adler, M. *Drawing Down the Moon*. p 34.

to David Miller, polytheism is a way of dealing with the issue of critical subjectivity on the part of religious practitioners. He writes,

> Polytheism is the name given to a specific religious situation characterised by plurality. Socially understood, polytheism is eternally in unresolvable conflict with social monotheism, which in its worst form is fascism and in its less destructive forms is imperialism, capitalism, feudalism and monarchy. Polytheism is not only a social reality; it is also a philosophical condition. It is that reality experienced by men and women when Truth with a capital "T" cannot be articulated reflexively according to a single grammar, a single logic or a single symbolic system.[47]

The importance of an ideological structure designed to promote tolerance and diversity was of critical importance in the creative, dynamic and diverse social and cultural formations of the sixties counter culture. Also of importance was the support for open eclecticism with regards to social forms, cultural symbols and rituals practised within the neo-Pagan movement. The appropriation of the beliefs, traditions and rituals of traditional societies, Buddhists, Hindus, Gnostics, Western philosophers and the religions of ancient civilizations led to substantial diversification of neo-Pagan beliefs and practices. To a large extent the primary theoretical perspective utilised to hold these extremely diverse cultural and religious traditions together under the banner of Paganism was a variation of the analytical psychological theories of Carl Jung.

Jung and the Neo-Pagan Movement

> There are many symbols that are not individual but collective in their nature and origin. These are chiefly religious images; their origin is so far buried in the mystery of the past that they seem to have no human source. But they are in fact, "collective representations" emanating from primeval dreams and fantasies. As such, these images are involuntary spontaneous manifestations and by no means intentional inventions.[48]

The adoption of Jungian analytical psychology by much of the neo-Pagan movement during the sixties and seventies led to profound changes in the na-

---

47. Miller, D. *The New Polytheism*. New York: Harper & Row, 1974. p 4.
48. Jung as cited by Drury. Drury, N. *Exploring the Labyrinth: Making Sense of the New Spirituality*. St Leonards: Allen & Unwin, 1999.

ture of neo-Pagan approaches to history, culture and spirituality. The focus of neo-Pagan approaches to history became a search for images that evoked strong emotion, a sense of affinity or cultural impact and could be interpreted via Jung's model of archetypes located within the collective unconscious. One of the most significant consequences of the neo-Pagan embracing of Jungian analytical psychology is that it laid the groundwork for the adoption of post-modernism and an almost complete rejection of empirical approaches to neo-Pagan history.

One particularly pertinent example is prominent Gardnerian, Vivianne Crowley's textbook for Witches called *The Old Religion in the New Age*. Whilst her book is certainly based on Gerald Gardner's Wiccan movement and the history of Murray's *Witch cult in Western Europe* she also incorporates Kundalini meditational practices and Hindu rituals into the practice of Witchcraft. As a practising Jungian psychoanalyst she bases the rationale for her work firmly in Jungian psychoanalytical theory. She argues that the capacity to integrate the practise of Wicca with the symbols, mythology and rituals of other traditions is, in Jungian terms, a signifier of a person's rise to self-fulfilment via the attainment of psychological integration.[49]

From the perspective of Jungian based neo-Pagan mythology, all symbolism and ritual serve as a metaphor of psychic development and the meaning and significance of these symbols is defined by their role as representations of the collective unconscious. Psychic development and human contentment cannot be achieved through will or intention alone. People require symbols and rituals to express realities beyond the scope of conscious thought in order to achieve wholeness. The collective unconscious, the wellspring of intentional and unintentional thought is, by definition, unknowable and cannot be grasped within the confines of conscious rational intent. The mediation of symbols is required to give a person's psychological development meaning beyond that of the purely rational. From this perspective, when a Jungian oriented neo-Pagan utilises ritual, it is as a metaphor to describe psychic realities in relation to certain archetypes, within the collective unconscious, that prescribe universal meaning to a person's psychological state. Jung describes the collective unconscious as follows.

> There exists a second psychic system of a collective, universal, and impersonal nature which is identical in all individuals. This collective

---

49. The entire text of The *Old Religion in the New Age* is replete with references to the work of Jung and the utilization of Wicca as a manifestation of Jungian analytical psychology in practice. Crowley, Vivian. *The Old Religion in the New Age*. New York: Harper Collins, 1989.

unconscious does not develop individually but is inherited. It consists of pre-existent forms, the archetypes, which can only become conscious secondarily and which give definite form to certain psychic contents.[50]

From the perspective of the neo-Pagan appropriation of Jung, the collective unconscious is a common, shared symbolic heritage to all human beings that gives meaning to people's experience. There are certain shared symbols or archetypes that are perceived to represent universals in all human psychic experience. Perhaps the most common example is the concept of *anima* and *animus*, the masculine and feminine components of the human mind, possessed by both men and women. In Jung's analysis there are certain aspects to social and cultural behaviour that can be ascribed to universal masculine and feminine qualities that are distinct from gender. These represent unique universal qualities common to both men and women. In other words, where a culture may have a legend about a knight and princess, from a Jungian perspective this may be interpreted in terms of the relationship between the masculine and feminine components of the psyche on the journey towards wholeness. Crowley illustrates the use of the archetypes of masculine (animus) and feminine (anima) from a neo-Pagan perspective as the underlying psychological truth of the Gardnerian postulate that divinity is focussed in an equally matched God and Goddess, espousing universal masculine and feminine qualities.

> The role of both anima and animus is to portray those functions which we have not yet brought into consciousness, but the goal of the spiritual quest is to absorb these qualities into our self-image, to own them as ours. For a man the goal is to find in the Goddess those aspects of himself that society has denied him. These qualities are necessary if we are to be creative people, for creativity comes from wholeness. The role of the Goddess was to act as a muse to inspire the man. The man finds the Goddess, the real muse, when he ceases to look for her in women and turns inward to seek her in himself.[51]

However, whilst the application of Jungian terms such as *animus, anima, archetype* and *collective unconscious* imply a direct correlation with Jungian ana-

50. Jung as cited by Drury. Drury, N. *Exploring the Labyrinth: Making Sense of the New Spirituality*. St Leonards: Allen & Unwin, 1999.

51. Crowley, V. *Wicca: The Old religion in the New Age*. p 169.

lytical psychology, the use of these terms by Jungian inspired neo-Pagans can be seen as a point of departure from Jungian analytical psychology. This is particularly significant with respect to the neo-Pagan movement's insistence that one can and should consciously create one's own images of divinity and psychological archetype and consciously ascribe them meaning. In his research, Jung attempted to take note of the symbol, its impact upon the culture and its cultural context. When a symbol is removed from its cultural context it's meaning is altered, for meaning is bound up with the symbols relationship to the collective, the community, the social grouping and context from which it derives its unconscious meaning. Symbol cannot exist in a cultural vacuum but becomes symbolic because of its cultural context. Consequently, the neo-Pagan penchant for consciously selecting and removing images from their cultural context fundamentally changes the nature and meaning of the symbol. Further, the selection of the symbols to be removed is based upon a person's own sense of affinity or rightness, which is itself perceived according to a consciously derived set of criteria. Thus, not only is the symbol's content altered in the process of removing it from its cultural and social womb, by virtue of deprivation of context. It is further altered by the imposition of another context in that it is transposed into a neo-Pagan culture.

It is one thing to acknowledge that symbols and archetypal images have a deep impact on the human psyche through religious experience. It is a profoundly different thing to believe that one can consciously and arbitrarily create and ascribe meaning to symbols, based upon that which is seen to be suited to consciously designated psychic needs. Jung clearly differentiates between symbols and archetypes embedded in culture and consciously constructed forms designed to have psycho-cultural impact or represent linkages with a constructed representation of the past. According to Jung, consciously constructed images are allegories and signs that give reference to psychological archetypes deeply buried in the unconscious mind. These do not represent the archetypes themselves and are thus not symbolic as such. Allegories and signs have a conscious and known meaning whereas a symbol must always and necessarily be an unknown quantity. If a symbol can be totally explained or rationalised within the confines of the conscious mind, then it ceases to exercise the power of a symbol and becomes an allegoric reference. From Jung's perspective, symbols represent those unquantifiable aspects of the unconscious that have a numinous quality, creating meaning for the individual or collective. These play an illuminating role, revealing hidden aspects of the psyche. However, when a symbol becomes a consciously apprehended and constructed image, it ceases to be a symbol and, although it may masquerade as a symbol, it becomes a representation of the persona. Therefore it ceases to be a union of opposites and becomes a collaborator in the suppression of the shadow. The shadow contains the parts of an individual and society that cannot be acknowledged and, as a consequence, these unconscious contents become projected onto individuals and representations in the external world.

Whilst Jung's works have had a profound effect upon the neo-Pagan movement in terms of providing a theoretical framework in which to function, it is also true that Jung would never have imagined his work becoming the means by which any religious movement might validate its own perception of the numinous. Jung was primarily concerned with exploring the role of the religious function within the human psyche. The process by which the neo-Pagan movement constructs its own symbols, archetypes and images of divinity is also reflected in the way in which it has adapted the works of Carl Jung. Even as it has utilized Jung's works in ways that it is doubtful Jung would have envisioned or condoned, it utilizes the symbols and rituals of other religions in ways, places, cultures and conceptual frameworks quite alien to those in which the symbols, images and rituals had evolved and previously served. In this sense, the nature of the symbols is fundamentally changed by their usage and makes the supposed symbolic impact of these signs as expressions of unconscious archetypes somewhat problematic. To this end it can be argued that the neo-Pagan appropriation of Jungian theory has become differentiated from its origins in Jungian analytical psychology and has become a unique interpretation of culture and religious experience in its own right.

However, despite these points of divergence, it is clear that the appropriation of Jungian philosophy and, in particular, the definitions of concepts like magic, miracles, Gods, Goddesses, masculinity, femininity, ritual, Enlightenment and symbols in Jungian analytical psychology has had a profound influence on the neo-Pagan movement. It provided both the theoretical basis for claims to legitimacy outside of the rapidly collapsing claims to historical antecedence, and the increasing irrelevance of English nationalism in Gardner's model of Witchcraft beliefs in an American cultural context, and also a clear ideological and cultural framework for integrating the increasingly diverse cultural, aesthetic and ritual expressions of Pagan faith in the post-sixties era. Thus derivations of Jungian theory became increasingly prevalent in the works of neo-Pagan writers such as Starhawk, Cassandra Carter, Aiden Kelly, Margot Adler and Laurie Cabot among others. The emphasis is on psychological truth, impact and Pagan consciousness rather than historical authenticity or adherence to doctrine. In many ways this represents a return to the origins of neo-Paganism in the Theosophical Society and nineteenth century Romanticism as opposed to the ideas expressed in Gerald Gardner's Wicca and the traditions of ritual secret societies and esoteric occultism that spawned the original Wiccan movement. This new perspective, prevalent in Wiccan/neo-Pagan movements after the sixties, is perhaps best illustrated by this passage from the Australian Pagan Alliance's manifesto in response to the question "What is Paganism?"

1: The idea that Divinity is immanent as well as transcendental. This is often phrased as "Thou art God" or "Thou art Goddess".

2: The belief that Divinity is just as likely to manifest itself as female. This has resulted in a large number of women being attracted to the faith and joining the clergy.

3: A belief in the multiplicity of Gods and Goddesses; whether as individual deities or facets of one or a few archetypes. This leads to multi-valued logic systems and increased tolerance towards other religions.

4: A respect and love for Nature as Divine in her own right. This makes ecological awareness and activity a religious and sacred duty.

5: A distaste for monolithic religious organizations and a distrust of would be messiahs or gurus. This makes Pagans hard to organize, even for their own good and leads to constant schisming, mutation and growth in the movement.

6: The firm conviction that human beings were meant to lead lives filled with joy, love, pleasure and humour. The traditional Western concepts of sin, guilt and divine retribution are seen as the misunderstandings of natural growth and experience.

7: A simple set of ethics and morality based on the avoidance of actual harm to other people and the living beings of this planet.

8: The knowledge that, with proper training and intent, human minds and hearts are fully capable of performing all the magic and "miracles" they are likely to ever need through the use of natural psychic powers.

9: A belief in the importance of celebrating the solar, lunar and other natural cycles in our lives. This has led to the investigation and revival of many ancient religious traditions.

10: A minimum amount of dogma and a maximum amount of eclecticism. Pagans are reluctant to accept any idea without personally experiencing and investigating it and are unwilling to use any concept not useful to their faith and spiritual fulfilment.

11: A strong faith in the ability to solve their current problems on all levels, public and private. This leads to ...

12: A strong commitment to personal and universal growth, evolution and balance. Pagans are expected to make continual effort in these directions.

13: A belief that one can progress towards achieving such growth, evolution and balance through the carefully planned alteration of one's normal consciousness using both ancient and modern methods of aiding concentration, meditation, reprogramming and ecstasy.

14: The knowledge that human independence implies community co-operation. Pagans are encouraged to use their talents to actually help each other as well as the local, national or international community at large.

15: An awareness that if they are to achieve any of these goals Pagans must practise what they preach. This leads to a concern with making one's lifestyle consistent with one's proclaimed belief.

In this manifesto the emphasis is not on proving the historical veracity of particular forms of Pagan belief or on adherence to ritual processes. The emphasis is instead focused upon a "Pagan consciousness" which manifests itself around prominent ideological, philosophical and aesthetic themes. Firstly, there is the belief that divinity is not solely manifested in an abstract deity who imposes his will from heaven. Secondly, that divinity has both masculine and feminine elements and is manifest in many different forms and symbols. And finally, it is manifested in the belief that Pagans should live in close concert with nature and natural rhythms and cycles rather than be part of techno centric culture. Form this perspective Paganism is based in the pursuit of cooperation with people in their community and is a constant struggle for personal growth and spiritual fulfilment.

Perhaps the most influential example of a prominent neo-Pagan who supports the Jungian approach to historico-cultural identity and claiming authenticity for various rituals and symbols within the neo-Pagan movement is Margot Adler. Her study of the neo-Pagan movement within the US, *Drawing Down the Moon,* is heavily oriented around the Jungian approach towards religious symbolism and the prioritizing of psychological and cultural significance within the collective unconscious as opposed to specific historical claims. For example, she claims that "Goddess worship has an ancient universality about it but it appeared in different places in different times" and that "The Old religion may not have existed geographically or historically but existed in the Jungian sense that people are tapping into a common source" are very clear examples of the Jungian approach to the significance and impact of symbols in religious belief and spiritual experience.[52]

According to Adler this perspective of history is very common throughout the neo-Pagan movement and has come to supplant the more empirical claims to historical legitimacy espoused by traditionalist neo-Pagans during the 1950s. In a series of interviews she found that many neo-Pagans focused on the symbolic experience as an indicator of past legitimacy, illustrated by statements like "When you are doing a ritual and you suddenly get the feeling that you are experiencing something generations of your forebears experienced it is probably true." Other neo-Pagans she interviewed claimed, "It doesn't matter whether the grandmother was a physical reality or a figment of our imagination. One is subjective the other objective but we experience both." What these statements indicate is that the fundamental issue of truth and legitimacy in many neo-Pagan truth claims is based upon symbolic impact, popular appeal and experiential reality in ritual. These psychological truths were perceived as existing in their own right independently of issues relating to empirical veracity.[53] From this perspective empirical history is perceived as largely irrelevant in comparison to the psychological truth of symbolic representations illustrative of the collective unconscious.

This paradigm shift in defining neo-Pagan identity is further illustrated by York's article *Defining Paganism*. Michael York argues that neo-Paganism, as a religious tradition, is particularly difficult as the sheer breadth of cultural forms utilised by Pagans and the quantity of different cultural associations of Paganism and Witchcraft in mainstream society are such that a definition rooted in the cultural forms and rituals of a particular movement is impossible. Instead he argues that what links neo-Pagan movements together is their shared attitude towards culture, nature and spirituality. Neo-Paganism and the legitimacy of Pagan rituals and symbols is not defined by any historical lineage but rather draws on the same source of the ineffable and recognizes that symbols and rituals represent multiple paths to Enlightenment. He defines Paganism as follows.

> Paganism is an affirmation of interactive and polymorphic sacred relationships, by individuals or communities, with the tangible sentient and/or non-empirical.[54]

The Jungian model of symbolic interpretation has proved to be an invaluable means of legitimating Pagan rituals, mythology and historical narratives. The prioritizing of the cultural significance of symbols within the collective unconscious has granted both a means for legitimating Pagan ritual outside of empirical history and a well-established philosophical and ethical structure for

52. Adler, M. *Drawing Down the Moon.* pp 56–58, 59 & 90.
53. Adler, M. *Drawing Down the Moon.* pp 56–58, 59 & 90.
54. York, Michael. "Defining Paganism." pp 6–9.

authenticating Pagan beliefs. From this Jungian perspective, the rituals and symbols of the neo-Pagan tradition are not so much valued in terms of their indexical relationship to a particular Pagan tradition of the past but rather as metaphors of a development into psychological maturity. If radically different cultural traditions are integrated together, such as Native Americans and pre-Roman Celts, it is not a violation of cultural authenticity but rather recognition of the common source of mythological symbolism in the collective unconscious and the universal search for psychological development. For example, prominent Australian neo-Pagan author Cassandra Carter comments on the significance of Pagan ritual in terms of its capacity to explain Jungian models of psychic development.

> In Jungian terms the descent of the Goddess teaches the need for a woman to go on her own quest in search of her *animus*—not waiting for the knight on a white charger who will rescue her from the need to make her own choices, but going to confront the Dark Lord and solve his mysteries—going of her own choice and will into the Kingdom of the Unconscious mind. For a man, he has been successful, with the help of the Goddess, his anima, in exploring and winning the battles within his own unconscious, and he and she are happily reunited in the underworld of the unconscious.[55]

The prioritising of symbolic significance of rituals and cultural forms over historicity in Jungian psychoanalytical theory has proven to be of immense importance for the neo-Pagan movement. In particular, the adoption of Jung's wholistic approach to culture, perceiving the historical origins of symbols as fundamentally interwoven and dependent on the transcendent significance within the collective unconscious, has given the neo-Pagan movement a theoretical model that can accommodate a diverse array of forms, symbols and rituals under the one body. Furthermore, the Jungian model of perceiving images of divinity and the sacred as representative of archetypes within the collective unconscious has given the neo-Pagan movement a ready made model for accommodating polytheistic religious belief. As Margot Adler writes,

> Much of the theoretical basis for a modern defence of polytheism comes from Jungian psychologists who have long argued that the gods and goddesses of myth, legend and fairy tale represent archetypes,

---

55. Carter, Cassandra. *The Old religion in the New Age*. Lecture Given to the C.G Jung Society. twentieth November 1992. p 6.

real potencies and potentialities deep within the psyche, which, when allowed to flower permit us to be more fully human.[56]

For Jungian oriented neo-Pagans the fact that the symbols and rituals utilised in the practice of their faith have a strong psycho-cultural impact is interpreted as evidence implying the existence of a divine universal source in a quasi-Platonic sense. However, it is worth noting that Jung's model arose out of a quasi-scientific attempt to chart a phenomenon found within the human psyche, that is the commonality of symbols within divergent cultural settings without previous contact. For Jung, the reality of that commonality which gave rise to his hypothesising the collective unconscious does not necessarily represent the existence of an external reality. Jung is far more concerned with the effect that this may have upon the human psyche and the way in which a model that takes account of its existence enables a better understanding and better way to effectively interact with the human condition. If there is an external numinous reality, the primary interest of Jungian analytical psychology is the extent to which it impacts on human existence and human experience. The actual existence of a divine source or its ultimate numinous or transcendent character is largely irrelevant.[57]

The adoption of a Jungian theoretical framework permitted many neo-Pagans to avoid confrontation with the problems raised by the empirical inaccuracy of many neo-Pagan truth claims regarding the "Burning Times" and pre-Christian Paganism. Perhaps the single most influential component of the adoption of Jungian theory by large sectors of the neo-Pagan movement was the shift from legitimising ritual and symbolism from history and ethnic/cultural identity to that of psychological impact and the representation of symbols in popular culture. Perhaps the most significant manifestation of this psycho-symbolic approach to religious belief is the increasing acceptance of the belief that ultimately one is responsible for one's own interpretation and experience of the divine beyond any external influences of dogma or tradition. The veracity of religious experience and its symbolic manifestations originates in the unconscious of the individual and whatever symbolic structures are utilised to make sense of that unconscious experience are legitimate manifestations of ultimate unconscious truth lying behind the phenomenology of spiritual experience. As Richard Noll author of the controversial critique of Jung *The Jung Cult* comments, "Through Jung's influence on New Age spiri-

---

56. Adler, M. *Drawing Down the Moon.* p 28.

57. Jung, Carl. *Symbols of Transformation.* Princeton: Princeton University Press. 1990. p 71.

tuality many now indeed believe it is an inalienable human right to personally choose the image of one's own God or Gods."[58]

The Integration of Neo-Paganism and the New Age

There is a certain degree of overlap between the New Age and neo-Pagan movements. Both traditions were fundamentally involved in the development of the counter cultural movements arising out of the sixties. They share a disdain for mainstream religious practices and draw upon the Western Romantic tradition and stereotypes of the religious practices of other cultures for inspiration. They share an eco-humanist perspective on society with links to the Green movement and alternative lifestyle practices. Many people cross the boundary between New Age and neo-Paganism and many new religious movements share elements of both traditions.[59] Both movements share a similar cultural base and, to some extent, share commercial support in similar shops and industries across the Western world.

The overlap between the New Age and neo-Pagan movement is perhaps most visible in the United States. Selena Fox, prominent US neo-Pagan Priestess and founder of the Pagan Spirit Alliance, moved away from a specifically Wiccan focus to embrace a much more eclectic version of nature mysticism that includes many elements of New Age spirituality. In particular Fox utilised an ideology of a search for planetary healing that incorporated elements of Native American, Sufi, Hindu, Buddhist, Christian and hermetic religious forms. She also openly encouraged all faiths to develop their own unique forms of spiritual expression so as to encourage religious Enlightenment and thus better personal empathy with the environment.[60]

According to Fox there are far too many similarities between neo-Paganism and the New Age movement to justify their segregation in matters of spiritual expression. She believes that both traditions share a deep and abiding concern for the earth, a recognition for both masculine and feminine expressions of divinity, a belief in reincarnation, a respect for astrology and the Tarot, use of shamanic ritual and a deep and abiding respect for pre-Christian and pre-industrial cultures. Fox also sees similarities with regards to the New Age and neo-Pagan support of organic food, herbs, natural medicine,

---

58. Noll, Richard. *The Jung Cult: The Origins of a Charismatic Movement.* London: Fontana Press, 1996. p 37.

59. York, M. *The Emerging Network.* pp 145–177.

60. York, M. *The Emerging Network.* p 156.

alternative energy sources and meditational practices. Given these similarities she believes that the distinction between the two movements is arbitrary and unnecessarily divisive.[61]

However, despite the many links and commonalities between them the neo-Pagan and New Age movements are quite distinct in many areas and there is a considerable body of criticism and tension between them. This is exacerbated by the fact that both sides of the movement have tended to underplay the once close links during the era of the sixties counter culture and deny the many similarities between them.[62] Purkiss argues that in the majority of cases members of the neo-Pagan movement tend to regard the New Age movement as a form of hypocritical "yuppie" consumerism which is very distinct from the search for union with the natural world and the Goddess espoused by neo-Pagans.[63] Some of these conflicts had appeared as early as the late 1960s with incidents of New Agers being accused by neo-Pagans of being hierarchical, divorced from nature and consumerist in their attitude to religion.[64] Some of the ambiguity felt towards the New Age movement by neo-Pagans is demonstrated by a survey conducted by the Pagan Spirit Alliance in 1990 which found that, whilst the majority of their respondents felt that there were similarities and useful insights to be found in the New Age movement, it was far more a fad and less of a religion. Terms such as goofy, phoney, looney, hypocritical, obnoxious, airhead, cultic and consumerist commonly occurred when respondents were asked to describe their perception of the New Age movements practitioners.[65]

According to Hutton the main difference between the neo-Pagan and New Age movements is that neo-Paganism is more overtly religious and precisely defined than the New Age. Neo-Paganism emphasises links with the Pagan religions of antiquity and Witches of Early Modern Europe, cyclical rituals and animistic/polytheistic forms of religious belief. It seeks an immanent source of the divine in the physical realm. The New Age movement, by contrast, emphasises karmic law, the inner self as the focus of spiritual expression and separation of the spirit from the limitations of the physical body.[66] According to

---

61. Fox, Selena. *Pagan Spirit Alliance Newsletter*. No. 37. Spring 2000. p 5.

62. Australian Pagan Survey Results (Australian Pagan Alliance). December 2000; Hutton, Ronald. *The Triumph of the Moon*. pp 411–412; Purkiss, Diane. *The Witch in History*. p 31; Starhawk. *The Spiral Dance*. p 26.

63. Purkiss, D. *The Witch in History*. Routledge: London. p 31.

64. Adler, M. *Drawing Down the Moon*. pp 246–247.

65. Fox, S. *Pagan Spirit Alliance Newsletter*. p 2.

66. Hutton, R. *The Triumph of the Moon*. pp 411–412.

this perspective the New Age movement is a diverse collection of alternative religious practices and spiritual beliefs that arose out of the sixties counter culture. It shares a focus on religious experience, personal Enlightenment and exploration of the inner self. Neo-Paganism represents a religious belief system that draws upon Romantic constructions of pre-Christian religion and contemporary images of Early Modern European Witchcraft.

One of the most visible differences between neo-Paganism and the New Age movement is the central role given to the figure of the Goddess in neo-Pagan thought. In the eco-feminist branches of the neo-Pagan tradition the Goddess is given an almost monotheistic role in the belief system. In Gardner's Wicca the central role of the Goddess is balanced with the male fertility God Cernunnos. However, the New Age movement does have examples of feminine images of divinity. Gaia is the perhaps the most prominent example. In contrast to the neo-Pagan tradition the New Age movement has tended to define the image of feminine divinity in terms of an eternal feminine principle or as a feminine aspect to the divine inner self rather than as an expression of feminine deity made manifest in the natural world.[67]

Another point of contention between the neo-Pagans and the New Age movement is the perceived commercialism and higher costs of New Age materials, rituals and seminars when compared to the more "earthy" expressions of Pagan belief. Adler describes this contention rather cynically when she comments that;

> The difference between Pagan and New Age is one decimal point. In other words, a two-day meditation by a New Age practitioner might cost $300, while the same course given by a Pagan might cost $30. While Pagan workshops still cost only a fraction of similar New Age seminars, there's no telling what could happen if, Goddess forbid, Paganism became really popular.[68]

According to York the New Age movement is considered by many Pagans to be more expensive, commercial, middle class and consumerist than neo-Paganism. It is perceived as a post-modern spiritual marketing machine aimed at middle class Yuppies for shock value, seeking a quick self-indulgent "fix" rather than a real religion. The New Age movement is also considered more elitist with a far lower level of spiritual commitment and a far higher finan-

---

67. Adler, M. *Drawing Down the Moon.* pp 35–36; Crowley, V. *The Old Religion in the New Age.* pp 163–182; Starhawk. *The Spiral Dance.* pp 22–25; York, M. *The Emerging Network.* p 146.

68. Adler, M. *Drawing Down the Moon.* p 420.

cial commitment than Paganism. Additionally, the narcissistic focus of many New Age searches for personal fulfilment, Enlightenment and religious experience seriously limits the potential for communion with the guiding spirit of nature and distracts from the practical task of healing the earth.[69]

However, it is difficult to gauge the verifiability of these complaints due to the fact that neither the New Age nor the neo-Pagan movements are homogenous bodies. There is also a degree of ambiguity in the fact that New Age and neo-Pagan material is supplied in the same shops and often shares the same festivals and markets, such as Australia's Confest and Nimbin festivals.[70] In fact there are significant variants of both traditions that actively seek to avoid homogeneity of religious practice and symbolic expression. This is particularly evident in the New Age movement, which is more a combination of similar attitudes and concepts than an organized faith. Variations of the New Age movement run the full gamut of class and cultural expression from the Ferals, a counter cultural movement that rejects consumerism and is closely linked to environmental activism, to urban middle class yuppies.[71]

There is a prominent wing of the New Age movement that is closely linked with the triumphalist capitalist consumerism that developed during the 1980s. There are increasing numbers of New Agers that have rejected links with the counter culture and are directing their attention to higher income households, mainstream social values and even big business.[72] One curious aspect of this shift is the adoption of New Age rhetoric and methodology in business management. These organizations promise to enlighten middle management staff to the possibilities of harnessing their true self in office management. However, as opposed to the self being conceived in religious terms, the self is conceived in terms of empowered business practices, creative energy and autonomy that can be utilised in the successful running of a business and acquisition of profit.[73] According to Heelas, one of the reasons the machinery of Western Capitalism has so easily appropriated the New Age movement is that the personalised and occasionally narcissistic individualised approach to spirituality

69. York, M. *The Emerging Network.* pp 158–159.

70. Newton, Janice. "Aborigines, Tribes and Counterculture." pp 50–56; St John, Graham. *Alternative Culture Heterotopia.* http://www.angelfire.com/pq/edgecentral/contents.html (25-3-2002).

71. Heelas, Paul. "The New Age in Cultural Context: The Premodern, the Modern and the Postmodern." *Religion.* Vol 23. 1993. pp 103–105. Australian Pagan Survey Results (Australian Pagan Alliance). December 2000.

72. Heelas, P. The New Age in Cultural Context. pp 106–107.

73. Jackson, Gerald. *The Inner Executive.* New York: Simon & Shuster, 1989.

by many sectors of the New Age movement is to some extent closely aligned with the discourse of individualistic enterprise culture and Western consumerism.[74] Furthermore, due to the conversion effect of the seminars and books marketed at higher income employees and clients, more and more individuals from the corporate heartland of Western capitalism are being orientated towards the New Age movement.[75]

However, despite the strong corporate and consumer component of the New Age movement, there are many New Agers who are quite hostile to this development and perceive it as a corruption of the search within that prostitutes the inner self to the needs of economic success.[76] There are also proponents of the neo-Pagan movement who feel that applying their beliefs, rituals, spells and practices to success in business, life, popularity and fashion is in no way incompatible with their identity as Pagans. Some Pagans go as far as to suggest that denial of desire and consumption for higher ends is a product of Christian asceticism and is in opposition to Pagan ideals.[77] As a result the relationship between consumerism and the New Age and neo-Pagan movements remains ambiguous and ill defined as means of differentiating the two sub-cultures.[78]

The Ambivalence to Nature in Neo-Pagan Discourse

One of the most critical components of both the New Age and neo-Pagan movements is their respective responses to Western modernity. Roszak sees

---

74. Heelas, Pl. The New Age in Cultural Context. pp 107–108.

75. Wenegrat, B & Yalom, I. Large Group Awareness Training. *Annual Review of Psychology*, 1982. pp 515–539.

76. Heelas, P. *The New Age Movement.* pp 30–32.

77. Cabot, Laurie. *The Power of the Witch.* New York: Arkana/Penguin, 1993. p 149–151.

78. The issues surrounding the neo-Pagan movement's rather ambivalent relationship to commodification, popular culture and late capitalism are far too complex to deal with here. The influence of late capitalism and commodification is instead dealt with in Chapter 6 where the underlying structures behind the growing influence of the sphere of commodification is dealt with specifically in relation to the rather ambivalent relationship between neo-Paganism as a Romantic social movement and a popular culture increasingly dominated by the market. At this point in time it is worth noting that there is a significant relationship between the New Age movement, neo-Pagans and the commodification of culture with forms a subtext to the evolution of neo-Pagan symbols, ideals and ideological configurations in the post-sixties era.

the development of the neo-Pagan tradition in the aftermath of the sixties counter culture as a response to the objectification, commodification and secularisation of society by the process of Western modernity.[79] The neo-Pagan tradition is the continuation of the critique of the urban-industrial imperative that began in the Romantic movement of the late eighteenth and early nineteenth centuries. The increasing artificiality of human experience in a human created world of technology and industrialism fundamentally disrupted the age-old communion between human experience and the natural world.[80]

There are many neo-Pagans who would share this perspective. Starhawk, for example, argues that contemporary Western society is dominated by a unique constellation of patriarchy, modernity, and industrialism that works to divorce Western society from nature, the feminine and the spiritual. This separation, combined with a dualistic worldview that defines reality in terms of polar opposites, leads to the objectification, hatred and exploitation of nature, women and dissident minorities.[81] This process of objectification and domination by technocratic patriarchal society has led to a collective experience of marginalisation and persecution by white patriarchal society towards those identified with femininity and the natural world: women, blacks, traditional societies and Witches.[82] The overcoming of inclusive, Goddess centred and nature oriented Paganism by the patriarchal and dualistic Judeo-Christian faiths has led to this deplorable situation from which the transformation of society by a re-embracing of Paganism is the most natural and authentic response.[83]

As previously discussed, these themes have been prominent within the neo-Pagan movement and its antecedents in the Western Romantic tradition. To a large extent this perspective forms a central component of neo-Pagan identity and its relationship with the past as a source of cultural authenticity and inspiration. However, there is a certain degree of ambiguity towards the role of technology in society from the perspective of neo-Pagans and New Agers. In her research into the beliefs and practices of American neo-Pagans, Adler initially anticipated her findings to suggest that most Pagans would support a Luddite or revolutionary response to technology, industrialism and scientific

---

79. Roszak, T. *Where the Wasteland Ends.* p viii.
80. Roszak, T. *Where the Wasteland Ends.* pp 6–13.
81. Starhawk. *The Spiral Dance.* pp 22–29.
82. Starhawk. *Truth or Dare.* San Francisco: Harper and Row. 1987. pp 6–7, 32–33, 106.
83. Starhawk. *The Spiral Dance.* pp 22–29.

progress. This would have meshed well with the neo-Pagan idealization of nature, pre-industrial societies and antagonism towards Christian and technocratic culture. However, the results of extensive interviews and surveys amongst neo-Pagan Americans indicated a much more ambivalent attitude towards technology. In many cases neo-Pagans were extremely familiar with and supported the application of high technology. Many respondents felt that through the application of ecologically sustainable technology, such as solar and wind power, many of the problems wrought by unrestricted exploitation of the natural environment could be overcome. However almost all recipients felt that technology and industry were abused by mainstream patriarchal and Christian centres of authority and thus Western civilization required a major structural, social and spiritual transformation of the human condition.[84] One typical respondent commented that,

> I'm all for technology, as long as it doesn't destroy the earth in the process. I'm very happy with technological advances. I'm very happy to climb in my car and drive 200 hundred miles to see my Pagan friends. [laugh] It's a bummer flying my broom in winter. Besides modern conveniences have eliminated a lot of drudgery. Modern technology has freed up time for philosophical pursuits.[85]

Another respondent commented that,

> There is a tendency among some Pagans to want to be back in, let us say, sixth-century Wales instead of wanting a transformed world. Going back to sixth-century Wales is a fantasy that is dear to me. It's part of the archetypal dream. But that's all it is. Nobody really wants to go back into the past, except a bunch of space cookies. It is not really modern technology that is desensitising. It is the misuse of it that is. I would not exchange my tape recorder for a lute.[86]

Heelas takes this ambiguity further by arguing that the New Age and neo-Pagan movements, despite protestations to the contrary, operate concurrently with mainstream Western society and modernity. According to Heelas, in many ways the New Age and neo-Pagan movements are not antithetical to the tradition of Western modernity but are, in fact, the culmination of long standing cultural trajectories. From this perspective the features of eclecticism, individualism, autonomy, a search for cultural authenticity and redefinitions of

---

84. Adler, M. *Drawing down the Moon.* p 21.
85. Adler, M. *Drawing down the Moon.* p 392.
86. Adler, M. *Drawing Down the Moon.* p 392.

the past to suit contemporary consumer identities are manifestations of the tradition of Western modernity. Many of these trajectories are not only visible in mainstream Western society but can also be found in the ideologies of the Free Market, propagated in the heartland of capitalism under Reagan and Thatcher.[87] This is not to deny the many critiques of modernity, industrialism and technocratic approaches to nature held by many neo-Pagans but rather it confirms that the neo-Pagan and New Age movements contain many common currents that emerged out of the traditions of Western modernity, individualism and humanism.

Play Power and Spirituality

One element of sixties counter cultural protests that has been extensively adopted by the neo-Pagan movement is the phenomenon of "Play Power." The phrase, coined by Richard Neville's book of the same name, describes a method of challenging political authority through harnessing the absurd, the nonsensical and the bizarre through the spirit of play and humour. This idea was posited by many sectors of the sixties counter culture, most notably the Yippies, as more subversive and challenging than traditional forms of protest as it attacked the very notions of rationality, conformity and normality that supported structures of hierarchy and authority.[88]

One of the most prominent examples of this form of protest action was the 1967 attempt to levitate the Pentagon and have it rotate and turn orange. The basis of the protest was not to actually cause this event to happen, nor was it a traditional activist protest. Rather it was designed to challenge the underlying system of logic behind government response to protests via the politics of display.[89] The WITCH movement on Wall Street in 1968 enacted a similar protest aimed at patriarchal authority.[90] According to the idea of "Play Power", protests of paradox, spectacle and play are more effective than traditional forms of activism because they are not rooted in coherent ideology. According to this theme, movements like the Yippies were a greater threat to the system precisely because they posed a total revolution to the very structure of

---

87. Heelas, P. *The New Age Movement*. p 154.
88. Stephens, J. *Anti-Disciplinary Protest*. pp 33, 35, 91–92, 96–98.
89. Neville, R. *Play Power*. pp 31–33; Stephens, J. *Anti-Disciplinary Protest*. pp 37–39.
90. The circumstances and background to WITCH is discussed in detail in the following chapter.

logic and rationality upon which mainstream society is based.[91] Throughout these kinds of movements lie a complex interwoven network of humour, spectacle and play connected with a serious attempt to challenge the social, cultural and political establishment. The perception of authority as serious, logical, rational and structured led to a perception that an alternative social order must be vibrant, creative, irrational, humorous and joyful.[92] This unique constellation of ideas was also adopted by many sectors of the neo-Pagan movement. Spectacles for shock value, parodies of mainstream religion and culture with an underlying serious attempt to challenge the dominant socio-cultural and religious order of Western society and a serious search for new forms of religious expression coalesced throughout many sectors of the neo-Pagan movement.

Many neo-Pagan religious organizations originating out of the sixties counter culture have rather comical or ironic histories. The Newly Reformed Orthodox Order Of the Golden Dawn or NROOGD was initially established as a joke and a parody of nineteenth century spiritualism.[93] An Egyptian oriented neo-Pagan movement called the Church of the Eternal Source began as an annual Egyptian themed student costume party.[94] The Reformed Druids of North America began as a protest against regulations at Carleton College requiring religious observance.[95] These movements, among others combined a serious search for spiritual expression with a sense of parody, humour and play in protest against mainstream societies fixation on the restrained, the ordered and the serious. Paganism is believed to represent joy, humour, irony and freedom in contrast to the perceived asceticism, authoritarianism and seriousness of mainstream religion. Starhawk, named one of her first covens "Compost" as both a reference to the image of all sorts of material coming together to create fertile soil and a humorous jibe at Wiccan pretentiousness.[96] In a statement designed to antagonize the intensely ritualistic and hierarchical traditionalist Wiccans and mainstream religions the Discordian Society gave as their guidelines for initiation into a Pagan religion that a hopeful mem-

---

91. Stephens, J. *Anti-Disciplinary Protest.* pp 96–97.

92. Neville, R. *Play Power.* pp 222–223.

93. Twilgus, Neal. "An Interview with Anton Wilson." *Science Fiction Review.* Vol 5. No 2. 1976. pp 32–33.

94. Moss, Harold. "Forum." *Green Egg.* Vol 5. No 51. 1972. pp 2–7.

95. Bonewitz, Isaac. *The Druids Chronicles.* Berkeley: Drunmeton Press, 1976. pp 1–12; Bonewitz, Isaac.. "Why and What is Reformed Druidism in the 1970s." *The Green Egg.* Vol 7. No 75. 1971. pp 15–17.

96. Starhawk. *The Spiral Dance.* pp 5, 52–54.

ber should simply "Decide the religion exists and include yourself in it."[97] The movement responded to claims by fundamentalist right wing Christians that their existence was part of a conspiracy to undermine American society and morals by setting up a chapter called "The Bavarian Illuminati" and then sending letters to the media to the effect that they were indeed secretly controlling the American youth through music, art and culture in preparation for communist invasion and had been since they had enlisted Beethoven in the eighteenth century.[98]

These variations of neo-Pagan practices were designed as both a protest against mainstream social conformity and a way of contrasting neo-Paganism as a religion of humour and joy against dour mainstream Christianity. Harvey Cox summarised this perspective as a natural response to the loss of true festivity, fantasy and communitas in Western culture. Neo-Paganism, as a religion developed largely in response to the development of Western modernity, has reclaimed the long lost ritual function of humour and play as part of religious focus. Its use of humour in constructing images, symbols and rituals may be ironic, flippant and spontaneous but this does not mean that it is trivial. To the contrary, the new forms of lost spiritual expression and the joy of play are being reclaimed as part of religious and social experience and the significance of play power in religion is now being fully realized.[99]

From Secret Society to Counter Culture Paganism Transformed

The impact of the sixties counter culture on the neo-Pagan movement can hardly be exaggerated. The very nature of what classifying oneself as a Witch or a Pagan meant was radically transformed. Similarly, the diverse range of Romantic recreationist religions that lay a claim to Pagan inspiration were integrated together in conjunction with a wave of counter cultural movements that gave the neo-Pagan tradition a mass appeal extending beyond the bounds of any specific organization. Paganism, as a spiritual concept, became fundamentally linked with social transformation or even revolutionary ideologies

---

97. Interview with Robert Anton Wilson cited in Adler, Margot. *Drawing Down the Moon.* p 332.

98. Twilgus, Neal. "An Interview with Anton Wilson." *Science Fiction Review.* Vol 5. No 2. 1976. pp 32–33.

99. Cox, Harvey. *The Feast of Fools.* Cambridge: Harvard University Press, 1969. pp 50–59.

designed to act as an antidote to the ills of Western modernity and industrialism. The neo-Pagan movement fundamentally shifted in orientation from an intense focus on ritual and esoteric practices linked to a recreation of distinctly national identity to an eclectic religion of play power and free flowing cultural expression defined in universalist terms.

Neo-Paganism, after the sixties, increasingly shifted towards a revolutionary perspective calling for a new era that would appropriate the purity, authenticity and freedom engendered by a re-embracing of a Pagan past. Such an orientation, it was believed, would inevitably lead to a new and better future. It is a fundamentally Romantic notion, looking backwards to an idealised construction of the past with an eye to a utopian future. However, unlike the traditionalist neo-Paganism or nineteenth century Romanticism, the neo-Paganism that was to emerge from the sixties rejected elitism and aimed for mass appeal and popularity. Images of powerful psycho-cultural impact were appropriated, reconstructed and reconfigured as new signs and symbols of counter-cultural identity. Witch and Pagan identity were images chosen on the basis of their impact in popular culture and utilised as symbols representing contemporary social, cultural and political issues. Similarly, for Jungian neo-Pagans empirical forms of historicity became abandoned in favour of metaphorical interpretations of symbols, myths and rituals that were perceived to illustrate the development towards maturity of a person's psyche. This embracing of eclecticism meant in practice that empirical claims to cultural identity could become discarded in favour of personally customised images of cultural identity, the divine and the spiritual. In this new paradigm of identity formation and cultural representation it is the semiotic structure of signs and signifiers that legitimised neo-Pagan identity and historicity became increasingly subjected to contemporary popular appeal rooted deeply in items of material culture.

7

Eco-Feminist Neo-Paganism: Marginalization and Romanticism

Though typically the object of childhood terror, Witches are ridiculed and dismissed by the large majority of adults in our society. But there is a new Witch at large in the west. She sups on tofu and organically grown vegetables rather than stolen penises and boiled babies, she lives in the suburbs rather than in a house of cake, she is limited to the same forms of transport as the rest of us, but she still flies in the face of Christians—at least her belief system does. She does not talk about the devil, but her invocation of ancient Goddesses, her wistful talk about the pre-Christian past, and her attempts to recreate Pagan rituals are unquestionably heretical. Why, we might ask ourselves, should any woman today see any point in calling herself a Witch when she knows full well that the Witch of mythology was a misogynistic invention and that the brutal process of Witch-labeling led, in Europe, to three centuries of gynocide? Who does this new Witch think she is?[1]

The WITCH Movement

In 1968, amongst a wide range of anti-modernist and counter cultural movements, the action wing of the New York Radical Women's movement staged a protest formed around the name WITCH or Women's International Terrorist Conspiracy from Hell. In a protest against capitalist patriarchal so-

---

1. Rountree, Kathryn. "The New Witch of the West: Feminists Reclaim the Crone." *Journal of Popular Culture*. Vol 30(4), Spring 1997. pp 213.

ciety they dressed themselves as Witches with black pointy hats, wands, crone masks and cloaks and converged on Wall Street. The stated aim was to pit their "ancient magic" against the center of the "Imperialist Phallic Society". They danced to the Federal Reserve Bank carrying a paper-mache pig's head on a silver platter. They went to the New York Stock exchange where they told guards at the door they had an appointment with the "Chief Executor of Wall Street—Satan". They then led a chant proclaiming the coming demise of stock prices. The "Great Glass Erection" of Chase Manhattan was circled and a ritual was performed calling for matriarchal insurrection and revolution. They continued this way throughout the city to various places including trendy nightclubs, restaurants, girl bars and burlesque houses chanting, "We are Witch, We are Women, We are liberation, We are We." and "Nine Million Women Burned as Witches."[2]

The WITCH movement described itself as predominantly Marxist in nature and selected the symbolism of the Witch for its value as a spectacle and as a figure represented on the outside of mainstream culture. Similarly, the use of ritual in these protests by Marxist feminists in the sixties was not focused on the idea of women channeling spiritual energy but was more orientated towards the use of ritual as public performance. The critical issue in the selection of the Witch symbology and use of ritual in the context of the sixties WITCH movements was the focus on creating crowd drawing theatricality in protests and the symbolic role of the Witch as a marginalized figure on the outside of mainstream Western culture.[3] The WITCH movement represented the historical Witch of the Early Modern period as the original proto-feminist engaged in a battle against patriarchal totalitarianism.

> Witches, it is pointed out, have been the original guerillas and resistance fighters against oppression down through the ages. Historically Witches are seen as non-conformist, free, intelligent, joyous, aggressive, creative, scientific and actively rebellious (birth controllers, abortionists, herbalists and pushers). These Witches knew not Marx and Engels but their conquerors knew Freud.[4]

---

2. Morgan, Robin. *Going too Far: The Personal Chronicle of a Feminist.* New York: Vintage Books. 1978. pp 70–79; Purkiss, D. *The Witch in History.* pp 8–9; Rountree, K. "The New Witch of the West." pp 214–216; Spretnak, Charlene (Ed.). *The Politics of Women's Spirituality: Essays on the Rise of Spiritual Power within the Feminist Movement.* New York: Doubleday, 1982. p 76.

3. Morgan, Robin. *Going too Far.* p 71–75; Neville, Richard. *Play Power.* p 72; Rountree, K. *The New Witch of the West,* p 216.

4. Neville, R. *Play Power.* p 72.

To the WITCH movement, and a number of other anti-establishment sub-cultures of the era, the Witch was representative of a long historical tradition of agrarian popular rebellion against white, scientific, religious and patriarchal oppression. Placed upon the Witch of history was a plethora of contemporary values and images peculiar to popular sixties activism. The creation of the Witch as a figure of resistance depended a great deal on the Witch's traditional role in Western European culture as a feminine figure on the outside of the political and cultural mainstream. However, it also came to rely extensively upon nineteenth century Romantic representations of the Witch such as Michelet's hypothesis that Witchcraft was a series of popular agrarian protests against religious, economic and political domination. The fact that these images and representations had little to do with the actual Witches of early modern Europe themselves meant little to the WITCH movement. The critical issue was that the Witch was a powerful symbol possessing psychological and cultural impact as a representation of feminine identity contrary to the forces of modernity, Christianity and patriarchy.

What makes the WITCH movement unique and so central to the development of modern eco-feminist Paganism is the strength of the Witch symbology for many American women in contemporary society. The symbol of the Witch exploits a long held Western theme of the Witch as representative of dark feminine power but its use here as an acronym for Women's International Terrorist Conspiracy from Hell is also quite significant. It represents an appropriation of the symbolic significance of the term "Witch", while creating for it a specific and localized new meaning in Western culture.

In the construction of the acronym WITCH, "Women's" denotes the neo-Pagan archetype of the Witch as both gendered and collective. This is to say that the symbol of the Witch is necessarily associated with the feminine and to the identity of women in general and within society rather than the isolated and ostracized figure of folklore on the edge of the established social order. "International" identifies this particular configuration of feminine identity as transcending national and cultural boundaries while "conspiracy" and "terrorist" are designed to characterize women as dark, secretive and possessing the capacity to bring terror to the established social order.[5] Also implicit and rather central to the 1968 WITCH protests was the following conception and idealization of the historical figure of the early modern Witch,

> They bowed to no man, being the living remnant of the oldest culture of all—one in which men and women were equal sharers in a

---

5. Purkiss, D. *The Witch in History.* p 9.

truly cooperative society before the death-dealing sexual, economic and spiritual oppression of the Imperialist Phallic Society took over and began to destroy nature and human society.[6]

The WITCH movement developed the image of the Witch crazes of the early modern period as a systematic pogrom against empowered women defined as the "Burning Times." This perspective held that Witches in the early modern period were the surviving remnants of a matriarchal agrarian utopia that was perceived as a threat and subsequently hunted down and persecuted by a burgeoning patriarchal alliance of conservative Christianity and Enlightenment Modernity.

The WITCH movement, in pursuing what it believed were significant issues related to women's identity and formation in society, utilized a number of powerful symbolic formations based upon the myriad of images associated with the figure of the Witch in contemporary society. One of these images is the pervasive representation of the Witch persecutions as synonymous with the pointless, unjust and prejudiced persecution of women. This practice is not limited to the WITCH and other eco-feminist movements. It is also integrally a part of other representations of the Witch crazes such as those of writers like Arthur Miller and historians like Norman Cohn and Jules Michelet. Another is manifested in the long traditions of Western Romanticism. Both the WITCH movement and Western Romanticism share a tradition of positing agrarian and utopian representations of the past against contemporary images of dystopian industrialism and violence against nature. This posture is also generally combined with a belief that the feminine body and spirit are inherently entwined with nature and masculinity with technology and industrialism.

Historically, the development of eco-feminist neo-Paganism is characterized by several stages. The first is the involvement of many American women in counter cultural movements in the aftermath of sixties radicalism. The second is a widespread eco-feminist appropriation of Romanticism. This approach was marked by many post-sixties feminist writers who posited a particular ideological construction which changed the focus of feminist activity and analysis from public sphere economic and political issues, to private sphere domestic, cultural and symbolic issues. The third is a paradigmatic shift in historical analysis and conceptions of authenticity, in the eco-feminist neo-Pagan movement, from reliance on traditional forms of empirical evidence and analysis to representations of history through the interpretation of

---

6. Spreknak, C. *The Politics of Women's Spirituality*. p 76.

contemporary symbols. Finally, the development of eco-feminist neo-Paganism is characterized by its interaction with broader trends of American social and cultural construction.

The Goddess and the Counter Culture

The impact of late sixties feminist movements and the aftermath of sixties radicalism, particularly during the sixties, represented a paradigmatic fulcrum in the development of eco-feminist neo-Paganism. The end of the sixties is often characterized in terms of political disillusionment, declining radicalism and the demise of hopes for social revolution and mass activism being replaced by a concentration on individualistic goals of personal fulfillment, wealth and career success. In this context, the demise of sixties radicalism and its failure to achieve social revolution in the mainstream political sense are interpreted in terms of a broader sense of failure and disillusionment with political activism in general. As Julie Stephens writes,

> This all too familiar slant on the sixties portrays this loss as marking a crisis of faith in apocalyptic revolutionary projects and is used to explain everything from the purported narcissism of the seventies, the consumerism of the eighties and the political landscape of the nineties.[7]

Not withstanding the problems involved in interpreting representations of sixties activism in the broader community, the experience of feminist activism and feminist orientated interpretations of sixties radicalism and the substantial development and growth of women's movements in the post sixties era are a critical aspect of the development of eco-feminist neo-Paganism. A common critique of dominant representations of the decline of sixties radicalism is the relegation of burgeoning women's activism to the periphery of analysis and interpretation. According to Echols, a central problem with representations of sixties radicalism is that the entirety of sixties activism is generally interpreted from the perspective of neo-leftist, white, middle class males.[8] According to Julie Stephens, the idea that despair and apathy followed the failure of sixties radicalism obscures the flourishing of radical and activist feminism in the seventies. Of particular importance is the militancy, political enthusiasm and

---

7. Stephens, J. *Anti-Disciplinary Protest.* p 120.
8. Echols, Alice. "We Gotta Get Out of this Place: Notes Towards Remapping the Sixties." *Socialist Review.* Vol 22. No 2. April/June, 1992. p 12.

strong tradition of radicalism in seventies and early eighties feminism, in sharp contrast to the supposed political quietism of the late seventies.[9]

What this indicates is that, at least in terms of contemporary representations of sixties activism in eco-feminist neo-Paganism, the experience of the sixties and its aftermath was very much an experience differentiated by gender. This is particularly interesting when representations of early sixties leftist activism are understood in rather negative terms from a gendered perspective. These range from Robin Morgan's description of the role of women in sixties leftist activism as incessantly rolling joints and cooking endless pots of stew,[10] to Starhawk's severe criticism of a patriarchal "Guru" mentality in many sixties spiritual and political movements[11] and Margot Alder's critique of the soulless condition of sixties Marxist feminism and other political ideologies.[12]

Critical interpretation of much of sixties activism by post sixties eco-feminists and neo-Pagans centered around its inability to escape the bonds of patriarchal power structures, to offer a salve to heal the wounds of profoundly spiritual social ailments or to offer a new uniquely feminine aspect to social revolution. Despite this, representations of sixties activism remain central to eco-feminist neo-Pagan ideological and socio-cultural construction. For example, Starhawk's representation of a future utopia in her novel "The Fifth Sacred Thing" is heavily based on images relating to sixties ideals of utopianism.

> She had adored the city ever since her first glimpse of it in the Summer of Love, more than eighty years before. She had been seventeen then, enchanted by the fog concealing and revealing mysteries like the veil of an exotic dancer, delighted by the crowded streets where people seemed to be perpetually in costume: gypsies, pirates, Indians, sorceresses skipping down the sidewalks to the strains of the Beatles singing "Love, Love, Love."[13]

Similarly, the strategies used in political activism and the mechanisms proposed for initiating social change in relation to gendered inequality, environmental degradation and social justice owe a large debt to experiences and representa-

---

9. Stephens, J. *Anti-Disciplinary Protest.* pp 121–123.

10. Morgan, Robin. *The Demon Lover: On the sexuality of Terrorism.* London: Methuen Press, 1989. pp 217–243.

11. Adler, M. *Drawing Down the Moon.* p 17–18.

12. Starhawk, *The Spiral Dance.* pp 116 & 207.

13. Starhawk. *The Fifth Sacred Thing.* New York: Harper-Collins Publishers. p 2.

tions of sixties radicalism. An example of this is Starhawk's representation of a popular matriarchal uprising against a patriarchal military dictatorship.

> On Shotwell Street, down below the slopes of the hill, which at the time was called Bernall Heights, lived a woman Maria Elena Gomes Garcia, whose grandmother grew fruit trees in the backyard from peach pits and avocado pits, and she saved her tomato seeds. While the steward's troops were massing down on the peninsula, commandeering all stockpiles of food, and the rest of us were debating what to do and trying to work up courage to do it, Maria gathered up together with her neighbors, Alice Black, Lily Fong and Greta Jeanne Margolis, four old women with nothing to lose. On the morning of the first of August, they marched out in the dawn with pick axes over their shoulders, straight out into the middle of Army Street, and all the traffic stopped, such cars as a few people could still afford to drive. Some of them were honking their horns, some of them were shouting threats, but when Amaria raised her pickaxe above her head, there came a silence like a great, shared, indrawn breath. Then she let it fall, with a thud that shuddered through the street, and the four old women began to dig.
> They tore up the pavement, blow by blow, and filled the holes with compost from the sack Greta carried, and planted them with seeds. By then a crowd had gathered, the word was carried through the streets, and we rushed from our houses to join them, bringing tools or only our bare hands, eager to build something new. And many of us were crying with joy or with fear, tears streaming enough to water the seeds.[14]

This representation of counter-cultural revolution illustrates several prominent features of eco-feminist neo-Pagan political representation shared with many counter-cultural movements and Western Romanticism. The protest represented is above all one of spectacle placing the forces of nature and agrarian ideals and symbols against modernity and modern civilization, epitomized by the technocratic military dictatorship. Of particular importance is the emphasis placed on femininity, intrinsically linked to nature and agrarian utopia and upon the power of the spectacle and the force of non-violent and therefore non-patriarchal protest. The source of both power and truth in this representation, as in most counter-cultural movements, is the impact of spectacle and

---

14. Starhawk. *The Fifth Sacred Thing.* p 25–26.

symbol over rationality, logic and traditional forms of state power. These features of popular protests of spectacle and symbolism are hallmarks of both sixties activism and the development of post-sixties eco-feminist neo-Paganism.

The Goddess and "The Burning Times"

There are several critical shifts involved in the political and historical location of post-sixties eco-feminist neo-Paganism. These issues are represented in a series of paradigmatic changes in feminist theory, interpretations of the nature of social and political transformation amongst activist movements and in the relationship between the neo-Pagan movement and its reliance on historical interpretation. The central feature underpinning these analytical and inspirational shifts in the ideological construction and development of eco-feminist neo-Paganism is the broader adoption of Romantic motifs, symbols and structures of analysis by feminist activists in the seventies and eighties. Where these changes are perhaps the most apparent are in the twin symbolic representations central to eco-feminist neo-Paganism, the symbol of a pre-Christian matriarchal utopia and its counter-part representation of the Witch crazes of the early modern period referred to as the "Burning Times". Throughout both these representations of history is the central figure of the Witch as a woman located on the outside of mainstream society yet representing universal values denied by that society to its own spiritual and ethical detriment.

The eco-feminist Witch and her role in representations of the past via the mythology of the "Burning Times" is particularly seductive because of her definition in learned social discourse as the ultimate victim. From the work of Norman Cohn to Margaret Murray and Jules Michelet to Arthur Millers representation of the Witch as synonymous with the victims of the House Committee for un-American Activities through "The Crucible", the Witch craze has become associated with the arbitrary persecution of innocents by aggressive ideology. Instead of simply recreating or redefining a narrative of feminine persecution the eco-feminist neo-Pagan movement, along with many other scholars involved in representations of Witch persecutions as a patriarchal pogrom against women, are following in the footsteps of liberal, Romantic and humanist historians who deplore the Witch crazes as a symbol of barbarity and injustice manifested in the contemporary injustices of the present.[15] The eco-

---

15. Purkiss, D. *The Witch in History.* p 15.

feminist Wiccan interpretation of the "Burning Times" of early modern Europe is well summarized by prominent neo-Pagan author Starhawk. It is a substantial quote but its significance in qualitatively illustrating the eco-feminist neo-Pagan model of the "Burning Times' warrants an extended passage.

In 1484, the Papal Bull of Innocent VIII unleashed the power of the inquisition against the old religion. With the publication of the *Malleus Maleficarum*, "The Hammer of the Witches" by Dominican's Kramer and Sprenger in 1486, the groundwork was laid for a reign of terror that was to hold all of Europe in its grip until well into the seventeenth century. The persecution was most strongly directed against women: Of an estimated nine million Witches executed, eighty percent were women, including children and young girls, who were believed to inherit the evil from their mothers. The asceticism of early Christianity, which turned its back on the world of the flesh, had degenerated, in some quarters of the Church, into hatred of those who had brought that flesh into being. Misogyny, the hatred of women, had become a strong element in medieval Christianity. Women who menstruate and give birth, were identified with sexuality and therefore with evil. "All Witchcraft stems from carnal lust, which in women is insatiable," stated the *Malleus Maleficarum*.

The terror was indescribable. Once denounced, by anyone from a spiteful neighbor to a fretful child, a suspect Witch was arrested suddenly without warning and not allowed to return home again. She was considered guilty until proven innocent. Common practice was to strip the subject naked, shave her completely in hopes of finding the Devil's "marks," which might be no more than moles or freckles. Often the accused were pricked all over their bodies with sharp needles; spots the devil had touched were said to feel no pain ... Most cruelly, they were tortured until they named others, until a full coven quota of thirteen were taken. Confession earned a merciful death: strangulation before the stake. Recalcitrant suspects, who maintained their innocence, were burned alive.

Witch hunters and informers were paid for convictions, and many found it a profitable career. The rising male medical establishment welcomed the chance to stamp out midwives and female herbalists, their major economic competitors. For others, the Witch trials offered opportunities to rid themselves of "uppity women" and disliked neighbors. Witches themselves say that few of those tried during the burning times actually belonged to members of the craft. The victims were the elderly, the senile, the mentally ill, women whose looks weren't pleasing or suffered from some handicap, village beauties who bruised the wrong egos by rejecting advances or had roused lust in a celibate priest or married man.[16]

This mythology is profoundly manifested at the personal level through the modern representation of the early modern Witch as is illustrated by the WITCH protests of the late sixties. A more personal representation of the identity of the early modern Witch in eco-feminist Wiccan mythology is characterized by Diane Purkiss.

Once upon a time, there was a woman who lived on the edge of a village. She lived alone, in her own house surrounded by her garden, in which she grew all manner of herbs and other healing plants. Though she was alone, she was never lonely; she had her garden and her animals for company, she took lovers when she wished and was always busy. The woman was a healer and midwife; she had practical knowledge taught to her by her mother, and mystical knowledge derived from her closeness to nature, or from a half submerged Pagan religion. She helped women give birth and she had healing hands; she used her knowledge of herbs to help the sick. However, her peaceful existence was disrupted. Even though this woman was harmless, she posed a threat to the fearful. Her medical knowledge threatened the doctor. Her simple, true spiritual values threatened the superstitious nonsense of the Catholic Church, as did the affirmation of the sensuous body. Her independence and freedom threatened men. So the inquisition descended on her, and cruelly tortured her into confessing lies about the devil. She was burned alive by men who hated women, along with millions of others just like her.[17]

This representation of women accused and persecuted by patriarchal society as Witches is a compelling and even horrifying story of domination, misogyny and cruelty. It has become a central driving influence behind many radical feminists like Mary Daly, Andrea Dworkins, Carolyn Merchant and Robin Morgan. Representation of contemporary Witch identity via the drawing of historical and socio-cultural links with the Witch crazes of early modern Europe have become central defining characteristics of much of the eco-feminist Wiccan movement through the work of writers and activists like Starhawk,

---

16. Starhawk. *The Spiral Dance.* pp 19–21.
17. Purkiss, D. *The Witch in History.* p 7.

Laurie Cabot, Naomi Goldenberg and Zsusanna Budapest.[18] The Witch identity in these narratives is invariably contained in the story of suffering and persecution of the innocent, pure, uncorrupted and natural feminine by the evils and corrupting influence of modernity/patriarchy seeking to objectify nature and, through natural association, the feminine. This representation of the burning times is heavily dependent on the aforementioned work of Margaret Murray and Jules Michelet and their analysis of the early modern Witch crazes as an attempt by the Church to stamp out the remnants of a surviving pre-Christian Witch cult.[19]

To summarize, whilst acknowledging the many differences of detail and emphasis in competing eco-feminist neo-Pagan interpretations of the Witch persecutions of the early modern period, there are several key points upon which most agree. These are essentially that,

1. Pagan women were the central targets of Witch persecutions perpetuated by patriarchal and Christian political structures.

2. The Witch burnings were the result of a systematic persecution of women and pre-Christian matriarchal social and religious structures by the Church, secular government, patriarchal society and early modern power structures in general.

3. There was an extremely antagonistic relationship between traditional healers and midwives and the rising male medical profession, who acted to deliberately foster antagonism and persecution against traditional healers and midwives.

4. The *Malleus Maleficarum* was central in defining the attitudes of the established political and religious authorities towards persecuting Witches.

However, this representation of what happened during the Witch crazes of early modern Europe and the Americas is, in purely empirical terms, simplistic and only partly accurate. There are many historical and empirical criticisms of this particular analysis of the Witch crazes as will be discussed below. My contention is that rather than relating specifically to issues of historical veracity, the eco-feminist Wiccan representation of the "Burning Times" is indicative of a modern mythological construction relating to contemporary American social and cultural issues. Furthermore, the issues in-

---

18. Purkiss, D. *The Witch in History.* p 9.

19. Adler, M. *Drawing Down the Moon.* p 47; Kephart, M.J. "Rationalist vs Romantics among Scholars of Witchcraft." pp 327–328.

volved in differing historical analyses are directly related to a two-part paradigm of a feminist appropriation of Romanticism combined with a particular means of interpreting history. Both of these features are defined within the context of a prioritization of symbolic impact over empirical analysis.

Europe during the early modern period was far from a homogenous culture. Cultural attitudes towards gender, Witchcraft, magic and the Church varied immensely from culture to culture and society to society. In addition, there were immense differences between folk beliefs of illegitimate use of magic, sorcery and Witchcraft held by the rural peasantry and the beliefs of the Church hierarchy. Furthermore, there were differences between the Church's attitudes towards Witchcraft as devil worship and its approaches to heresy, local sorcerers and surviving Pagans. This is particularly evidenced by the inquisition's confusion and comparatively ambiguous approach to the Bennandanti Witches of Northern Italy and the Witch/healers of Sicily. Similarly, whilst in England, Germany and many parts of France, Spain, Scotland and Italy Witch persecutions were generally oriented towards women, in Eastern Europe, Scandinavia, Normandy and several other parts of Europe, persecution was generally focused on male Witches. This is not to discredit the claim that early modern Europe had a patriarchal social and political structure or that misogyny was strongly involved in Witch prosecutions, but rather that there was far more to the Witch crazes than simply the persecution of dissident women by patriarchal institutions of authority. For that matter it is worth noting that women were commonly central in making Witchcraft accusations and in making depositions supporting charges of Witchcraft.[20]

Witch crazes were never systematic or coherent in application. Whilst large-scale edicts against the practices of Witchcraft and the works of the devil were common enough in the Church hierarchy, their application was normally localized and derived from specific local political and cultural issues. Similarly, the specific characteristics and mythology surrounding Witches and their supposed *maleficium* varied a great deal from culture to culture and were commonly a mix of local mythology, use of illegitimate magic, malevolent creatures of local myth and folklore and of Church doctrine. This stands in sharp contrast to the mass execution and military action by the Church and state

---

20. Weisner, Mary. *Women in Gender in Early Modern Europe.* Cambridge: Cambridge University Press, 1993; Evans, Richard. *The German Underworld: Deviants and Outcasts in German History.* London: Routledge, 1988. pp 57–74; Monter, William. "The Witches of Normandy." *Journal of French History.* Vol 20. No 4. Fall 1997. pp 563–595.

against heresy and large scale political and religious movement like the Albigensians, Bogomils and Paulicans who challenged the spiritual legitimacy of the Church's role in politics and the obtaining of wealth and threatened to undermine the power of the Papacy in the Middle Ages.[21]

Midwives and traditional healers were not overtly in direct competition and conflict with the Western medical profession until the modern period. Despite claims that the male medical profession was motivated to attack traditional healers and midwives in order to establish their own professional territory, there is little evidence of conflict between the fledgling male medical profession and traditional healers, herbalists and midwives until the late eighteenth century. In fact, in England, midwives were perceived to be extremely important in ascertaining the truth of Witchcraft accusations because of their intimate knowledge of the local community. Similarly there is little evidence to suggest that healers and herbalists in early modern Europe, aside from midwives and home remedies, were exclusively or even predominantly female prior to the establishment of the Western medical profession.[22]

Whilst undoubtedly excessive, barbaric and unjust, the methods of Witch prosecution and persecution would not have been necessarily incongruous with judicial proceedings of the era. In today's society a confession obtained under duress is nonsensical, except as a means to assure a conviction in a corrupt judicial system. But in the early modern period the role of torture in obtaining a confession had somewhat different overtones. The role of interrogation was in many cases perceived less as a means of establishing an objective fact than as a test of will between the subject and the power of the Church or sovereign. Consequently, the judicial procedure revolved around the processes of accusation and forced confession as opposed to modern ideals of justice or truth differentiated from the will of the sovereign or Church as representative of the higher power of God. Torture, misleading questions and forced confessions were utilized extensively in a range of judicial proceedings until well

---

21. Adler, M. *Drawing Down the Moon.* pp 49–52; Cohn, N. *Europe's Inner Demons.* pp 1–4, 16–17, 22, 55–58 & 229–230; Mayer, P. "Witches." In Marwick, Max (Ed.) *Witchcraft and Sorcery.* London: Penguin Books, 1970. pp 54–71.

22. Briggs, R. *Witches and Neighbors.* pp 77–78, 217–218, 279–281; George, Janet and Davis Alan. *States of Health.* 3rd Edition. London: Addison, Wesley & Longman Australia, 1997. pp 113–118; Griggs, Barbara. *The New Green Pharmacy.* New York: Random House Publishing , 1997. Ch 4; Harley, David. "Historians as Demonologists: The Myth of the Midwife Witch." *Journal for the Society of the Social History of Medicine.* vol 3, 1990. pp 1–26; Marland, Hillary (Ed.) *The Art of Midwifery: Early Modern Midwives in Europe.* London: Routledge, 1993. pp 45, 50, 88, 119 & 159.

into the eighteenth century. As late as the nineteenth century there was debate as to the legitimacy of forced confession and misleading depositions in the interrogation of accused persons.[23]

The *Malleus Maleficarum,* often the primary source of the belief that Witch hunting was empowered woman hunting, was not the dominant guide for Witchcraft prosecution in Europe. Whilst popular with some extremists the *Malleus* was far from universally accepted by the Church and political mainstream. Many considered it degrading to piety of men. Others felt it degraded the works of female saints and nuns and many felt that it ignored much of the established lore of demonology and Witchcraft. Many clergy and inquisitors openly disdained the *Malleus* as a rabidly misogynist and paranoid text which diverted attention away from the finding of "true Witches". Similarly, whilst heretics and people practicing Pagan religious and cultural beliefs were often accused of fomenting the work of the devil, the secular and religious authorities commonly distinguished between these activities.[24] There was a complex methodology used by the inquisition and Church authorities to determine the nature and veracity of claims of Witchcraft practices ranging from accusations that fitted into established demonological doctrine, simple *Maleficium* or evil magical practice, heretical doctrinal beliefs and Paganism. The methods used to ascertain the truth of these claims varied greatly as did the punishments assigned to each transgression. These ranged from hanging, to lashes, to burning at the stake, to short term imprisonment. Often those who were accused were comparatively leniently treated in exchange for an oath of fealty to the Church and a recanting of previously held beliefs. Others were used as examples against those who challenged Church authority.[25]

---

23. Briggs, R. *Witches and Neighbors.* pp 17–18, 32, 58, 216–217, 326; Foucault, Michel. *Discipline and Punish: The Birth of the Prison.* New York: Random House Publishing, 1977. pp 10–22, 32–34, 38–44 & 49–55; Russell, S. *Foucault Genealogy and Witchcraft.* pp 1–5.

24. Anglo, Sydney. "Evident Authority and Authoritative Evidence: The Malleus Maleficarum." In *The Damned Art: Essays in the Literature of Witchcraft.* Routledge: London. 1977. pp 152–153; Ankarloo, B. & Henningsen, G. *Early Modern Witchcraft.* ch 6; Cohn, Norman. *Europe's Inner Demons.* pp 1–4, 11, 30, 34, 117–122, 225, 262; Kevin, Robin. "Magical Emasculation and the Limits of Popular Anti-Clericism in Early Modern Europe." *Journal of Social History.* Vol 31. No 1. Fall 1997. pp 61–83.

25. Briggs, R. *Witches and Neighbours.* pp 92, 148–156, 166, 237. Carlo, Ginzberg. *The Night Battles: Witchcraft and Agrarian Cults in the Sixteenth and Seventeenth Centuries.* London: Oxford University Press 1983. pp 14, 32–39; Ankarloo, B. & Henningsen, G., *Early Modern European Witchcraft.* pp 7–16, 47, 191–215, 266–276, 431.

What these issues indicate is that whilst gender conflict and the patriarchal nature of the various early modern European societies were central to what occurred during this period, the actual empirical phenomena are far more localized and socio-culturally fragmented than is generally acknowledged. The Witch crazes occurred over a long period of time, a broadly diverse social, political and cultural expanse of territory and in separate localized areas interconnected with the social, cultural and political formations of the time. Similarly, perceptions of Witchcraft varied according to class and culture in a variety of ways manifested in differences and even conflicts between local beliefs of Witchcraft activity and learned Church doctrine. This is perhaps best demonstrated by the Catholic Church's repeated attempts to establish learned doctrine over Scandinavian, Sicilian, Portuguese and Basque Witch prosecutions, only to be foiled by a conflicting understanding of *Maleficium* among the local populace.[26]

The issue of empirical veracity is an area of extreme tension for the many eco-feminists, neo-Pagans and others who support this particular perspective. Despite its many empirical difficulties, the mythology of the burning times has come to be a powerful symbol, defining the nature of patriarchal exploitation linked to modernity and ecological destructiveness. Consequently, attempts to disprove this perspective are often met with hostility, for example Mary Daly's claim that criticism of feminist histories are equivalent to Nazi book burnings.[27] Another response is typified by the statement that "The arguments as to whether our Witchcraft traditions are authentic seems to be the usual male posturing, debating the number of angels on a pinhead."[28] However, this issue of historical authenticity in witchcraft traditions still appears to be an area of some tension as illustrated by Starhawk, who after, rather blatantly, utilizing narratives based on the above narratives, almost apologetically includes an appendix in her text *Dreaming the Dark* which gives a far more thorough and empirically oriented historical interpretation of the "Burning Times" including many of the ambiguities involved in this representation. These included the influence of local social and political disputes, the social impact of the growing market economy, increasing levels of class conflict, localized beliefs of *Maleficium*, the conflict between the Church and secularism

---

26. Ankarloo, B. & Henningsen, G. *Early Modern European Witchcraft.* pp 7–16, 191–215, 266–276.

27. Daly, M. *Gyn/Ecology.* pp 196, 208, 217, 298, 306.

28. Kelly, Aiden. "An Update on Neo-Pagan Witchcraft." in Isaac Bonewits, *Real Magic: An Introductory Treatise on the Principles of Yellow Magic.* London: Open Gate Publishing, 1972. p 136.

and the fact that the localized persecution of women in parts of Europe during this period of history was in context with a larger phenomenon of the persecution of Jews, heretics, dissident intellectuals and secularists.[29]

This myth has become important, not because of its historical and empirical veracity, but because of its social and cultural impact on the psyche of modern Western women. In a society full of social and ethical ambiguity and difficulties with traditional forms of defining meaning and values in cultural forms and symbols, the myth of the patriarchal pogrom against liberated women is a story with clear unambiguous oppositions. Good and Evil are rigidly defined and the narratives of Witch persecution offer both a means of identifying with oppression and also a symbolic identity of modern women in a patriarchal industrial society. It is a recreation of humanist and Romantic utopian mythology; how perfect life could be, how perfect society could be if not for the mistakes of the past and the distancing from our authentic origins, created by the corrupting effects of technology and civilization.

Like other histories, the eco-feminist neo-Pagan interpretation of that portion of history referred to as the "Burning Times", is based upon a variety of myths, ideals and political struggles. The movement's ideological and symbolic approach to the past essentially attempts to erase the issue of their own historicity in order to present eco-feminist neo-Pagans as having access to a transcendent, unmediated perspective on historical authenticity. By focusing representations on the personal narratives of individuals and representations designed to evoke a strong emotive response in individuals in a post-Enlightenment and humanist society, a sense of empathy with the past and an unambiguous sense of personal social identity and source of values can be derived from the construction of historico-cultural identity.

A central example of the mutability of representations of the past is manifested in the all too common use of the *Malleus Maleficarum* as the central representation of chronic misogyny lying behind the Witch crazes without justifying its centrality in Witch persecutions. Very rarely does one find any other early texts or actual trial records being utilized. There are many reasons for this extremely narrow focus but central to its use as the primary analysis of Witch persecutions is its ability to create strong emotive reaction from its readers raised in an Enlightenment humanist culture. It is quoted not for its accuracy in defining popular Witchcraft beliefs in the late Renaissance period but because of its striking confrontational qualities. For example, it contains repeated reference to stolen *Phalloi* and continual representation of the sexual

---

29. Starhawk. *Dreaming the Dark*. Appendix 1.

weakness and manipulative ability of women as a source of evil and corruption. Similarly, its representations of Witchcraft stand for ideals fundamentally against traditional Enlightenment humanist values, illustrated by its casual attitudes towards torture, execution and imprisonment in adherence to "evidence" based on superstition, religious values and denial of secularist logic and science in defining a person's guilt.[30]

The central issue here is that whilst it is important in the eco-feminist representation of the Witch burnings, the *Malleus* is not necessarily representative of beliefs relating to Witchcraft in the early modern period in a broad European context. A text like the *Malleus* is analyzed according to a criteria defined by powerful symbolism, compelling narrative and powerfully striking anecdotes rather than an empirically supported historical interpretation. History, in this case, is perceived as a personal narrative designed to illustrate contemporary social, cultural and political issues. Postmodern historical narratives are representative of a quite conscious attempt to redefine historical interpretations in terms of a mythology symbolically representing the social, cultural and political issues of the present. In this case, the issue is to represent the circumstances of patriarchal domination in Western society, social justice and environmental degradation as integrated together in opposition to modernity. Similarly, this perspective attempts to justify the acceptance of the historical model of the "Burning Times" by claiming it represents an unambiguous representations of past repression by patriarchy, modernity, Christianity and mainstream Western society.

An example of how narratives, anecdotes and symbolism have overwhelmed historicity and empirical variability in the "Burning Times" mythology is given by Diane Purkiss' analysis of Robin Morgan's poem *The Network of the Imaginary Mother* also utilized by noted feminist author Mary Daly in her critique of patriarchal culture in *Gynecology*.

> Repeat the syllables
> before the lesson hemorrhages through the brain:
> Margaret Barclay, crushed to death with stones, 1618.
> Peronette, seated on hot iron as torture
> and then buried alive, 1642.
> Sister Maria Renata Sanger, sub-prioress
> of the Premonstratension Convent of Unter-Zell,

---

30. Robins, Kevin. "Magical Emasculation and the Limits of Popular Anti-Clericism in Early Modern Europe." pp 61–83; Sydney, A. "Evident Authority and Authoritative Evidence."

accused of being a lesbian;
the document certifying her torture
is inscribed with the seal of the Jesuits,
and the words Ad Majorem Dei Gloriam-
To the greater glory of God.
What have they done to us?[31]

According to Purkiss' analysis, the entire purpose of this poem is to insist on the reader's participation and to direct their attention to a series of names, means of death and dates. The list symbolizes untold stories, lost peoples and memories. Their death and persecution reduces their individual stories to mere names and dates in the context of personal suffering. The poem utilizes similar methods to that of memorials to war and to the holocaust, oblivious to the fact that these memorials can afford the luxury of anecdotal method as they were designed to remind and serve as a memorial to living people who can remember the names, stories, memories and personalities attached. From this perspective, Purkiss argues that there is an intrinsic paradox in representing the stories of people, long forgotten and buried under history as icons devoid of historical, contextual and personal specificity. However, ironically this very paradox it is a central component of the poem's symbolic impact. These people have been buried under oblivion and forgotten, illustrating the means by which the persecution and history of women has been similarly buried in Western patriarchal society. However, the poem also relies extensively on the fact that the reader is assuredly ignorant of the personal narratives and identities of the people involved. To recognize these people as individuals with individual histories and identities in the context of the social and cultural milieu of the era troubles the central purpose and focus of the poem: that these people were the same and integrally linked with each other and the women of contemporary Western society with a common social and cultural identity.

In Daly's use of Morgan's poem in Gynecology it is paradoxically her symbolic use of the memorial in illustrating this blurring of past and present, subject and object to describe the events of early modern Europe as a contemporary atrocity in contemporary Western terms. This is reinforced by her emphasis of Morgan's line "What have they done to us". The entire poem is designed to enjoin the reader to claim collective identity with the "us" of the poem, to lead the reader into the position where they feel identified with long dead Witches

---

31. Morgan, Robin. "The Network of the Imaginary Mother." Cited by Daly, M. *Gyn/Ecology.*

as a symbol of modern patriarchal oppression.[32] What is particularly interesting about this poem is that it represents an attempt to draw out the narrative of the disenfranchised and dis-empowered individuals of history whilst simultaneously attempting to categorize and define these figures in terms of contemporary constructions of socio-political identity, cultural structure and ideology.

The use of Morgan's poem mirrors Daly's utilization of the "Burning Times" in that it utilizes emotive and symbolic impact to both conceals and appropriates the voices of silenced women from the past for ideological goals. There is a certain contradictory problematic in this methodology of defining historical narrative through contemporary symbolic impact. These figures from the past are appropriated on the basis that they are representative of the voices of the disenfranchised and oppressed of the past that give meaning to the contemporary experience of oppression. However, the actual historical experiences of these figures are concealed behind a method of representation and categorization that perceives the legitimacy of these historical representations purely in relation to contemporary social, cultural and political issues and structures. Consequently the actual impact of the experiences and events surrounding the deaths of these disenfranchised and oppressed individuals remain buried in the past and the light the actual experiences of these individuals could shed on contemporary experiences of oppression remain buried under layers of cultural and ideological constructions.

This particular phenomenon of appropriation and concealment is illustrated in Mary Daly's utilization of the "Burning Times" narrative as a symbol of patriarchal oppression. In her representation of the Witch crazes she describes the narratives of only three Witches. In the only story to which she enters in any depth, that of a woman named Agnes, she describes the exact weights and measures utilized in her torture and execution but leaves out any reference to what Agnes actually said, did or even the events leading to her being caught up in that situation.[33] As in the above memorial/poem, this silence is particularly significant as it prevents the historical context and individuality of the woman persecuted, or the socio-cultural and historical context in which it occurred from interfering with the meta-narrative extracted from its representation. By this method, the narrative is used to define issues located in modern Western society and culture. The ultimate justification of the ideological project becomes located in the suffering body of a faceless in-

---

32. Purkiss, D. *The Witch in History.* p 12.
33. Daly, M. *Gyn/Ecology.* pp 181, 190 & 214.

dividual; a metaphor constructed to give meaning and inspiration for modern Western women. As all people have a physical body and fear persecution, torture and death, the focus on the details of pain and suffering without acknowledging the specificity of the individuals represented, creates a strong emotive and very visceral means of identifying modern women with that of long dead Witches from early modern Europe and America. However, acknowledging the cultural and social individuality of the people represented or the extent to which social discursive practices mediated the circumstances surrounding these people's deaths, could shatter this illusion of government backed systemic pogroms against women.

A central issue of these representations of the past in terms of individual pain and suffering isolated from the socio-cultural structure in which it occurred and the lived experience of those individuals afflicted, is that the people are represented as glorified spectacles of pain and torment selected for their visceral impact on reader as opposed to an attempt to create a sense of empathy and understanding with appropriated individuals and events of the past. The reduction of these individuals to voiceless tortured bodies removes the very possibility of subjectivity for the victims who actually lived through this appropriated era of history. Instead these people become instructive spectacles of pain and torment offering no room for the possibility of a sense of empathy or understanding of the events that occurred or the figure of the Witch as a historical figure. An example of this disassociation of the image of the Witch from the actual lived experiences of those tormented is illustrated by Elizabeth Brooke's representation of Witch burnings as repressed memories.

> I remember, how I remember the smell of burning flesh, the hair catching alight, the awful agony of your feet slowly burning up. I remember the jeers of the men who watched, and the frozen dread of the women and children who were forced to watch my ending.[34]

The ultimate result of this method of historical appropriation is that the figure of the Witch is transformed from an individual located in the life experiences of her time and place to that of an ahistorical symbol deeply entrenched in the social, cultural and political construction of modern Western society. This raises an important issue in terms of what fantasies, contemporary issues and symbolic/cultural structures are displaced on the Witch burning narrative. It also raises questions as to the validity of projecting a

---

34. Brooke, Elizabeth. *A Woman's book of Shadows: Witchcraft : A Celebration.* London: Women's Press, 1993. p 46.

constructed Witch identity as a symbol of patriarchal oppression if its role is that of a target of social and cultural projection upon a fictional historical narrative whilst relying upon the appropriated symbols of deliberately silenced personal narratives. Consequently, the fundamental issue in examining the development of the figure of the Witch in eco-feminist neo-Paganism is not so much the empirical veracity of its claimed historical origins but rather, the contemporary social, political and cultural features that were involved in its formation.

The Witch and the Feminine

From this perspective, the image of the Witch itself is a particularly illuminating area of study. The Witch in eco-feminist neo-Pagan discourse is invariably rustic, wise, nurturing and has a close empathy with nature. Often the Witch is beautiful but is sometimes a wise old lady, is sexually liberated and is loved by her local community with the exception of patriarchal men and political patriarchal authorities. Invariably the Witch is also a source of feminine continuity having learned or inherited skills from a long line of matriarchal ancestors. As Starhawk writes,

> The old woman carries a basket of herbs and roots she has dug; it feels heavy as time on her arm. Her feet on the ground are her mother's feet, her grandmother's, her great grandmother's; for centuries she has walked under these oaks and pines, culled the herbs and brought them back to dry under the eaves of her cottage on the common. Always, the people of the village have come to her; her hands are healing hands, they can turn a child in the womb; her murmuring voice can charm away pain, can croon the restless to sleep.[35]

The identity of the Witch represents an earthy contrast to the experience of the fragmented post-modern self. It is a symbol of continuity, it stands for a connection with nature and agrarian life, it stands for feminine nurturing and it represents a desire for a society where traditional female skills and roles in the community are highly regarded and are relied upon as much as traditional male oriented professional skills. In essence, it represents a fantasy of feminine identity where aspirations to profession, traditional female domestic roles and feminine sexuality are blended together in a way that engenders images

---

35. Starhawk, *Dreaming the Dark.* p 183.

of power and respect in the community. It also inherently integrates the "natural" ideal of feminine identity with nature and an agrarian existence.

Central to this representation of the Witch figure as the ideal feminine archetype is the creation of an image of a feminine *imago dei* which is inherently linked with nature, diversity and agrarian lifestyle in opposition to the objectification of nature, the exploitation of the disenfranchised and the destructiveness of capitalist modernity. As Starhawk writes,

> The Judeo-Christian heritage has left us with the view of a universe composed of warring opposites, which are either good or evil. They cannot co-exist. A valuable insight of Witchcraft is that the polarities are in balance not at war ... The Goddess is ourselves and the world—to link with her is to engage in the world and all its problems ... A matrifocal culture, based on nature, celebrates diversity, because diversity assures survival and continuing evolution. Nature creates thousands of species, not just one; and each is different.[36]

Similarly, Elizabeth Brooke also demonstrates the association between sexuality, agrarian lifestyle, nurturing motherhood and feminine identity,

> Behind the lesser gods was the cosmic mother of all, whose breasts poured milk into the firmament and who birthed new stars, whose curved and luscious body was the very earth they trod on ... Priestesses of the Goddess, who had many names, presided over birth and death, the blessing of fields and the building of cities.[37]

This representation of feminine identity is grounded in the belief that femininity, nature and inclusivity are essentially linked through the manifestation of a feminine essence in the figure of the Witch. In other words it is precisely because matriarchal-based social structures are inherently inclusive and integrated with the natural world and are geared towards a matriarchal agrarian utopia that their ontological, ideological and cultural structures are validated. Correspondingly, patriarchal identity is associated with that which is defined as oppositional to the ideals of this feminine essence. Patriarchy is therefore linked with dogmatism, technocratic society, ecological destructiveness, socially exploitative industrialism and is orientated towards a patriarchal industrialized dystopia. This is perhaps well illustrated in Starhawk's novel "The Fifth Sacred Thing" which posits a future where patriarchal society has col-

---

36. Starhawk, *The Spiral Dance*. p 201.
37. Brooke, E. *A Woman's Book of Shadows*. p 9.

lapsed into a Nazi style dictatorship based on the exploitation of women and the environment while a competing matriarchal society, through a non-violent revolution, has evolved into an agrarian, spiritual utopia promoting strength through collective diversity and ecological sensitivity.[38]

This particular perspective attempts to link together the disempowerment of women with images of agrarian utopia and thus join together the dual social constructs of femininity with the crisis of Western modernity in a clear easily accessible way. However, it also presents problems relating to its insistence on the universality of the eco-feminist perspective and its denial of historicity and subjectivity. As Diane Purkiss writes,

> The problem with the Goddess is that she remains mired in the thinking of "Images of women feminism." This thinking can be annihilatingly prescriptive demanding that all women recognize themselves as lactating mothers for example. Its insistence that positive images of women are positive for all women and in all contexts can seem cozily unaware of difficulty or difference. Just what might constitute strength and authority for an exhausted working mother? Might there not be a time when she wants to acknowledge aspects to herself which are not maternal? If she is already a mother, what kind of mother goddess does she need? What about cultures in which maternity has different meanings? The myth of the Goddess betrays its origins in male fantasy.[39]

The Goddess and History

The image of the Goddess herself, as a central figure in the construction of eco-feminist neo-Paganism, is a symbol that actively attempts to disassociate feminine identity from the trappings of power, progress and rationality in Western culture. Consequently it serves to make images of the feminine in the context of political and social power problematic and associated with patriarchal identity as a corrupted form of masculinity. A logical derivative of this representation of femininity, as that which is not associated with the supposed inherently masculine traits of progress, technocratic rationality and industrialism, is that cultures which also do not fit contemporary Western representations of masculinity associated with technocratic power are defined as fem-

---

38. Starhawk, *The Fifth Sacred Thing.*
39. Purkiss, D. *The Witch in History.* p 33.

inine or at least non patriarchal. Ironically enough this often includes the west's own pre-history. This particular representation of Western pre-capital-ist history as a matriarchal agrarian utopia bereft of the problems and cor-ruption of modernity is utilized extensively by modern eco-feminist neo-Pa-gans as a representation of their own history in a pre-Christian/patriarchal society. As Laurie Cabot writes,

> What were these women centered, Goddess worshiping cultures like? Many European scholars have noted their strong resemblance to the many European myths and legends about a Golden Age, suggesting that the myths arose as latter day accounts of what must have been a reality. The absence of military fortifications and weaponry indicates that they were peace-loving cultures. There seems to have been no large-scale organized warfare, only the minor personal skirmishes and conflicts that arise in any human society. Weapons were small, per-sonal instruments which suggests they were used for primarily for de-fense and symbolic value.
> Goddess centers also lacked a bureaucratic political structure; people lived in a clan like extended families run by mothers. There was no slavery. Women functioned as priestesses, artists, agriculturalists, small game huntresses and later large-scale farmers. In short these neolithic Goddess cultures seem to have laid the seed for Western thinker's fascination with Utopia, not as a futures possibility but as a dream about a reality we have lost.[40]

In a similar way, Zsussana Budapest writes of pre-patriarchal society that,

> Matriarchal women had no defense systems. They didn't even have swords although they did use wands. All they had was superior sewage systems, elaborate baths, beautiful wall paintings and exqui-site jewelry. They were beauty oriented, not war obsessed, and thus were easily overrun and sacked in the cruelest sense of the word.[41]

This particular representation of pre-industrial society relies extensively upon the work of male nineteenth century writers and is part of the long tradition of Romantic idealization of medieval Witches. French Historian Jules Michelet, for example, describes Witchcraft as a religion of the peasantry who adapted the ancient fertility cult of the goddess into a protest movement

---

40. Cabot, L. *The Power of the Witch.* pp 34–35.
41. Budapest, Zsuzsanna. *The Holy Women's Book of Mysteries.* Oakland: Wingbow Press, 1989. p 284.

against the Church and state. His image of the priestess representing the Goddess, as stated previously, was that of "A face of Medea, a beauty born of suffering, a deep tragic, feverish gaze, with a torrent of black untamable hair." This combination of objectification of the feminine in the context of a sexualization of the suffering feminine body is extensively used in the creation of the mythology of the burning times. It is also important to note that Michelet makes the assumption that because he is describing a fertility cult it must necessarily be associated with the feminine in terms of sexuality, mature and nurturing. This also assumes a certain degree of cultural and societal universality with regards to gender images and socio-cultural constructions of gendered identity. The fundamental basis of this representation is that the feminine, like nature and the primitive culture, reified the primitive and instinctual. Consequently, women became represented as the dark shadowy projection of civilization that, in a patriarchal society, becomes associated with a concept of masculinity characterized as representing Enlightenment values, rationality and the power of knowledge.

The belief in an ancient matriarch of pre-history dominated by a great mother or goddess is one shared by many nineteenth century Romantic writers. Perhaps the most central to the development of this perspective are the writings of Rousseau, in which the trappings of civilization serve to corrupt and confine the spiritual, cultural and intellectual verities of the primitive. In this context myths like that of the Romantic "Prometheus" or Michelet's Pagan peasant religion come to represent underlying truths about the nature of human identity differentiated from the corrupting ideals of Western technocratic industrial civilization. In other words, the quasi-spiritual construction of representations manifested in recreations of past history, according to specifically contemporary social, cultural and political issues, comes to represent ideals, beliefs and symbols fundamental to a natural essence of human identity buried under artificial layers of Western society. These buried ideals, images and representations of the past were thus believed to be beyond those of culture, knowledge and lived experience, within the discourse of Western socio-cultural formations, and thus represent the universal cultural and social infrastructure upon which our identity is based. Subsequently, those categorized by mainstream Western society through patriarchal and colonial social formations as lacking the refinements of progress, civilization, technology and rational objectivity, such as women and traditional societies, are also commonly caricatured as having access to the lived experience of a universal truth of human identity, uncorrupted by the artificial formative power of Western modernity. As a consequence, the images of women, traditional societies and agrarian cultures were created from the symbolic cultural and social projections of individuals in Western society.

The concept of images of femininity linked to nature dates back to the nineteenth century. As previously stated, in its contemporary form it is strongly dependent on images and ideals of nineteenth century Romanticism that were subsequently adopted in a broad trend of feminist appropriation of Romanticism in post sixties feminism. Whilst many Romantic writers intrinsically linked femininity to nature via the opposing association of masculinity with the values of modernity, rationality and progress, many post sixties feminist writers began to interpret the perceived natural feminine-nature association as intrinsic to the development of gender equality. This occurred through a variety of ways. Some believed that patriarchy represents a certain kind of socio-cultural structure which categorizes women and nature as objects. Other writers sought the linkages between femininity and nature in biology through the act of birthing and the belief that women are more in touch with their bodies (and therefore the physical world) than men. In either case the result is an embracement of femininity linked with nature as a means to alleviate the inequalities and exploitation suffered by Western women. As King writes,

> We can nonetheless consciously choose not to sever the woman nature connection by joining male culture. Rather, we can use it as a vantage point for creating a different kind of culture and politics that integrate intuitive, spiritual and rational forms of knowledge, embracing both science and magic insofar as they enable us to transform the nature-culture distinction to create a free and ecological society.[42]

Feminist Critique of the Burning Times and Goddess Religions

Not all feminist writers agree with this particular theoretical standpoint. Many feminist writers, such as Naomi Wolf, Rebecca Grant, Diane Purkiss, Angela Carter and Cecile Jackson are quite critical of this perspective. Naomi Wolf in particular is quite scathing of what she describes as "Victim Feminism" which seeks to identify feminine identity passively with the victims of history and the exploitation of nature.[43] The Romantic approach to feminism has also

---

42. King, Y. "The Ecology of Feminism and the Feminism of Ecology." In J. Plant ed. *Healing the Wounds: The Promise of Eco-Feminism.* Philadelphia: New Society Publishers, 1987. p 19.

43. Wolf, Naomi. *Fire with Fire: The New Female Power and How it Will Change the 21st Century.* London: Chatto & Windus Ltd, 1993. pp 147–149.

come under criticism for potentially denying the validity of women playing a more direct political and economic role in the context of mainstream society in the workplace or having greater control over their reproductive rights by virtue of its adherence to universal images based in nineteenth century models of gendered identity. As Angela Carter writes,

> If women allow themselves to be consoled ... by the invocation of hypothetical great goddesses, they are simply flattering themselves into submission (a technique often used on them by men) ... Mother goddesses are just as silly a notion as father gods. If a revival of these cults gives women an emotional satisfaction, it does so at the price of obscuring the real conditions of life. That is why they were invented in the first place.[44]

Another difficulty with this perspective is that it is fundamentally mired in images of femininity being passive, nurturing and disassociated from social power and, in the case of the "Burning Times" mythology, always relegated to the role of powerless victim. In other words, feminine identity is still defined passively by what masculinity is not. Even if this representation is presented in a positive light it still has the fundamental difficulty of being a creation of patriarchal society defining women as objects. Consequently, rather than allowing the creation of new forms of society, it is claimed that Romantic models of femininity are ultimately defined in the context of images of femininity created by modern Western patriarchal society. As Rosalind Coward writes,

> The issue is not really whether a woman's genitals are revered or reviled, but the fact that women by virtue of their bodies are rendered as symbols. Far from being a new ethic, this is a time-honored way in which women have always been treated. When any group (Whether it be sexual or ethnic) becomes a symbol the individual in that group will be defined from the outside and suffer from that identity.[45]

Suffice to say that there are serious concerns regarding the feminine/nature connection as a model for feminist liberation from patriarchal domination within various sectors of the feminist movement. As a consequence it should be noted that the eco-feminist approach to the issue of gendered identity does not appear to be synonymous with the feminist movement in general. Rather

---

44. Rountree, Kathryn. "The Politics of the Goddess: Feminist Spirituality and the Essentialism Debate." *Social Analysis,* Issue 43(2), July 1999. p 147.

45. Coward, Rosalind. *The Myth of Alternative Health.* New York: Faber Publishing, 1989.

than a feminist approach to the Goddess there are feminisms of which the eco-feminist model is but one example.[46]

Romanticism and the Goddess

The eco-feminist neo-Pagan conception of feminine is critically dependent on the ideology of the feminine link with nature and the ultimate expression of femininity being located in a mother Goddess image. The ideal is an intrinsically Romantic one, not merely through the application of images utilized by Romantic writers of the past such as Michelet or Rousseau. Central to this ideal is the precedence of "traditional" values disassociated from the corrupting influence of Western rationality, industrialism and its corresponding association, in a technocratic patriarchal society, with masculinity.

The essential links between modern eco-feminist neo-Paganism and Romanticism are belief in the necessity to gaze inwards and into representations of the past to find forms of identity and symbols of meaning which are quintessentially perceived as natural and in opposition to the forces of modernity and industrialism. Conversely this also involves a belief in the veracity of symbols, images and feelings over empirical experience and logic. Like much of Western Romantic literature, eco-feminist neo-Paganism is fundamentally dominated by a belief in authenticity of beliefs and images. Quintessentially modern ideological and symbolic socio-cultural formations are reinforced by interpretations of the past which are dogmatically protected. In the post sixties era of mass culture and commodity fetishism however, this belief in the legitimizing power of historical and cultural authenticity underwent a subtle transformation. While pre-sixties neo-Pagan movements were involved in extremely dedicated studies of folklore and mythology as a source of accurate rituals and practices, post-sixties eco-feminist neo-Paganism, along with other new age and neo-Pagan subcultures, became focused upon the veracity of popular images which had a powerful impact on mass culture, representing fundamental psychic truths beyond the dictates of empirical accuracy.

---

46. The author is aware of the problematic nature of a masculine critique of feminism. No claim to the legitimacy or illegitimacy of the eco-feminist approach to liberating women from patriarchal control is made here. Rather, alternative approaches and critique from within the feminist movement are being illustrated to contrast the eco-feminist model and demonstrate that it is not uncontested within the context of competing feminisms.

The ambiguity of the relationship between eco-feminist neo-Paganism as a protest sub-culture and mainstream American capitalist society is perhaps best illustrated by Starhawk's call for Paganism to aid a return to traditional American values for modern American society.

> Yet these good old "American Values," the values we have preached and never practiced, are still worth fighting for. They are, perhaps, the magical challenge we have set ourselves, the illusion we now must make real. We must call to account our country, ourselves, to become what we say we are.[47]

Similarly, Laurie Cabot, despite her promotion of Paganism as source of world peace and her claims that matriarchal social structures are intrinsically non violent and lack the political and military means to instigate warfare, claims that an American Pagan matriarchy could utilize magic to aid the defeat of US enemies and the defense of U.S soil.

> Witches must make peace an important goal. We must do magic and spells to work for a war free world. Using the spells in this book for peace may be one of our most important contributions to our children's and grand children's futures. We can do binding spells, using white light to neutralize soldiers, their weapons, and especially the military leaders who send them into battle. We can put protective shields around our armies and civilian populations, who, more now than in the past, are the major victims of war. We must also protect the land, its crops, and its animals, which are also the innocent casualties of war.[48]

Furthermore, Laurie Cabot also strongly promotes the idea of magic and traditional medicine being taught and treated as a science despite her previous claim of scientific rationality being inherently linked with patriarchal epistemological structures and a tradition of dominating nature.

> The new Science Tradition that I founded and have been teaching in Salem for twenty years draws on both ancient wisdom and the latest developments in theoretical physics. It blends the new science with the old laws in magic, now largely forgotten, and certainly not taught in twentieth-century school systems ... Science is our country; it is where we feel most at home. In spite of the dazzling, almost unbe-

---

47. Starhawk. *The Spiral Dance.* p 315.
48. Cabot, L. *The Power of the Witch.* p 293.

lievable discoveries on the subatomic level, science describes a world that makes sense.[49]

These ambiguities indicate that there is much more going on within the eco-feminist neo-Pagan subculture than simply a protest against Western modernity, capitalism or patriarchal power structures. Many of the values extolled by eco-feminist neo-Pagans are intrinsically based in Enlightenment rationality and humanism and many of the symbols of femininity and patriarchal persecution are also derived from sources located in Western traditions of patriarchy and modernity. Starhawk's definitive patriarchal enemy in her novel "The Fifth Sacred Thing" is not exploitative capitalism, commodification of social formations or even Enlightenment rationality, but an anti-capitalist military dictatorship, America's long held traditional enemy. This heavy reliance on traditional Enlightenment and American propagandic ideals, values and symbols demonstrate that, like Western Romantic traditions, eco-feminist neo-Paganism consists of more than just latent traditions of femininity or anti-patriarchal/modernist protests, but is instead a curious offshoot of critical modernism.

There has always been far more involved in the development of Romanticism than latent traditionalism acting in response to the ideals of modern technocratic rationality and this similarly applies to eco-feminist neo-Paganism. Modernity has never been an entirely coherent or unified project and Enlightenment rationality has never been accepted as the uncontested paradigm of social and cultural coherency. The development of modernity in post-industrial Europe was characterized from the beginning by the dual development of rationalist classicism and Romanticism historicism. These two fields emerged as competing but overlapping epistemological discourses which fed upon each other while simultaneously attacking and hardening each other's ideological positions. The images, which have sustained the Western Romantic episteme, have been formed in the context of a society dominated by ethical, ontological and cultural structures of Western modernity. It is these structures that have created the framework from which the social and cultural configurations of counter cultural movements have emerged.[50]

The Romantic counter culture of the eco-feminist neo-Pagan movement has formed a countervailing tradition of meaning and introspection to the issues of Western modernity. This has occurred primarily from the perspective of a unique integration of Western conceptions of femininity with consumerist

---

49. Cabot, L. *The Power of the Witch.* p 149–151.
50. Hansen, Thomas. "Inside the Romanticist Episteme." pp 24–27.

mass culture. What has been formed in the interaction between these two overlapping cultural and social traditions is a symbolic and intellectual structure of conceptual and symbolic opposition between mutually conditioned ontological and epistemological poles. These representations of difference stress either historical and contextual horizons of meaning, cultural authenticity and legitimacy of socio/cultural formations or rationalist and universalist traditions of logic and faith in ideal of human progress. What these Romantic sub-cultures have done is provide a constant opposition and critique from within the socio-cultural construction of Western modernity against the pressures of objectification of nature and social forms by the dominant rationalist and technocratic episteme. Romanticist counter cultural movements, like that of eco-feminist neo-Paganism have thus been characterized by nonconformity, individualism, a search for truth and cultural authenticity and at the same time have been plagued by issues of essentialism and their origins within the modernist sphere of Western capitalism and Enlightenment sociocultural and epistemological structures.

8

ECLECTIC PAGANISM:
THE OLD RELIGION IN THE
POST-MODERN AGE

Has not this society, glutted with aestheticism, already integrated former Romanticism, surrealism, existentialism and even Marxism up
to a point? It has, indeed, through trade, in the form of commodities. That which yesterday was reviled becomes tomorrow's cultural
consumer goods, consumption thus engulfs what was intended to
give meaning and direction.[1]

Since the inception of the neo-Pagan movement in the 1930s and 1940s the
processes by which symbols, ideologies and historical interpretation have been
utilised to construct neo-Pagan socio-cultural identity have undergone a series of paradigmatic shifts. Firstly, as indicated in the previous two chapters,
the neo-Pagan movement has largely abandoned the somewhat conservative
and nationalist inclined perspectives of its founders and become more inclined
to embrace the libertarian and leftist values espoused by the sixties counter
culture and eco-feminist movement. Secondly, the structures by which historical narratives of Paganism are authenticated and legitimised within the
neo-Pagan movement are no longer solely entrenched in claims to empirical
legitimacy and lineage. Instead, neo-Pagan approaches to historicity and cultural identity have become increasingly oriented towards eclectic and constructed models and symbols perceived to be associated with Pagan beliefs and
attitudes to nature and society. There are several reasons for this change of
perspective towards culture, history and identity. The impact of recent historical scholarship into the Early Modern Witch crazes has led to an increasing crisis with regards to neo-Pagan claims to empirical legitimacy in the con-

---

1. Cited in Hebdige, Dick. *Subculture: The meaning of style.* p 92.

struction of their historical narratives. For antiquarian and traditionalist neo-Pagans this has largely resulted in the alteration of historical claims to authenticity in accordance with new historical findings. However, the adoption of Jungian and post-Modern rhetoric in the aftermath of the 1960s has led many neo-Pagans to abandon empirical claims to authenticity. Rather they have tended to focus on the psycho-cultural impact of the symbols, narratives and rituals on the individual. Finally, the increasing growth of Witchcraft and Pagan related branches of the new age industry has heavily impacted upon the social structure and cultural framework of the neo-Pagan movement. Out of the increasing popularisation and marketability of Witch and neo-Pagan identity has developed a form of neo-Pagan practice that has become highly commodified and culturally oriented around mass marketed purchasable symbols and positive media representations of Witchcraft that are deeply rooted in popular culture. Similarly, and perhaps more importantly, the corresponding networks of social and economic relationships underlying cultural configuration have also been irretrievably transformed via the impact of cultural commodification upon neo-Pagan cultural identity.

The Empirical Challenge to Witchcraft Beliefs

Since the late 1970s, a quiet revolution has taken place in the study of historical Witchcraft and the Great European Witch Hunt. The revolution wasn't quite as dramatic as the development of radiocarbon dating, but many theories which reigned supreme thirty years ago have vanished, swept away by a flood of new data. Unfortunately, little of the new information has made it into popular history. Many articles in Pagan magazines contain almost no accurate information about the "Burning Times", primarily because we rely so heavily on out-dated research.[2]

Despite the early attempts to legitimize and entrench Wicca and the neo-Pagan revival as empirically verifiable religious movements dating from antiquity, the legitimacy of neo-Pagan representations of the past quickly came under serious challenge. A central component of Gardner's model of Witchcraft history was the support of members of the Folklore Society, Frazer and Murray in particular, and the work of Romantic historians such as Jules

---

2. Gibbons, Jenny. Recent Developments in the Study of The Great European Witch Hunt. *The Pomegranate*. No 5. Summer 1998.

Michelet. The close relationship between Murray and Gardner and the role their friendship played in the formation of Wicca is particularly well documented. However, from the 1960s onward the empirical veracity of the neo-Pagan histories presented by Murray and Michelet have come increasingly under threat. This transformation of popular and academic interpretation of Witchcraft history also threw the claims to legitimacy and cultural identity of many sectors of the neo-Pagan movement into turmoil. Furthermore, the very methodology of the Folklore Societies came under serious and sustained attack, damaging the very foundations of Wiccan and neo-Pagan claims to antiquity and historical legitimacy in ritual, symbols and historical identity.

The 1980s saw a major transformation in the historical study of Witchcraft that in turn led to major shifts in the construction of historical legitimacy within the neo-Pagan movement. Prior to the mid 1980s, Anglophone Witchcraft histories were predominantly concerned with universalist arguments about magic and the primitive, the nature of mass persecution and the dangers of superstition compared to scientific rationality. In addition, Anglophone histories of Witchcraft were heavily influenced by a fixation upon the English and American experience of Witch-hunts with only a peripheral interest in the Witch crazes and Witchcraft beliefs of continental Europe. During the 1980s a series of conferences were held in Paris and Schleswig by a collection of continental Witchcraft historians. These historians were examining the history of Witchcraft from the perspective of local history rather than broad pan-European studies based in a search for evidence revealing the nature of mass persecution. What was perhaps the most significant outcome of their research was the finding that popular beliefs of Witchcraft and the nature of the early modern Witch crazes arose out of an immensely varied and diverse period of history. The social class, gender and cultural background of those persecuted varied immensely according to location and time. Furthermore, it was found that the nature of the charges placed against those accused of Witchcraft and the socio-cultural identity of those charged also varied immensely. Similarly, there was an apparent difference between learned doctrine of Witchcraft practices, as represented by the *Malleus Maleficarum* and the *Demonomonaire*, and that which was believed and manifested in Witchcraft accusations at the local level in European society.[3]

Aside from revolutionizing and granting renewed credibility to the study of Witchcraft as a historical discipline, the conclusions reached by historians examining the Witchcraft beliefs of the early modern period increasingly

---

3. Ankarloo, B. and Henningsen, G. *Early Modern European Witchcraft.* pp 1–7.

placed the empirical veracity of the historical claims of the neo-Pagan move-ment under threat. Furthermore, the claims of several of the primary leaders of the neo-Pagan movement, most notably Gerald Gardner, also came under question. It was found that much of the material that he claimed had origi-nated with a secret coven of Witches in rural England was in fact derived from his interpretations of Hindu manuscripts, the ritual magic of Aleister Crow-ley and other nineteenth century occultists.[4] It became increasingly doubtful whether he had actually met with any surviving Witches at all. Even Gardner's closest associates, such as Doreen Valiente and Ray Buckland, began to claim that whilst they believed the core of his ideas came from an actual experience with a surviving cult of Witches, much of his writings were an attempt to fill the gaps in his experience with his own knowledge of ritual magic obtained through his studies in anthropology and ritual magic. These critiques were also supported by the fact that once local empirical studies of Witchcraft be-liefs and practices came to be generally recognized in the Anglophone world, the representation of Witchcraft described by the neo-Pagan movement and Romantic historians like Margaret Murray and Jules Michelet bore very little resemblance to that suggested by the empirical data available.[5]

The Post-Modern Response

These challenges to neo-Pagan claims to historical legitimacy formed the underlying structure behind the transformation of neo-Pagan claims to cul-tural authenticity. The transformation of neo-Paganism during the sixties counter culture and its subsequent appropriation by branches of the feminist movement led many sectors of the neo-Pagan movement to abandon empir-ical approaches to authenticity and construct cultural formations within the context of an eclectic methodology deeply rooted in popular culture and Jun-gian symbolism. Within this new structure of cultural association the ultimate value of cultural formations, rituals, symbols and historical claims became that of psycho-cultural impact upon the individual rather than claims to em-pirical legitimacy. Within the context of neo-Pagan "Play Power" and eco-fem-

---

4. Guiley, Elizabeth. 'Witchcraft as Goddess Worship'. In *The Feminist Companion to Mythology*. Ed. Larrington, Carolyne. Pandora Press: London. 1992. pp 411–424; Hutton, Ronald. *The Triumph of the Moon*. pp 217–220; Bishop, C. & Bishop, P. "Embarrassed by our Origins." pp 48–55.

5. Ankarloo, B. and Henningsen, G. *Early Modern European Witchcraft*. pp 1–7; Ginzberg, C. *Ecstasies: Deciphering the Witch's Sabbat*. pp 9–15.

inist narratives of Witchcraft persecutions, empirical veracity had become largely abandoned in favour of post-modern approaches to history and culture. However, despite the eclectic attitude to culture, historicity and identity formation, the ideological structure of neo-Paganism and Witchcraft came to be perceived as universal and in opposition to the destructive impact of modernity, patriarchy and industrialism. In other words, the underlying cultural and ideological structure remains firmly within the discourse of the Western Romantic episteme. In this light what was important in Witchcraft histories was not the empirical veracity of historical claims but the psychological impact and universality of images like the Witch, the crone and the Witch persecutions of the early modern era and their representation according to Romantic and Enlightenment ideologies.[6]

It is worth noting that the appropriation of Jungian ontology and the post-modern mood by large sectors of the neo-Pagan movement did not occur simply as a passive response to a crisis in neo-Pagan empirical historicity. These trends had been developing within the neo-Pagan movement for a long time. For example, the belief in a universal basis upon which all religions could be redefined in terms of their value in the search for ultimate truth and personal development was one of the central tenets of the theosophical movement. Similarly, the influence of Jungian analytical psychology through much of the sixties counter culture and its influence on the development of post-sixties new spirituality movements is well documented and became a significant component of neo-Pagan approaches to culture, ritual and symbolic representation.

The crisis of historicity amongst neo-Pagan claims to lineage and empirically verifiable history strengthened support for eclectic approaches to neo-Pagan identity. Simultaneously, this crisis severely weakened the claims of those sectors of the neo-Pagan movement whose primary claim to legitimacy was a perceived empirically justified lineage to the paganism of antiquity or the Witches of the Early Modern period. The threat posed by challenges to the empirical accuracy of neo-Pagan claims to historical authenticity also led to some extreme reactionary comments against empirical critique of neo-Pagan histories by some sectors of the eco-feminist branch of the neo-Pagan movement, as illustrated by Mary Daly's claim that critique of feminist histories of Witchcraft are equivalent to Nazi book burnings. Additionally, the counter cultural penchant for appropriating images that have strong psycho-cultural impact as a means of drawing attention to protests and as a metaphorical rep-

---

6. Adler, M. *Drawing Down the Moon*. pp 28, 30, 31, 44 & 88; Starhawk. *The Spiral Dance*. pp 22–24.

resentation of contemporary political, social and cultural struggles further strengthened popular support for the adoption of an eclectic and non empirical approach to defining neo-Pagan identity and historical claims.[7]

An important side effect of this adoption of eclecticism and the concomitant rejection of empirical history in defining neo-Pagan identity is that it led to a renewed search for a unifying ideological basis to legitimate claims to neo-Pagan identity. Aside from the common appropriation of Romantic anti-modernism, one of the most critical aspects to this new structure of neo-Pagan identity was that it centred the ultimate source of legitimacy in defining neo-Pagan identity within an individual's relationship with the natural, social and cultural world. One of the most significant implications of this approach to defining values and the role of the sacred is that it centres the locus of the divine within the existential experience of the individual. For many neo-Pagans this perception of the divine made manifest in the physical world is the quintessential component of neo-Pagan identity. The rituals and symbols may vary but paganism retains a sense of homogeneity via a common existential relationship to the divine as located within the world and human experience. As York writes,

> So in answer to the question how does the contemporary Western Pagan recognize that Chinese folk religion, Confucianism, Shinto, Siberian shamanism, Kahuna, Australian Aboriginal religion, Amerindianism, the Afro Atlantic practices of Santeria, Macumba and Voodoo, various tribalism of sub-Saharan Africa and so forth are Pagan is because they are Pagan. They all share in an essential this worldliness. Earth is sacred, the sacred source of mother existence. The material is understood as the matrix in which and from which the world, the human and the gods have their being, though not necessarily their end. In each of these religions we have the implicit pantheism, animism and polytheism that Margot Adler recognized as the constituent features of paganism.[8]

The Jungian model, widely adopted by many neo-Pagans in the nineteen sixties, seventies and eighties implied that the very fact that the images and symbols of neo-Paganism had such a strong impact on the psyche and within the collective unconscious, legitimated the belief in the existence of a divine source manifested in the minds of human beings. One of the strongest im-

---

7. Stephens, J. *Anti-Disciplinary Protests.* p 34.
8. York, M. "Defining Paganism." p 7.

ports of this belief system for neo-Pagans was that it located the manifestation of the divine within human experience and the physical world as opposed to being a divine source located, in a neo-Platonic sense, outside of the realm of the physical. The Goddess is immanent in the world and consequently the ultimate source of value must also lie within the individual's experience and comprehension of the physical world. As Starhawk writes,

> Immanence means that the Goddess, the Gods, are embodied, that we are each a manifestation of the living being of earth, that nature, culture and life in all their diversity are sacred. Immanence calls us to live our spirituality here in the world, to take action to preserve the life of the earth, to live with integrity and responsibility.[9]

These eclectic approaches to defining neo-Pagan identity ultimately had the effect of reorienting the definition of neo-Pagan identity into the realms of the ideological inasmuch as the inherently subjective nature of cultural interpretation increasingly dislodged the Jungian paradigm in which neo-Pagan identity appeared "natural", an eclecticism in which an essential centre of identity was no longer needed. Subsequently, culture and history became relegated to the role of symbolic trappings that could be utilised as metaphors in symbolic representations of contemporary social, cultural and political issues. The most obvious example is the use of the Witch trials of the early modern period as a model for expressing the contemporary plight of women in patriarchal society. In this light culture and material culture was no longer appropriated as a means of proving empirical historicity but was instead derived from popular and mainstream representations for psycho-cultural impact and metaphorical significance. From this perspective the kinds of representations of culture defined by movements such as the Discordian Society, described by Richard Neville as playpower, gained increasing predominance as the ultimate expression of neo-Pagan identity. Eclecticism and human experience became the ultimate sources of meaning and value. In this environment the Jungian interpretative approach increasingly came under threat. Conceptions of ritual, symbolism and belief, that reified the aesthetic and the creative as a transcendent source of meaning beyond the prescriptive model of Jung's collective unconscious, bombarded neo-Pagan representations of Witch and Pagan identity. The sheer diversity of symbolic interpretations came to represent an ultimate source of meaning in and of itself, beyond the universalist assumptions of Enlightenment historicity and Jungian analytical psychology.

---

9. Starhawk. *The Spiral Dance*. pp 10–11.

During the 1980s neo-Pagans who had adopted the Jungian analytical psychology came under increasing criticism from a variety of neo-Pagan and academic sources. In particular post-modern critiques of the universalism of Jungian psycho-analytical theory, post-colonial critiques of the Euro-centric bias in Jungian interpretations of myth and symbolism, feminist critiques of the gendered implications of Jungian theory and gay critiques of Jungian assumptions of male/female polarity inflicted telling blows against Jungian oriented neo-Paganism. A movement that perceived itself as closely linked to feminism, indigenous societies and anti-Enlightenment rationalism had considerable difficulties accommodating charges of sexism, Euro-centrism, homophobia and universalism. Noted Jungian eco-feminist neo-Pagan Starhawk commented in her ten year revised edition of Spiral Dance that,

> I would no longer describe the essential quality of the erotic energy
> flow that sustains the universe as one of male/female polarity. To do
> so enshrines heterosexual human relationships as the basic pattern of
> all being, relegating other sorts of attraction and desire as deviant ...

Post-modern theory stepped into the void created by the weakening of Jungian analytical psychology as the dominant philosophical basis of neo-Pagan thought. By abandoning meta-narratives in the interpretation of symbols, ritual and culture neo-Pagans could focus their attention almost exclusively on the experience of ritual and significance given to symbols via their own creative process. If symbols, rituals and history have no universal interpretive framework then their usage becomes inherently flexible and may be shaped by Pagans themselves. Instead of needing to argue the veracity of historical interpretations empirically, neo-Pagans could deconstruct and re-read historical narratives on the basis of their underlying assumptions. From this perspective symbols and rituals become a process of creatively giving meaning to experiences rather than an attempt to appropriate myth or history.[10]

One of the most prominent indicators of the appropriation of post-modern methods by many neo-Pagans was the increasing rejection of historicity and interpretive structure, beyond individual experience, in defining the legitimacy of neo-Pagan ritual, symbolism and foundation myths. Perhaps some of the most prominent examples of this are Margot Adler's comment that "everything in the Craft, even the Great Metaphor of the Goddess, is still only a metaphor" and Miriam Simos(Starhawk), stating that "I have spoken of the Goddess as psychological symbol and manifest reality. She is both. She

---

10. Purkiss, D. *The Witch in History*. pp 41–45.

exists and we create her."[11] One may even encounter statements like, "It does not matter if the first religion of most societies was Goddess worship or even if the Goddess had the characteristics that paganism now ascribes to her ..."[12]

Jim Wafer describes this abandonment of both empirical history and Jungian analytical psychology by large sectors of the neo-Pagan movement as a shift from foundationalism to post-modernism, utilizing Lyotard's description of post-modernism as "A recognition of the futility of seeking an absolute foundation for knowledge."[13] In other words this definition of neo-Pagan identity implies a denial of the existence of any transcendent teleological structure on which to base our conception of a true theory or just society.[14] Consequently, the increasing permeation of the post-modern mood into neo-Pagan conceptions of identity, authenticity and historicity offers a model by which the new post-modern era can be navigated by a social movement without recourse to empirically based claims to authenticity. As Diane Purkiss comments, "The entirety of modern Witchcraft offers a unique opportunity to see a religion being made from readings and rereadings of texts and histories. No one person is in charge of the process, so modern Witchcraft is not a unified set of beliefs. Every interpretation is subject to reinvention by others."[15] According to this ideology, even the interpretive framework of Jung may be abandoned and the ultimate value in rituals, symbols and history for neo-Pagans becomes the experience of its practitioners and the meanings they ascribe to arbitrarily devised signs. Consequently the critical issue is the experiential impact of symbols and rituals on the practitioner as opposed to any sense of historicity or cultural context. As Roberta James comments with regards to the primacy given to experiential reality in ritual amongst post-modern oriented neo-Pagan groups.

---

11. Starhawk. *The Spiral Dance*. p 95.

12. Mary Ellen Brown (ed.) *Neo-Paganism: A Search for Religious Alternatives*. Bloomington: Indiana University Women's Studies Program. 1988. pp 106–108.

13. Wafer, Jim. *Gay and Lesbian Alternative Religious Movements: Do you have to have foundations before you can rock them*. Australian Anthropological Society Annual Conference: Alternative Culture Panel. 10 July 1999. University of New South Wales. p 3. Wafer is of course referring to Lyotard's famous definition in his ground breaking work *The Post-Modern Condition*. "I will use the term modern to designate any science that legitimates itself with reference to a meta-discourse making explicit appeal to some grand narrative, such as the dialectic of the spirit, the hermeneutics of meaning, the emancipation of the rational or working subject or the creation of wealth." Post modernity, in contrast is defined as "an incredulity towards meta-narratives." Lyotard, Jean. *The Post-Modern Condition*. Minneapolis: University of Minnesota Press, 1984. pp xxii–xxiv.

14. Callinicos, Alex. *Against Post-Modernism*. London: Polity Press, 1989. p 3.

15. Purkiss, D. *The Witch in History*. p 52.

Though Women's Spirituality rituals rely to some extent on the notion of Pagan 'tradition' and the acceptance and authority of the Pagan festival calendar, they are invented, created, made anew each year by different people using different materials. Only the most general details of structure and content could be anticipated. No one creating a ritual would expect that even they would know or could predict the eventual character of a ritual that they themselves had crafted. The ritual's 'right-nature' is made moment by moment of its instantiation ... Ritual is a *physic* experience in which the senses are deliberately stimulated to bring about an experience of the sacred; things acting on encultured corporealities that encourage ongoing commitment to Women's Spirituality and any other spiritual or religious formation. The very corporeality of this plexus of apprehendings offered by ritual engenders ongoing commitment. Self-esteem or feeling good *about* the self stems from good feeling *through* the (sensing) self. In the absence of *doxa*, experience is both the foundation and test of faith in Anglophone capitalist liberal democracies.[16]

The adoption of post-modern approaches to culture and historicity by many sectors of the neo-Pagan movement became not only a means of rationalizing a particular conception of history; it also became a statement of ideological identity. The very fact that history was defined in accordance with alternative perspectives of historical legitimacy became a means of illustrating fundamental differences in the nature of neo-Pagan epistemology and cultural structure. This was placed in comparison to the linear empirical perspectives of Enlightenment and traditional historiographical discourses of Witchcraft history. This perspective is illustrated by Diane Purkiss' comment that "Modern Witches' histories of Witchcraft present a much cleaner break with academic values than anything feminist historians have ever produced or wished to produce. Far more than Derrida or Foucault, popular history disregards the assumptions that make Enlightenment history possible."[17] Neo-Paganism, particularly those eco-feminist branches that embrace cultural eclecticism, offers a means by which the totalizing project of patriarchal modernity can be overcome by new forms of socio-political activism that embrace the decentred nature of the post-modern condition and whose socio-political identity

---

16. James, Roberta. *Spirit Shifts.* p 1. Unpublished manuscript obtained, and cited with permission, at the Australian Anthropological Society Annual Conference: Alternative Culture Panel. 10 July 1999. University of New South Wales.

17. Purkiss, D. *The Witch in History.* p 52.

are rooted in the fragmented organic construction of self created images rather than in the quantifiable struggles of traditional politics.

The construction of neo-Pagan identity and cultural representation as an example of a post-modern social movement closely echoes the theoretical structure of Baudrillard. It implies a circumstance in which reality and representation, as defined by empirical or Enlightenment definitions, have become circumvented by the culture of the simulacra. That is to say that the underlying basis of neo-Pagan culture, historical identity and representations have ceased to be defined in terms of derivations of an objective reality but have instead become self perpetuating representations that have no relationship to any objective reality; the representation has itself become the underlying basis of experiential reality surpassing the impact of any empirically verifiable history. As Baudrillard writes,

> Abstraction today is no longer that of the map, the double, the mirror or the concept. Simulation is no longer that of a territory, a referential being or a substance. It is the generation by models without origin or reality: a hypereal. The territory no longer precedes the map, nor survives it. Henceforth it is the map that precedes the territory—*precession of simalcra*—it is the map that engenders the territory and if it were to revive the fable today, it would be the territory whose shreds are slowly rotting across the map. It is the real, and not the map, whose vestiges subsist here and there, in the deserts which are no longer those of the empire, but our own. *The desert of the real itself*.[18]

According, to many post-modern academic studies of neo-Paganism by such writers as Purkiss, Wafer, Starhawk and James this reification of cultural signifiers, supposedly bereft of universalist interpretative or ideological structures, is perceived to be an immensely liberating component of the neo-Pagan movement. By dissolving the link between fact and fiction, post-modern history and culture are believed to become the property of those who create them and thus challenge the epistemological dominance of technocratic, patriarchal, Enlightenment rationality. If culture can be divested of its essential meaning in relation to universalist ideologies of empirical history, tradition or national identity then the consumption and reconstruction of these images can be perceived as a means of escaping these ideologies and the correspon-

---

18. Baudrillard, Jean. *Simulcra and Simulation*. Michigan: University of Michigan Press, 1981. pp 1–2.

ding social formations and power relations on which they are based. This is ultimately a model of knowledge linked to the power of societal discourse that closely echoes Foucault's postulate that power is intrinsically based and inter-related with corresponding epistemological structures that give it meaning and significance. Purkiss, in particular, perceives the adoption of post-modern approaches to culture by many neo-Pagans, especially within the eco-feminist tradition, to represent a complete break with previously assumed relationships between experience, culture and history altogether.[19] Furthermore, the close links between legitimacy in knowledge and power structures implies an inherent push towards social activism. She comments that,

> The valorization of historical creativity rather than historical authority no doubt explains why women have been able to be so prominent in modern Witchcraft; individual histories obviate the need to battle with institutional and social understandings of whose word goes, understandings that are invariably gendered.[20]

From this perspective, the post-modern pastiche allows history, culture and social identity to avoid the homogenizing effect of meta-narratives that define reality in accordance with dominant power structures and cultural formations in society; structures and formations that are inherently exclusive and restrictive of people's freedoms. The challenge against the domination of Enlightenment thought over the legitimacy of knowledge is thus a struggle for freedom. Eagleton describes this perception of the post-modern as follows,

> Post-modernism signals the death of such "meta-narratives" whose secret terroristic function was to ground and legitimate the illusion of a "universal" human history. We are now in the process of wakening from the nightmare of modernity, with its manipulative reason and fetish of the totality, into the laid back pluralism of the post modern, that heterogeneous range of life-styles and language games which has renounced the urge to totalize and legitimate itself.[21]

This construction of post-modernism postulates a model of modernity and the Enlightenment that is characterized by a totalizing project of universal reason, science and industrialism that objectifies the human condition and alienates human experience from the natural world and spiritual fulfillment. The

---

19. Purkiss, D. *The Witch in History.* p 40.
20. Purkiss, D. *The Witch in History.* p 40.
21. Eagleton, Terry, cited in Harvey, David. *The Condition of Post-Modernity: An enquiry into the Origins of Cultural Change.* Blackwell Press. 1990.

model does not so much argue that we are now in a post-modern era characterized by fragmentation and impermanence, as argued by Lyotard, Baudrillard and Derrida, as much as proposing that an acceptance of the ideals of post-modern decentralization, fragmentation and flexibility can offset and overwhelm the totalizing project of modernity. This conflict, between supposed diametrical opposites, is not that of a struggle for social equity or political representation but against alienation and rationalization. The enemy is not so much defined by control of wealth and power or social class but by adherence to the Enlightenment goals of science, reason and progress. Consequently, by adopting new and unruly forms of protest, histories and identities that flout logic, reason and traditional definitions of culture it is believed that the overarching episteme of modernity and progress can be sabotaged from within. This form of post-modern resistance is thus configured as the antidote to the destruction wrought by the totalizing universal project of modernity.

Post-Modernism or Romantic Anti-Modernism

Thomas Hansen argues that the construction of post-modernism which postulates modernity as universalist and totalizing reason is intrinsically based in Romantic philosophies of language, culture, history and identity that constructed the image of modernity as objectifying rationalism and unrestrained industrialism in the late eighteenth and early nineteenth centuries. In other words it represents a contemporary manifestation of Romantic anti-modernism. From this perspective, far from representing a new epistemological and ontological paradigm, the definition of post-modernism in opposition to the "terroristic" function of Enlightenment reason is a manifestation of the Romanticist episteme in the context of Western modernity. It is an episteme which,

> Posits knowledge and meaning as being culturally differentiated, as always mediated by a specific language, as always situated in unique historical settings. It presupposes a fundamental culturalist ontology, positing human beings and human subjectivity, first and foremost, as being produced within discrete and distinct cultural horizons of meaning.[22]

For Hansen, the Romantic construction of modernity permeates almost every aspect of the post-modernist critique of modernity as universal reason or faith

---

22. Hansen, T. "The Romanticist Episteme." p 23.

in meta-narratives; almost invariably constructed as faith in meta-narratives that are supported by Enlightenment definitions of knowledge and truth. Of particular importance in Hansen's perspective of post-modern critiques of modernity as universalist reason is the work of Foucault. As Hansen describes it, Foucault's primary objective was to create a system of tools by which empirical history, knowledge and identity formation could be made subjective and so dissolve the overarching meta-narrative of Enlightenment progress, science and rationality into "unruly histories of dissent and heterogeneity."[23] The individuals located within the boundaries of history, such as Witches, constitute the boundaries of mainstream bourgeois history and society and are the principle targets of normalizing strategies based in structures of knowledge defined by the mechanisms of power. Essential to this project, developed by Foucault and taken up by the aforementioned neo-Pagan idealization of the post-modern critique of modernity, is an implicit identification of modernity with the normalizing and objectifying power of mainstream christo-centric, patriarchal and industrialized society that is associated with Enlightenment thought in Romantic discourse. This particular conception of modernity rendered it the appearance of a coherent systematized project manifested in an emerging and irresistible will to order and control through positivist constructions of knowledge. Hansen describes this process as "An emerging episteme bent on explanation and taxonimization, and a drive to discipline bodies and social agency through scientific discourses and state institutions."[24]

Interestingly, Foucault came to reject this dualist model of modernity versus human freedom and autonomy and came to support what he described as "A critical ontology of ourselves as a historico-practical test of the limits that we may go beyond, and thus as work carried out upon ourselves as free beings."[25] From this perspective, particularly well illustrated in his response to Kant's essay *What is Enlightenment,* modernity is instead defined by a faith in Enlightenment as a search for intellectual autonomy and freedom from dogma as well as faith in the possibility of creating ourselves as autonomous beings.[26] Thus by drawing upon both the Romantic belief in creative and cultural autonomy and Enlightenment faith in the potential for autonomy in the critical application of reason, Foucault could redefine his project firmly within the sphere of modernity. This enabled both critique and progress without neces-

---

23. Hansen, T. "The Romanticist Episteme." p 22.

24. Hansen, T. "The Romanticist Episteme." p 22.

25. Foucault, Michel. "What is Enlightenment?" In Rainbow, P. (ed.) *The Foucault Reader.* Penguin: New York, 1984. pp 46–47.

26. Foucault, M. "What is Enlightenment?" pp 46–47.

sarily being dependent on the dogmatic application of a single universalist discursive structure or the taxonimization of the human experience.

In this particular configuration, the dominant strain of epistemological conflict in Western society is not modernity, configured as universalist reason, in opposition to traditionalism but is instead located in differing conceptions of Enlightenment and human autonomy located within the discursive sphere of Western modernity. This is particularly important with regards to the adoption of post-modern rhetoric by sectors of the neo-Pagan movement in identify formation and in the critique of mainstream Western culture. Rather than representing a fundamental break with modernity the appropriation of cultural laissez faire and the abandoning of empirical veracity in constructing histories according to the dictates of psycho-cultural impact is essentially a manifestation of the Romantic opposition to modernity configured as universalist reason. Certainly it is impossible to sustain the claim that the adoption of cultural *laissez faire* and the abandoning of historicity in identity formation represent an abandonment of meta-narratives. Rather, this model of modernity and post-modernity is a fundamentally dualist interpretation of the socio-political and cultural order. It posits a monolithic homogenizing and controlling alliance of traditionalism, conservatism and Enlightenment modernity in eternal opposition to a heterogeneous combination of anti-rationalist, dissident movements. It is a model of Manichean conflict combined in the context of a worldview dominated by a millenarian struggle for the end of meta-narratives and is a far grander and universalist ideology than the models of reason, science and humanist ethics promoted by Kant or Marx. As Eagleton comments,

> Post-modern culture is much taken with change, mobility, open-endedness, instability, while some of its theory flattens everything from Socrates to Sartre to the same tedious saga. A supposedly homogenizing Western history is violently homogenized.[27]

The development of post-modern styled histories and the embracing of cultural eclecticism are intrinsically based on the adoption of universalist assumptions about human nature, modernity and culture that are deeply rooted in the Romantic episteme and the socio-political context of popular culture. These intertwining structures of Romanticism and popular culture form the underlying basis for subsequent universal ideologies of nature, the feminine, pre-industrial civilization and the significance of symbols in forming human

---

27. Eagleton, Terry. *The Illusions of Postmodernism*. Oxford: Blackwell Publishers, 1996. p 34.

identity and a sense of cultural authenticity and autonomy. This position that history, culture and symbolic representation only have significance in relation to their capacity to aid contemporary political struggles in opposition to the totalizing project of patriarchal Enlightenment reason implies the existence of a universalist ideological configuration and a corresponding teleological narrative of human progress and freedom; albeit from the Romantic rather than Enlightenment interpretation of Western modernity.

This construct of modernity, empirical history and the Enlightenment is not so much an expression of post-modernism, as configured by Lyotard and Baudrillard, but perhaps better perceived as an expression of Romantic anti-modernism. In this light the conflict between post-modern and empirical history within the neo-Pagan movement is representative of the conflict between Romantic and Enlightenment perspectives of human autonomy and creativity in conflict with dogma and traditionalism. In other words, the issue centers on debate as to whether it is the Romantic or the Enlightenment episteme which is truly modern. Is the potential for human freedom, authenticity and autonomy better represented through the struggle for autonomy from nature via the application of science, reason and progress or is it manifested in the struggle for creativity and cultural authenticity and autonomy? Romantic anti-modernism caricatures modernity as an alienating, industrialized, scientific dystopia. It is depicted as the universal other against which an alliance of heterogeneous dissident sectors of society are in constant opposition. It is a conflict based in language and structures of thought rather than in overt political power. It is a very seductive and idealistic approach for a society faced by environmental devastation, alienation and an exponential rate of scientific progress. It is an approach that draws on the symbolic impact of a mythologized past and postulates a utopian future if the spiritual values ascribed to the mythologized past could be applied in the vales and cultural representations of the social and cultural order. While the details surrounding the symbols and cultural specificity may have become defined according to an eclectic perspective the sense of history as a source of ideals uncorrupted by the influence of Enlightenment modernism is taken as given.

The perception that aesthetic experience, as manifested through symbolic representation and ritual, represents a higher form of consciousness and understanding than Enlightenment values of science and progress is also an ideological theme that can be traced back to the origins of Romantic movement. By focusing on the creative process and aesthetic experience as an end in itself, a sense of sublime, unity and identity can be injected into the material artifacts of culture and thus counteract the sense of alienation and fragmentation common to contemporary life. This also offers a universal basis from which to critique the destructive impact of modernity, as configured by post-modern/Romantic models of universal and objectifying reason, science and industrialism. It is in this light that the past, as an eclectic *bricolage* of symbols and cultural artifacts evoking a sense of nostalgia, becomes particularly important. The past is the cultural resource from which visions of alternative approaches to modernity can be constructed. It promotes the ideal that by appropriating and constructing images of the past and its associated constructions of societal values and aesthetic experience a new socio-cultural order can be developed for the betterment of an alienated and industrialized society. Consequently, models of protest that are perceived to reject and satirize values associated with the Romantic construction of modernity such as the play power protests of the sixties, the WITCH movement, eclectically constructed aesthetic histories and images of the historically disenfranchised, can be construed as challenging the very foundations of modernity. The constructions of new self-created identities that reject empirical history are seen to be a legitimate challenge to the very fabric of the Enlightenment ideology sustaining the Romantic anti-modern caricature of Western modernity.

Accordingly, the claim that neo-Paganism represents a model of post-modern resistance against the totalizing project of patriarchal modernity is difficult to substantiate beyond a penchant for cultural eclecticism and a belief that history should form a mythological rather than an empirical role in defining socio-cultural identity. The blend of symbols, images and histories may well be eclectically constructed but they are appropriated on the basis of their cultural impact which is itself a product of a variety of power structures, cultural formations and historical narratives located within the dominant paradigm of Western society and culture. In this light the increasing acceptance of cultural eclecticism that has come to be defined as an example of post-modernism is perhaps better defined as an expression of Romantic anti-modernism in an era where culture has increasingly come to be defined by the processes of commodity exchange. In other words, eclectic neo-Paganism is an example of the Romantic episteme operating in an era where culture has increasingly become dominated by the commodifying impact of late capitalism. Thus what is defined as post-modernism, with regards to the embracing of eclecticism and rejection of historicity amongst neo-Pagans, may be better perceived as a Romantic manifestation symptomatic of the culmination of the project of modernity. As Heelas writes with regards to the claim that the New Age and neo-Pagan movements are representative of a new post-modern form of religion and social activism,

> Currently, the New Age is not post-modern. To make that claim is to essentialize modernity, contradicting the non-essentializing outlook

of the (supposedly) post-modern condition, and, by treating modernity as one thing, failing to recognize that the New Age is a perpetuation—thinking of perhaps the most pertinent of cultural trajectories—of the counter-Enlightenment Romantic Movement.[28]

Witchcraft, Commodification and Popular Culture

In a society where popular culture has been increasingly dominated by the processes of fashion and consumer capitalism, it is logical to expect that the sources from which neo-Pagans draw their inspiration, symbols and histories should also be dominated by symbols appropriated from consumer culture. The popularization of novels like *The Mists of Avalon*, the film *The Craft* or even the television series *Buffy the Vampire Slayer* are examples of the growing number of popular representations of neo-Paganism. Neo-Pagan attitudes to culture have undergone significant transformation but it is not driven by either incredulity towards meta-narratives nor can it be described as representation supplanting the real as per Baudrillard's model of a culture defined by the simulacra. Rather, the shift in the meaning of culture may be better interpreted as the appropriation of culture and history into the process of commodity exchange. History, or more specifically a sense of historical antecedence, continues to play a formative role in the construction of historical and cultural identity. However, the mechanisms by which that history is constructed and the corresponding symbols, rituals and artifacts associated with that history have increasingly come to be defined by their role in a matrix of popular culture dominated by the impact of consumer capitalism. The very process that assumes that culture is simply a resource for the obtaining of aesthetic experience and identity formation implies definition of culture as a consumable commodity. Similarly, the approach to radical cultural eclecticism implies an ideological configuration that defines culture as a resource or commodity to be consumed in line with market trends.

It can be argued that the commodification of culture and the conception of culture as something to be purchased and consumed as a source of aesthetic experience and identity formation have very deep historical roots rather than being simply a creation of post-sixties narcissism. Critiques of cultural commodification can be seen as early as the nineteenth century. Marx, for exam-

---

28. Heelas, P. *The New Age Movement*. pp 216–217.

ple, argued that in a system of commodity production and consumption, where the social activity of production is mediated by the circulation and consumption of products in the labor market, the social relationship between people can become dominated by a perception of an almost numinous value attributed to particular artifacts of cultural significance. Ultimately this relationship between cultural artifacts and production is a privileging of the exchange value over the use value of cultural commodities in the realm of aesthetic experience. Thus by treating culture and aesthetic experience as commodities, the production of human creativity becomes private property and a person's creative potential is reduced to labor power to be bought and sold on the market. The entire symbolic construction of a culture within the sphere of commodification, such as that of Western representations of Native Americans, ancient Celts or medieval Witches, can become a cultural resource for the production of symbolic artifacts and the acquisition of profit according to the phenomenon of defining human relationships and identity via the process of commodity fetishism.[29] Thus as more and more of human experience and the natural world become incorporated into the system of production and exchange, culture increasingly comes to dominate nature and the process by which symbolic significance is attached to cultural commodities. This process occludes the underlying structure of social relationships beneath a bewildering array of purchased cultural artifacts and fashions symbolically representing a wide array of socio-political relationships.[30]

Similarly, the commodification and commercialization of cultural artifacts during the nineteenth century has its own examples of consumer based cultural eclecticism. This is most commonly manifested in a consumer driven competitive struggle to constantly "cannibalize" and reconstruct cultural artifacts in order to sell cultural products as novel examples of aesthetic experience. Reminiscent of the claims that post-modern culture has led to a situation in which "integrated into production is a general economic urgency to produce wave after wave of novel seeming goods, assigning an essential economic function to aesthetic innovation,"[31] 19th century economic production also shared many of the hallmarks of commodification, niche marketing and cultural consumption. As David Harvey comments on the plight of nineteenth

---

29. Callinicos, A. *Against Postmodernism*. p 149; Gare, Arran. *Postmodernism and the Environmental Crisis*. London: Routledge, 1995. p 79; Marx, Karl. *Capital*. Vol 1. London: Harmondsworth. 1976.

30. Marx, Karl. *Grundrisse*. Harmondsworth: Penguin, 1973. p 409.

31. Jameson, Fredrik. *Postmodernism or the Cultural Logic of Late Capitalism*. Durham: Duke University Press, 1999. p 4.

century artists forced by economic demands to create and sustain their own niche markets,

> The commodification and commercialization of a market for cultural products during the nineteenth century (and the concomitant decline of the aristocratic, state or institutional patronage) forced cultural producers into a market form of competition that was bound to re-inforce processes of creative destruction within the aesthetic field it-self. Each and every artist sought to change the basis of aesthetic judg-ment, if only to sell his or her product. It also depended on the formation of a distinctive class of cultural consumers. Artists, for all their predilection for anti-establishment and anti-bourgeois rhetoric, spent much more energy struggling with each other and against their own traditions in order to sell more products than they did in en-gaging in real political action.[32]

The claim that the late twentieth century experience of cultural commodifi-cation and niche markets actually represents a fundamentally new form of cul-tural formation and economic exchange is somewhat tenuous. Alex Callini-cos, for example, argues that this process is better described as simply the continuation and expansion of a process already well established in nineteenth century Europe.[33] The full details surrounding this debate are well beyond the scope of this book. However, in reference to the neo-Pagan movement's ap-proach to culture, history, identity formation, social demographics and po-litical orientation, there has been a substantial transformation in the mecha-nism by which culture is appropriated and the ideology by which historico-cultural identity is legitimized. To a large extent these changes par-allel the development of the sixties counter culture and the New Age move-ment discussed earlier. However, the increasingly eclectic approach to culture and the prominence of popular culture in the formation of neo-Pagan sym-bolism and identity formation is well described by Fredrick Jameson's defini-tion of post-modernism as a restructuring of the role of culture in society con-comitant with the development of what he defines as "late capitalism."

According to Jameson, the recent development and expansion of Western capitalism and its corresponding process of cultural commodification has led

---

32. Harvey, David. *The Condition of Postmodernity: An Enquiry into the Origins of Cul-tural Change.* Cambridge: Blackwell, 1990. p 22.

33. For more information on this debate please see Callinicos, A. *Against Postmod-ernism*; Harvey David. *The Condition of Postmodernity.* pp 39–65; Jameson, F. *Postmod-ernism or the Cultural Logic of Late Capitalism*; Eagleton, T. *The Illusions of Postmodernity.*

to a paradigm shift in the role of history and culture in formulating human identity and cultural representation. He argues that capitalism was initially characterized by a process of bureaucratization through which the heterogeneous social and political order was reconstructed into a rationalized and bureaucratized structure to better serve the needs of production and the new social order that replaced the old aristocratic regime. In other words, it is the development and subsequent establishment of the regime of taxonimization and rationalization of the experiential world that so inspired the Romantic critique of modernization and formed the basis of Foucault's model of modernity. This system is characterized by the,

> Desacralization of the world, the decoding and secularization of the older forms of the sacred or the transcendent, the slow colonization of use value by exchange value, the realistic demystification of the older kinds of transcendent narratives in novels like Don Quixote, the standardization of both subject and object, the denaturalization of desire and its ultimate displacement by commodification (or, in other words, "success") and so on.[34]

Late capitalism, however, is defined by the prodigious expansion of commodification into almost all aspects of human social and cultural experience and the recasting of symbolic meaning to that of its place in the cultural market. Culture, as a purchasable and consumable commodity becomes an end in itself and ultimately replaces empirical interpretations of historicity and socio-cultural identity. The aesthetic becomes dominated by the role of symbols in the market and the copious consumption of images becomes an end in itself. From this perspective, what is defined as post-modernism is not incredulity towards meta-narratives or the fragmentation of the human socio-cultural experience but is instead manifested in the encapsulation of human social and psychical experience within the human social and cultural order of cultural consumerism.[35] The final triumph of a modernity dominated by the process of commodity production and exchange is an almost complete domination of humanity's experience with the natural world and the triumph of a human created system of cultural production and commodity exchange. In other words, the embracing of eclecticism characterized as post-modernism is not so much a rejection of modernity but of a triumph of modernity in terms of the cultural supplanting the social and physical. As Jameson argues,

---

34. Jameson, F. *Postmodernism or the Cultural Logic of Late Capitalism.* p 410.
35. Jameson, F. *Postmodernism or the Cultural Logic of Late Capitalism.* p 3.

Post-modernism is what you get when the modernization process is complete and nature is gone for good. It is a more fully human world than the older one, but one in which "culture" has become a veritable second "nature." Indeed, what happened to culture may well be one of the most important clues for tracking the post-modern; an immense dilation of its sphere (the sphere of commodification), an immense leap in the aestheticization of reality ... a prodigious exhilaration with the new order of things ... our representation of things tending to arouse an enthusiasm and a mood swing not necessarily inspired by the things in themselves.[36]

Consequently, in the context of Jameson's model of post-modernity the eclecticism of neo-Pagan histories can be interpreted as a pastiche of symbols designed to evoke a feeling of pastness and ideological identity via the appropriation of symbols from mainstream consumer culture.[37] History, as represented via this process of appropriation and reconstruction, is manifested as nostalgia for a feeling of permanence and history and the eclectic appropriation of images associated with a particular sense of ideological correlation or opposition to mainstream bourgeois social values. Nostalgia refers to the past as idealized and imagined through a combination of memory, metaphor, symbolism and desire and as such is dependent on the irrecoverable nature of the actual past for its emotional impact and appeal. Nostalgia does not sim-

---

36. Jameson, F. *Postmodernism and the Cultural Logic of Late Capitalism*. p 1.

37. It is worth noting that Jameson's model of post-modernism being a product of late capitalism is not uncontested. Linda Hutcheon for example, argues that Jameson ignores the cultural specificity of post-modernism by equating it with the phenomena of late capitalism and thus equating it with contemporaneity. She also argues that the loss of historicity is a product of the medium used to present the past rather than post-modernism. However, this critique is as much a problem caused by slippage in the meanings ascribed to the term post-modernism as it is a critique of Jameson's argument that what is defined as post-modernism is more a product of the influence of late-capitalism on culture than it is a collapse of the universal narratives of the Enlightenment. Furthermore, there is little evidence that the neo-Pagan movement is representative of post-modernism defined as "Recognition of the futility of seeking an absolute grounding for knowledge." Rather, as has been discussed, the growth of eclecticism within the neo-Pagan movement is better defined as a continuation of the Romantic episteme within the context of a trajectory of Western modernity increasingly dominated by the sphere of commodification. For more information of critiques of Jameson's model of the post modern see, Hutcheon, Linda. *A Poetics of Post-Modernism: History, Theory, Fiction*. New York: Routledge, 1987; Hutcheon, Linda. *Irony, Nostalgia and the Post-Modern*. http://www.library.utoronto.ca/utel/criticism/hutchinp.html 17/8/2002; Friedberg, Anne. *Cinema and the Post-modern Condition*. PMLA, Issue 106: 3, 1991.

ply replicate memory but rather by denying and degrading the present it is symbolically constructed brings the idealized past, as imagined from the present, into the site of immediacy, presence and authenticity. It is essentially a Romantic ideal; the past is replicated and reconstructed according to psycho-symbolic and metaphorical impact and thus serves as means to reconstruct and redefine the relationship to the present with an eye to the future. History is thus redefined as an expression of consumable cultural identity or ideological fashion manifested through a feeling of pastness rather than a sense of historicity or identification with an actual past. As Jameson writes,

> Nostalgia ... restructures the whole issue of pastiche and projects it onto a collective and social level, where the desperate attempt to appropriate a missing past is now refracted through the iron laws of fashion, change and the ideology of the generation ... More interesting and more problematic are the ultimate attempts, through this new discourse to lay the siege either to our own present and immediate past or to a more distant history that escapes individual memory.[38]

Consequently, for Jameson, the abandonment of traditional historiography, empirically based claims to links with the past or even the illusion of continuity created through repetition, as illustrated by Hobsbawm's model of invented traditions, becomes irrelevant. They are ultimately supplanted by a cyclical struggle to cannibalize and consume the past as a source of seemingly novel aesthetic experience, making attempts at genuine historicity problematic and requiring new approaches to historico-cultural identity formation. As Jameson writes,

> Faced with these immediate objects—our social, historical and existential present and the past as a referent—the incompatibility of a post-modern nostalgia with genuine historicity becomes dramatically apparent. This contradiction propels this mode into complex and new formal inventiveness, it being understood that the nostalgia was never a matter of some representation of historical content but instead approached the past via a stylistic connotation implying a sense of pastness.[39]

According to Jameson, the most significant effect of this nostalgia on society and culture is the subsuming of identity, politics and historicity to the all-per-

---

38. Jameson, F. *Postmodernism and the Cultural Logic of Late Capitalism.* p 19.
39. Jameson, F. *Postmodernism and the Cultural Logic of Late Capitalism.* p 19.

vading influence of culture as manifested via consumable and ultimately purchasable symbols from popular culture. In effect, this defines Witch identity
in terms of appropriation of images defined via purchasable symbols. If the
Romantic critique of modernity involves the privileging of the aesthetic over
the empirical, linked to a reconfiguration of the modern as a search for cultural autonomy and authenticity, then it makes more sense to define post-
modern eclecticism in terms of the Romantic episteme within the sphere of a
Western modernity dominated by the influence of late capitalism. Similarly,
if history is defined through its aesthetic experience according to the psycho-
cultural impact of its symbolism then the reconstruction of historicity into an
aesthetically defined nostalgia for the past is also an example of the permeation of the sphere of commodification within the context of the Romantic
episteme. Romanticism is inherently shaped and defined by its relationship to
the Enlightenment and the subsequent influence of capitalist industrialism in
Western modernity. Similarly, the transcendent imagination, the central component of Romantic thought as defined by Richard Kearney, does not occur
in isolation from the economic, epistemological and social formations in
which it develops. The meaning, significance and identity of the social and
cultural structures from which the Romantic episteme defines social and cultural significance are fundamentally characterized by the dominant economic
and socio-political structures from which these symbols are appropriated.

Given that the Romantic episteme and the cultural forms they appropriate
are the products of particular national, economic and political configurations,
it is not surprising that as the structure of Western modernity and its inter-
relationship with capitalism has changed, so too has the Romantic counter
episteme. Romanticism is a quintessentially modern movement based in the
continual process of reshaping cultural meaning in a social order dominated
by capitalist industrialism and the commodification of social value in terms
of both symbolic significance and in terms of labor and production. From this
perspective, the shift from "Foundationalist" to "Post-modernist" in the neo-
Pagan movement, as described by Jim Wafer and Diane Purkiss, is not brought
about by the realization of the "Futility of seeking an absolute foundation for
knowledge".[40] Rather, the shift from foundationalism to post-modernism in
the neo-Pagan movement is perhaps more appropriately defined in terms of
a shift in the nature of Western modernity in the era of late capitalism. Such
a shift is inevitably attenuated by corresponding structures of symbolic ap-

---

40. Hebdidge, D. *Subculture: The Meaning of Style.* p 92; Stephens, J. *Anti-disciplinary Protest.* p 76.

propriation and discourses of cultural meaning within the Romantic counter episteme.

In this context, neo-Paganism and its relationship with historical representations is perhaps best described as an expression of the Romantic episteme located within the sphere of Western modernity. The cultural symbols it appropriates and the ideological basis of social and cultural identity are fundamentally defined by the overarching structure of Western modernity in which it exists and is given meaning. What we are seeing in the shift from foundationalism to post-modernism in neo-Pagan histories is representative of several issues. Firstly, it is representative of the inter-relationship between popular history and academic history. The two areas are often in conflict, particularly with regard to cultural signs of strong symbolic impact in Western culture. The means by which this tension has been transformed over the course of recent history is indicative of broader trends of popular and academic historiography in Western society. Secondly, the development of neo-Pagan histories is illustrative of how academic debates about the nature of historiographical validity and the interpretation of empirical evidence impact in popular representations of history. It is also representative of the means by which these ideological constructions of legitimacy in historical construction are utilized in defining symbolic cultural and social identity. Finally, the shifts in neo-Pagan historiographical method are also indicative of the inter-relationship between Romantic and Enlightenment epistemes in Western culture. This is particularly significant in the era of late capitalism where the increasing commodification of cultural symbols has become a strong influence in the construction of popular history and the reabsorption of counter-cultural identities into mainstream society as consumable and purchasable symbols of identity.[41]

---

41. Hebdidge, D. *Subculture: The Meaning of Style.* p 92; Stephens, J. *Anti-disciplinary Protest.* p 76.

9

Commodified Paganism: Where to From Here?

In creating the WIKID WITCH KIT I hope to take you on a magickal
and exciting journey! Through ritual, music, song and spoken word
I will help you unleash your inner magick and discover the wonder-
ful and positively empowering world of Witchcraft.
As part of this journey you will discover your WIKID magickal name,
giving you access to our exclusive website and online coven. There
you can meet up with other WIKID Witches to swap spells stories and
ideas. And every full moon I will personally join you for an online
gathering—which will be truly WIKID.
WIKID Witch Kit features WIKID magic Fizz/ WIKID Magick Po-
tions/ WIKID magick fire/ WIKID magic Star/ WIKID Magick cord/
WIKID magick audio CD.
(The web page of musician and Pagan celebrity Fiona Horne)[1]

Being a diverse and fragmented movement that overlaps a wide array of cultural phenomenon it is difficult to ascertain the size of the neo-Pagan related
industry or the extent to which the process of commodification impacts on
the process of identity formation and ritual within the neo-Pagan movement.
While there are figures that indicate a growing industry, such as the claim by
the American Booksellers Association that sales of neo-Pagan related books
has increased to 10 million in 2000 from 4.5 million in 1990,[2] it is difficult to
determine how these statistics directly impact on commodification of the neo-
Pagan movement. Even at the most pragmatic level, differentiating where the

---

1. Fiona Horne's Web page. Fiona Horne is the lead singer of the band Def FX and is
the author of several neo-Pagan texts aimed at 12–17 year old women. http://www.fiona-
horne.com (15-3-2002).

2. American Booksellers Association website. http://news.bookweb.org/news/ (10-2-
2001).

neo-Pagan movement begins and the New Age movement ends in terms of the symbolic significance of purchasable paraphernalia is a problematic exercise, as is defining what constitutes specifically constitutes neo-Pagan cultural artifacts from the New Age movement. Is a packet of scented candles or a Goddess statue a purchase of neo-Pagan or New Age paraphernalia or simply aesthetics not necessarily linked to any claims to neo-Pagan identity? Similarly, even with figures indicating the sales of *Witchcraft* Magazine in Australia[3] there is little relevant information as to the symbolic significance of these items or in what context are they purchased and consumed. Consequently, in attempting to ascertain the extent to which the process of commodification has impacted on the neo-Pagan movement the central issue is the social significance of the consumption of these materials by neo-Pagans and the mechanisms by which producers of neo-Pagan materials market themselves to their consumer base as opposed to market statistics on the number of items sold. In other words, how are neo-Pagans defining their cultural identity with regards to the increasingly diverse array of consumable products available to them and to what extent is neo-Pagan identity rooted in representations of Witchcraft in popular culture?

As post-modern approaches to cultural and ideological identity have come to prominence within the neo-Pagan movement, the extent to which neo-Pagans have become willing to draw on the material culture of consumer capitalism has developed accordingly. Increasingly, images and identities drawn from popular culture have come to dominate neo-Pagan identity formation and this trend has been paralleled by the development of forms of highly commodified neo-Paganism; that is items which are heavily linked to the New Age industry and the process of commodity exchange. The number of commercial books on Paganism and Wicca, fee paying courses on Witchcraft, magazines promoting Witchcraft and paganism, movies and television programs featuring neo-Pagans and the rise of the new age industry have increased exponentially since the 1980s and the neo-Pagan related branch of the New Age industry and its influence in popular culture continues to grow. While books, conferences and ritual tools have always been available for purchase, these forms of participation have been largely peripheral to the practice of neo-Pagan religious systems. However, according to Doug Ezzy, as neo-Paganism becomes increasingly popularized the opportunity for participation are becoming dominated by the process of market exchange such as the purchasing

---

3. According to personal communication with Christine Froebel, Editor and advertising manager, the Australian version of *Witchcraft* magazine has a print run of approximately 16,000 per month.

of "how to" books and videos, fee paying courses, purchasable tools, trendy accessories and the mastering of Witchcraft and New Age fashion.[4] While neo-Pagans have always published and consumed books or artwork and attended seminars these aspects of neo-Pagan culture have tended to be peripheral to the social networks, historical claims and ideological agenda involved in adopting neo-Pagan identity. Consequently, the increasing significance placed on purchasable items and symbols in defining neo-Pagan identity is indicative of broader changes in the socio-cultural basis of neo-Pagan identity formation. Similarly, it can be argued that implicit in the adoption of an aesthetic based cultural eclecticism, as manifested in the consumption of purchasable items, is the embracing of an individualist consumerist ideology rooted in the consumption of purchasable cultural capital.

Post-modern approaches to neo-Paganism, as illustrated above, have tended to hail the increasing adoption of eclecticism as liberation from the tyranny of Enlightenment, patriarchal and traditionalist approaches to religion, culture and identity. Apart from the argument that a post-modern approach to neo-Pagan identity offers a means for marginalized sectors of society to construct their own identities and mentally break free of the pre-suppositions and ideologies that support forms of social control, there is also an argument that an individualist eclectic approach to cultural consumption can bring a whole new variety of aesthetic experience to religion. In other words, neo-Paganism can represent a religion that can be designed to suit the needs of the religious consumer instead of coercing the individual to conform to an established ideological and cultural position. It could also be implied that a flexible approach to culture is necessary for any religious movement to accommodate new forms of social relationships as traditional work place and community identities disintegrate under the strain of a post-Fordist economy. [5] Finally, it can be argued that a post-modern individualist and consumerist approach to religion can liberate religious expression from the constraints of traditionalism. As Moore comments,

> When people think of religion as something to be sold rather than as
> something imposed—something advanced in the prospect of a mu-

---

4. Ezzy, Doug. "The Commodification of Witchcraft." *Australian Religious Studies.* Volume 14, No 1, p 32.

5. Ezzy, D. "The Commodification of Witchcraft." p 33; Heelas, Paul. "The New Age in Cultural Context." *Religion.* Vol 23, 1993. pp 106–107; Heelas, Paul. *The New Age Movement.* Oxford: Blackwell Publishers: Oxford, 1996. p 75; Lyon, D *Jesus in Disneyland: Religion in Post-Modern Times.* Cambridge: Polity Press, 2000. p 75.

tually beneficial contract, which parties are free to accept or reject—religious toleration advances.[6]

There are certainly neo-Pagans who openly embrace the popularization and marketization of neo-Paganism and Witchcraft. Neo-Pagan writer Dana Kramer argues that the consumerist approach normally attributed to the New Age movement has been enormously beneficial for the neo-Pagan movement in terms of public acceptance, ease of access to neo-Pagan materials and the growth of the movement. As she writes,

> If it wasn't for the New Agers and White Lighters we wouldn't be finding Tarot decks at Barnes and Noble and aromatherapy candles at Target. And a lot of the people buying these things on the mass market are also becoming a whole lot more open to any sort of non-Judeo-Christian (and now we should add Islamic) theological paradigm (one big god who demands submission).[7]

Similarly, some neo-Pagan writers argue that attitudes to Witchcraft that deny material gain are in fact a corruption caused by the influence of Judeo-Christian belief on Pagan ideals.[8] From this perspective the pursuit of self-aggrandizement, though not at the expense of others or through dishonest practices, is perceived to be entirely legitimate objective for the practice of neo-Paganism. Consequently, the adoption of a consumerist ideology is perceived to be entirely compatible with neo-Pagan belief. An example of this is neo-Pagan writer D.J. Conway's claim that,

> Some schools of Witchcraft will tell you that doing magic for financial benefit is selfish and wrong. This is an erroneous idea held over from Judeo Christian beliefs and has nothing whatsoever to do with ritual magic and spellworking. The truth is, if you cannot manifest for yourself, you have little chance of manifesting for others.[9]

It is worth noting that this approach to wealth is far from universally accepted within the neo-Pagan movement. Scott Cunningham for example in *Wicca: A*

---

6. Ezzy, D. "The Commodification of Witchcraft." p 33 Citing Moore, R. *Selling God: American Religions in the Market Place of Culture.* New York: Oxford University Press. 1994. pp 272.

7. Personal Communication Dana Kramer-Rolls a Neo-Pagan Fantasy writer who holds a PhD from the Berkley Theological Union for her folkloric analysis of the "legends of Mary in Medieval Europe", Natrel E-list 17-5-2002.

8. Starhawk. *The Spiral Dance.* pp 124.

9. Conway, D.J. *Celtic Magic.* New York: Llewellyn Press, 1990. p 10.

guide for the Solitary Practitioner gives this stern warning against using the practice or teaching of Witchcraft for financial benefit "It is unwise to accept money for the use of the power, for it quickly controls its taker. Be not as those from other religions."[10]

The idealization of a post-modernism defined as an unfettered cultural supermarket of aesthetic experience ignores the many problems raised by a wholesale adoption of cultural consumerism and the significant changes wrought by an adoption of commodification as the primary basis of cultural exchange. The neo-Pagan response to the increasing influence of popular culture has been extremely ambiguous. On the one hand popularization and marketization has led to increased acceptance and proliferation of their ideals and cultural identity. On the other hand the social, cultural and political character of the movement is also becoming transformed. As neo-Pagan author Lucie de Fresne comments,

> Witchcraft is marketed through *Buffy, Charmed, Sabrina, Blair Witch, Llewellyn* and even cheesy little books at the supermarket on love spells. Some of these ideas are interesting, even realistic, while others at best rival the story lines and plots of pornographic cinema with their shallow treatment of the subject and 2 dimensional characters. When does this cease to be a journey for knowledge and degenerate into pure entertainment and narcissistic hedonism? Does our embracing of popular culture really strengthen our movement and public acceptance of Witchcraft or does it eat away at the edges of our credibility and draw others to the community for the wrong reason.[11]

According to Ezzy, one of the most significant aspects of the increased influence of commodification in the neo-Pagan movement is the changing structure of social relationships and sense of community that are concomitant with the embracing of an individualist and consumption based approach to cultural property. Rather than the post-modern argument that the consumption of symbols, rituals and cultural artifacts is arbitrary beyond the meaning given to them by the consumer, the process by which culture is appropriated implies an array of social and political relationships. Drawing heavily on the work of anthropologists Gregory and Mauss, Ezzy argues that the perceiving of cultural resources as objects of consumption has very different socio-economic implications to cultural property shared by a community or exchanged as a gift.[12]

---

10. Cunningham, Scott. *Wicca: A Guide for the Solitary Practitioner.* New York: Llewellyn publications, 1988. p 145.

11. Personal Communication Lucie du Fresne, Natrel e-mail list 23 April, 2002.

12. Ezzy, Doug. "The Commodification of Witchcraft." pp 34–35.

Apart from the influence of the profit motive and fashion in defining the value of cultural artifacts and symbols used to formulate neo-Pagan identity, there is a fundamentally different set of social relationships embedded in commodity exchange compared to gifts or resources communally distributed. In particular, gifts often imply a social connection that is reminiscent of family or community structure and is *geimenschaft* in character. By contrast a commodity transaction is performed between self interested and independent individuals and there are, usually, little or no enduring links or obligations between them.[13] As Gregory writes,

> Commodity exchange establishes a relationship between the objects exchanged, whereas gift exchange establishes a relationship between the subjects. In other words commodity exchange is a price forming process, a system of purchase and sale. Gift exchange is not. As Mauss noted, they replace our system of sale and purchase with one of gifts and return gifts. With gift exchange it is wrong to speak of alienation, for these things are loaned rather than sold and ceded. An inalienable thing that is given away must be returned. Thus a gift creates a debt that has to be repaid.[14]

There are important connotations to this notion of gifts and commodities. In part gifts, particularly in the context of shared ritual activity, knowledge, initiation and craft activities implies a basis of communication in shared knowledge. To partake of the exchange of knowledge in a community setting is a statement of shared common identity and an expression of community solidarity. In this sense, the gift binds people together through the statement of shared identity, history, culture and values that the gift exchange symbolically represents. In a sense it ties the community together through webs of shared reciprocity and obligation and a sense of shared historical consciousness.[15]

The approach to cultural eclecticism practiced by post-modern styled Wiccan practitioners often characterizes culture, rituals and artifacts as commodities. There is little or no perceived relationship or obligation between the source of the material consumed and the uses and interpretations to which it is placed. The relationship between the source of the material and the consumer is dissolved on the completion of the transaction. In essence, the perception that there is no overarching structure to culture, ideology and iden-

---

13. Gregory, C. A. *Gifts and Commodities.* London: Academic Press, 1982. pp 10–15; Maus, Marcel. *The Gift.* London: Routledge, 1974. pp 9–10 & 62.

14. Gregory, C.A. *Gifts and Commodities.* p 19.

15. Sykes, Karen. *Arguing with Anthropology: An Introduction to Critical Theories of the Gift.* Routledge: New York 2004.

tity formation implies that culture fits within the realm of the commodity. Thus the intrusion of commodity exchange into social relations, ritual and neo-Pagan identity can be particularly discordant for many neo-Pagans who perceive themselves in ideological opposition to the perceived objectifying and commodifying impact of western capitalism. Romantic nostalgia and the ideal of a community and cultural identity that can transcend crass materialism is a central component of the romantic critique of modernity embraced by many neo-Pagans. In this sense, the ideologically implications of the perceived cultural and social significance of gift exchange and the passage of culture becomes a flash point of conflict amongst many neo-Pagan communities.[16]

As a result, the exchanges of objects, information, rituals and symbols are fundamentally perceived to be representative of the socio-political structure from which they originate. Material exchanged as a commodity implies the social relationship of commodity exchange and consumer capitalism whereas that which is exchanged as a gift or shared resource implies a sense of shared community. With regards to the ideological and community basis of neo-Paganism the process of exchange and the intrusion of commodity into community obligation have important connotations for its socio-political structure and the significance of its rituals, artifacts, symbolism and other cultural resources. In the model of traditionalist neo-Paganism, skills and knowledge are transferable as part of a personal relationship between a priest/priestess and student, an individual and their role in a broader neo-Pagan close knit community. This is an exchange of knowledge passed on through an established social structure and is deeply based in personal relationship and reciprocal obligations. The exchange of knowledge and culture involves the creation of a personal inalienable relationship between the individual and the coven that is part of a deeper structure of social relationships. Knowledge and culture are not arbitrarily exchanged but are directly connected to a particular structure of social relationships.[17] Neo-Pagan author Alicia writes against the transformation of neo-Paganism through the influence of the ideology of commodity exchange in her unpublished manuscript *Craft for Sale* arguing that,

> In the way that I was taught Witchcraft, straight and old fashioned as it was, you did not sell what you were taught, just as you did not pay

---

16. Anderson, E. "Is Women's Labour a Commodity." *Philosophy and Public Affairs*. Vol 19. 1990. p 72.

17. Ezzy, D. "The Commodification of Witchcraft." pp 33–35; Sykes, Karen. *Arguing with Anthropology: An Introduction to Critical Theories of the Gift*. Routledge: New York 2004.

to learn it. The idea of money never entered into it. Trust, love and personal dedication to the services of the Old Ones—all these things were demanded and freely given, but money?" Hardly! Those relationships between teacher and student should be like shining stars of experience—not the grubby, commercial, limited, production-line feed-out of pre paid rituals.[18]

While the impact of commodification and cultural consumerism may well have led to a proliferation of choice in identity formation and symbolic interpretation, it most certainly does not imply that neo-Paganism is a religion of free and unfettered belief. A religion based in the institutions and ideology of market exchange and socio-cultural formations of popular consumer culture is intrinsically shaped and oriented by its relationship to the broader context of cultural commodification. Consequently, the embracing of consumerist eclecticism does not simply free neo-Paganism from authoritarian political structures, kinship systems of familial control or hierarchical traditionalism. Indeed, as Sykes argues, the idea that the belief that capitalist patterns of wealth accumulation equate to search for individual freedom is predicated on the dubious premise of freedom existing outside of social relations and patterns of reciprocal obligation. To the contrary a religious system based in the process of market exchange is intensely shaped by values, priorities and ideological configuration of the secular institutions of the broader society in which it is founded.[19] This is not to claim that neo-Pagan eclecticism based in an ideology of aesthetic cultural consumerism necessarily implies an ideological alliance with free market capitalist ideology, but rather that the claims that neo-Paganism is inherently linked to a liberation from the alienating and destructive aspects of a modernity characterized by patriarchy, destruction of the natural world and the objectifying gaze of science, are much more ambiguous and circumspect than may at first appear.

The rise of commodified Witchcraft and the adoption of an eclecticism based in the rhetoric of cultural consumerism has led to increasing social disruption between differing sectors of the neo-Pagan movement over questions of authenticity, ideology, authority and publicity. This is a particularly important issue when some sectors of the neo-Pagan movement, particularly traditionalist and antiquarian neo-Pagans feel that their public identity is be-

---

18. Alicia. *Craft for Sale.* Unpublished manuscript. p 1. Cited in Ezzy, Doug. "The Commodification of Witchcraft." p 34.

19. Hanegraff, P. New Age Spiritualities as Secular Religion. *Social Compass.* Issue 46. 1999. p 148.

coming subverted and dominated by higher profile branches with better access to the media and greater input into mainstream representations through the New Age and neo-Pagan industry.[20] The problem of who speaks and represents a movement as diverse and ideologically heterogeneous as neo-Paganism becomes especially vexing when almost all sectors of the movement claim to be pluralist and supportive of religious diversity. As Sian Reid writes,

> Clearly, the decentralized nature of neo-Paganism in general acts as a crucible for conflict. However, the ideology of neo-Pagan Witchcraft is such that conflict "should" not occur, because a whole range of beliefs and practices are accepted as valid and legitimate. Individuals are supposed to develop their own understanding of the meaning of their practise, and come to the conclusions about appropriate morality and ways of "being" in the world.[21]

The higher profile nature of major neo-Pagan organizations and authors allied to large publishers and New Age businesses are often perceived to dominate public perceptions of the movement. Apart from increased input into the milieu of popular culture through film, novels, television and marketing major media outlets frequently use these higher profile organizations as their source of Pagan culture and ideology with the result that their highly marketable version of the craft is presented as the true or legitimate version of neo-Paganism usually without acknowledging that alternative perspectives exist. Similarly, with the high profile of the eco-feminist branches of neo-Paganism tied to a specific ideological and political agenda other forms of Paganism can feel coerced or categorized by someone else's political agenda. Sometimes this can be result of deliberate attempts at hegemony, poaching new members or the absorption of other versions of neo-Paganism but it can also be the result of the journalists or publishers own agenda.[22] However, underlying these conflicts of representation is a fundamental difference between those branches of neo-Paganism that embrace eclecticism as a means of asserting a particular ideological perspective and traditionalist neo-Pagans that situate neo-Pagan identity within the boundaries of history and lineage and to whom politics is largely a secondary personal decision independent of religious belief. As Kevin Marron comments,

---

20. Reid, Sian. "Witch Wars: Factors contributing to Conflict in Canadian neo-Pagan communities." *The Pomegranate*. Issue 11. February 2000. pp 10–21.

21. Reid, S. "Witch Wars." p 14.

22. Reid, S. "Witch Wars." p 12.

These two groups are on a collision course. The radicals tend to see the traditionalists as failing to live out the principles of a religion based on respect for nature, which should oppose a society that exploits the earth. The traditionals regard the radicals as people who have latched onto Wicca as for their own political purposes.[23]

To a large extent these conflicts revolve around the issue of legitimacy and authenticity of various traditions of neo-Pagan belief. Whilst some branches have fully adopted and accepted post-modern styled ideologies of eclecticism, some link Paganism to a particular political project, some argue that belief and ritual should have an empirically verifiable historical heritage while others argue the for the importance of initiation and lineage to a recognized tradition such as Gardnerian or Alexandrian Wicca. These differences can disrupt and obfuscate the sense of neo-Pagan community. Sian Reid essentially sees this problem as a conflict between the eclectic and traditionalist branches of the movement, particularly since eclectic and commodified approaches to neo-Pagan identity are on the rise and increasing exponentially compared with the more static numbers of traditionalists. As she comments,

> Traditional craft constructs itself very much as a mystery religion and puts a relatively greater emphasis on the esoteric and mystical aspects that are highlighted in their received material than do most eclectics. Eclectics are far more likely to focus on the creative and celebratory aspects of the practice, with the esoteric components being available but not essential … This leads to tension between the two groups because of the way in which each constructs and construes the other's practice. Eclectics often perceive traditionals as hide bound, hierarchical and slavishly adhering to received material, while traditionals view eclectics as fundamentally missing the point of the whole practice, diluting the mystery tradition to the point of unrecognizability in superficial rituals. Because the numbers of people involved in eclectic practice are increasing at a much greater rate than those involved in traditional groups, these tensions are unlikley to vanish.[24]

The development of a sense of community requires a loci or sense of focus around which a communal identity is shared. This sense of focus can have a social, economic, political, religious or ritual basis or a combination of all or

---

23. Marron, Kevin. *Witches, Pagans and Magic in the New Age.* Toronto: Seal Books, 1989. p 94.

24. Reid, S. "Witch Wars." p 18–19.

any of them. Historically, what has linked the diverse branches of the neo-Pagan movement together is a shared embracing of the Romantic episteme and the Romantic anti-modernist caricature of Enlightenment modernity and Christianity. However, as the structure of the Romantic episteme has changed in the context of Western modernity the means by which the ideology of Romantic anti-modernism is applied, in terms of the sense of cultural authenticity and historical legitimacy given to neo-Pagan symbolic representations, has become extremely diverse. The form of Neo-Paganism that was to emerge in the context of the sixties counter culture and in its eco-feminist branch appropriated the image of the Witch as a symbol held to represent the ultimate antithesis of patriarchy, Enlightenment reason and Christian conservatism. Witches make an ideal symbol of Romantic anti-modernist and feminist activism, and have been utilized as such since Michelet wrote *La Sorciere* in the 1850s. The Romantic movement solidified the image of the Witch as associated with nature, chaos, disorder, sexuality and the feminine in popular culture and artistic and literary representations and for many people antagonized and alienated by industrialism, patriarchy, social conservatism and scientific rationalism, the persecuted but powerful Witch forms an identifiable and empowering symbol in opposition to the dominant cultural matrix of contemporary society. The image of the Witch disrupts the symbolic structure underlying the ideology of Western modernity and patriarchy. Counter cultures typically construct their symbolic opposition in an attempt to create semantic disruption through appropriating and reconstructing images and symbols held to be antithetical to the dominant socio-cultural order.[25] The counter-cultural and political activist branches of neo-Paganism are little different in that respect.

The perception that political activism can be based in the politics of image and the adoption and recasting of meaning associated with images perceived to be inimical to the socio-political mainstream has been severely criticized. Naomi Klein for example, writes extensively on the problems created by the embracing of a political activism that ignored issues of class, income and political power in favor of a struggle for political change through cultural representations. She argues that the construction of identity configured through embracing and reconfiguring images, symbols and representations to serve a particular ethical or ideological imperative can only have a limited success in transforming power structure because it refuses to challenge the underlying political and economic basis of oppression and exploitation. Consequently,

---

25. Purkiss, D. *The Witch in History.* pp 24–25.

the politics of image are inherently vulnerable to the process of co-optation, trivialization and marketability.[26] She argues that for all the apparent challenge to the established social order via the politics of image the development of counter cultures rooted in reconstructing cultural imagery do not necessarily challenge the socio-economic but are instead integrated into the process of commodification through the creation of niche markets based around the perception of feminist radicalism.[27] As she writes with regards to the feminist adoption of the rhetoric of identity politics,

> In this new globalized context, the victories of identity politics have amounted to a rearranging of the furniture while the house burned down. And though girls may indeed rule in North America, they are still sweating in Latin America, making t-shirts with the "Girls Rule" slogan on them and Nike running shoes that will finally let girls into the game. This oversight isn't simply a failure of feminism but a betrayal of the feminist movements founding principles ... The abandonment of the radical economic foundations of the women's and civil rights movements by the conflation of causes that came to be called political correctness successfully trained a generation of activists in the politics of image not action ... We were too busy analyzing the pictures on the wall to notice that the wall itself had been sold.[28]

The basing of political activism in a symbolic configuration based in the promulgation and reconfiguration of images, fashion and cultural artifacts is inherently vulnerable to the effects of cultural commodification and cooptation into a niche market. This process is a common phenomenon in counter cultures oriented around symbolic representation and visual spectacle as the main form of political activism and identity formation and has been the subject of research for many writers on the phenomenon of counter cultures such as Michael York, Julie Stephens, Paul Heelas and Dick Hebdidge.[29] Dick Hebdidge's analysis is particularly pertinent to the phenomenon of commodifica-

---

26. Klein, Naomi. *No Logo: No Space, No Choice, No Jobs.* New York: Harper Collins, 2001. pp 108–112 & 123–124.

27. Klein, N. *No Logo.* pp 111–113.

28. Klein, N. *No Logo.* pp 123–124.

29. A full debate regarding the impact of popular culture on the phenomenon of counter cultures is beyond the scope of this thesis and has already been well covered by a wide variety of researchers. For more information see, Hebdidge, D. *Subculture*; Heelas, Paul. "The New Age in Cultural Context."; Stephens J. *Anti-disciplinary protest*; Jameson, F. *Periodising the sixties*; York, Michael. *The Emerging Network.*

tion in his argument that while the violations and disruption of established structures of symbolic representation by a counter cultural movement like the activist branches of neo-Paganism have immense power to disturb and challenge the social order, they are also extremely vulnerable to becoming reincorporated and depoliticised through the process of commodification and cooptation.[30] As he writes,

> As the subculture begins to strike its own eminently marketable pose, as its vocabulary (both visual and verbal) becomes more and more familiar, so the referential context to which it can be conveniently assigned is made increasingly apparent. Eventually the mods, the punks, the glitter rockers can be incorporated, brought back into line, located on the preferred map of problematic social reality ... the fractured order is repaired and the subculture incorporated as a diverting hedonistic spectacle within the dominant mythology from which it in part emanates.[31]

The danger, in terms of the longevity and continued social and political relevance of a counter culture, is that a movement, after an initial rise as vibrant counter-culture can become incorporated within the structure of the market and co-opted back into the dominant socio-cultural order as a niche market based on fashion and consumer driven identity. This is exacerbated by the fact that the images that defined the counter-cultural identity were consumed and reconstructed according to an ideology that perceives culture as a consumable aesthetic commodity according to popularity and psycho-cultural impact. As the cultural artifacts and symbols associated with neo-Paganism increasingly become defined by their role in niche marketing and popular culture the struggle to maintain a sense of common purpose and socio-political and cultural identity will increasingly come to forefront of conflicts within the movement. The extent to which images of Witchcraft move into the realm of K-Mart and *Buffy the Vampire Slayer* cannot help but challenge the claims to cultural authenticity and historical/ideological legitimacy on behalf of a movement which is intrinsically defined by the inter-relationship of the Romantic episteme with the broader current of Western modernity. In a society where Western modernity is increasingly becoming dominated by the commodifying effects of late capitalism the issues raised by the changing role of culture and identity will continue to shape the development of the neo-Pagan movement in the foreseeable future.

---

30. Hebdidge, Dick. *Subculture*. pp 92–100.
31. Hebdidge, Dick. *Subculture*. p 94.

THE OLD RELIGION IN A POST-MODERN AGE?

The primary contention of this book is that the process by which the image of the Witch has been constructed is symptomatic of the relationship between the Romantic and Enlightenment epistemes in Western culture. Indeed, representations of Witches, Witchcraft and Paganism and their evolution into contemporary postmodern and consumerist variants serve as a window into the interaction of these broader philosophical themes. They are also manifested in the associated symbols of femininity, the supernatural, the anti-human, nature, religion and industry. That is to say that the symbols that coalesce into the signifier of the "Witch" and the "Pagan", stand astride the romantic and enlightenment configuration of modernity in western culture. In this sense, the significance of the neo-Pagan movement, as both a counter culture and a religious movement, becomes particularly apparent when utilized as a model to comprehend the Romantic reinterpretation of symbols construed as the antithesis of enlightenment patriarchal modernity.

The Witch is thus a particularly unique and important signifier of modernity as it is the quintessential symbol that stands astride the Romantic/Enlightenment cultural divide in Western culture. For some sectors of society the Witch represents superstition, evil, irrationality and the primitive; that which limits the potential for human progress and autonomy from nature. To others, the Witch represents beauty, nature, freedom and cultural autonomy from the corrupting and limiting influences of patriarchy, scientific rationalism, commodification and industrialization. In this context, the construction of the Witch and of Witchcraft within the neo-Pagan movement is indicative of a broader underlying trend of Romantic thought in Western society. The rise of neo-Paganism also serves to give us insight into the means by which social movements and religious communities appropriate images and symbols in the construction of identity, values and community.

Given that Romantic epistemes and the cultural forms they appropriate, are the products of particular national, ethnic, economic and political configurations it is not surprising that as the structure of Western modernity and its inter-relationship with capitalism has changed so too has the Romantic counter episteme in its manifestation of counter-cultural and religious movements. Subsequently, the changes in the processes by which neo-Pagan identity has been formed and legitimized are part of the broader context of the inter-relationship between Romanticism and the overarching structure of Western modernity. Thus the neo-Pagan movement's multi-faceted approach to culture illustrates the continual process of reshaping cultural meaning and conceptualizing cultural authenticity within the broader context of Western modernity.

It is also here that we see the particular pertinence of a historical approach to the development of neo-Paganism. Whilst there are numerous breaks between the paganism of antiquity and the contemporary pagan revivals, the construction of the image of the Witch in the Anglo-phone world still revolve around issues developed both during and in the aftermath of the English experience of witchcrazes during the civil war and the English experience of the enlightenment era. The witch as the iconic representation of the feminine "anti-human" combined with the enlightenment response to the deep emotional scars left in East Anglia during the witch crazes became the foundation of the English Pagan revival. Similarly, the romantic reconstruction of the witch as the persecuted feminine other remain closely linked, albeit often antithetically, to the enlightenment caricaturization of a Early Modern England dominated by a superstitious and primitive medieval world view. This perception is reinforced through the concomitant idealization of pre-industrial "merry" England and the extent to which the folklore emerging from modern representations of Witchcraft were construed as cultural fossils within the myth ritual school of folkloric studies pioneed by Frazer and Tylor.

In this sense, the historical origins of English representations of Witchcraft are particularly pertinent as they establish how the lived experience of witchcraft during the Early modern period constructed the groundwork for its contemporary interpretations and the associated themes of folklore and ritual that formed the foundation of the Pagan revival. Examining the historical experience of Witchcraft also throws into stark relief the numerous points of divergence between the historical witch and its reconstruction by the eco-feminist and new age manifestations of the pagan revival. This also serves to serves to give us enormous insight into the process of symbolic appropriation and identity construction with the social and cultural formations of romanticism in contemporary society.

However, it is worth noting that neo-Paganism is not a homogenous entity any more than the early modern Witchcraft it purports to emulate. It is a movement characterized by an extremely diverse range of social and cultural demographics. Commonality is defined primarily by an appropriation of one of the various symbolic representations of the Witch in history as a form of social identity in Western culture which is manifested in a sense of belonging with images of the past, femininity and nature. The fact that new approaches to culture, history and politics, and thus the means by which socio-cultural identity is authenticated, have co-existed with their predecessors within the neo-Pagan movement rather than supplanting them indicates that the evolution of the Romantic counter-episteme of Western modernity is both somewhat fragmented whilst remaining integrated within the context of the Romantic episteme.

The new legitimacy granted to Witchcraft and Pagan studies within academia, which to some extent has made this book possible, has also had a significant impact on the construction of historico-cultural identity within the neo-Pagan movement. By studying the development of historical interpretations of Witchcraft and Paganism, important insight is given to the complexities of the relationship between popular and academic interpretations of history and socio-cultural identity. Academic history and popular culture are two streams of representations of the past that are often in conflict, particularly with regards to cultural signs of strong socio-symbolic impact. The means by which this tension has been transformed over the course of recent history is indicative of broader trends in popular and academic historiography in Western society. Secondly, the development of neo-Pagan histories is illustrative of how academic debates about the nature of historiographical validity and the interpretation of empirical evidence impact in popular representations of history. It is also representative of the means by which these ideological constructions of legitimacy in historicity are utilized in defining symbolic cultural and social identity. Finally, the shifts in neo-Pagan historiographical method are also indicative of the inter-relationship between the Romantic and Enlightenment epistemes in Western culture. This is particularly significant in the era of late capitalism where the increasing commodification of cultural symbols has become a strong influence in the construction of popular history and thus the reabsorption of counter-cultural identities into mainstream society as consumable and purchasable symbols of identity.

BIBLIOGRAPHY

Ackerman, Robert. *J.G. Frazer: His Life and Work.* Cambridge: Cambridge University Press, 1987.

Ackerman, Robert. *The myth and ritual school: J.G. Frazer and the Cambridge ritualists.* New York: Garland Pub, 1991.

Adler, Margot. *Drawing Down the Moon: Witches, Druids, Goddess worshipers and other Pagans in America Today.* 2nd Ed. New York: Penguin Group Publishing, 1986.

Ahlstrom, Sydney. *A Religious History of the American People.* London: Yale University Press, 1972.

Anderson, E. "Is Women's Labour a Commodity." *Philosophy and Public Affairs.* Vol 19. 1990. pp 70–92.

Ross, Andrew. "Cultural Preservation in the Polynesia of Latter-day Saints." In Bennet, David. *Cultural Studies: Pluralism and theory.* Melbourne: Melbourne University Press. 1993.

Anglo, Sydney. *The Damned Art: Essays in the Literature of Witchcraft.* London: Routledge, 1977.

Ankarloo, Bengt & Henningsen, Gustav. *Early Modern European Witchcraft: Centres and Peripheries.* Oxford: Clarendon Press, 1990.

Ankarloo, Bengt & Clark, Stuart (Ed.). *Witchcraft and Magic in Europe.* Athlone History of Witchcraft. Vol 5. London: Athlone Press, 1999.

Ankarloo, Bengt & Clark, Stuart (Ed.). *Witchcraft and Magic in Europe: The Twentieth Century.* The Athlone history of Witchcraft. Vol 6. London: Athlone Press, 1999.

Australian Pagan Survey Results (Australian Pagan Alliance). December 2000.

Baker, James. "White Witches: Historic Fact or Romantic Fantasy." In Lewis, James (Ed.) *Magical Religion and Modern Witchcraft.* New York: State University of New York Press. 1996.

Barzun, Jacques. *Classic, Romantic and Modern.* Chicago: University of Chicago Press, 1961.

Baudrillard, Jean. *Simulacra and Simulation*. Michigan: University of Michigan Press, 1981.

Beard, Mary. Frazer, Leach and Virgil, "The Popularity (and Unpopularity) of 'The Golden Bough.'" *Comparative Studies in Society and History*. No 34. 1992. pp 203–224.

Beilharz, Peter. *Postmodern Socialism: Romanticism, City and State*. Melbourne: Melbourne University Press, 1994.

Bennet, David. *Cultural Studies: Pluralism and theory*. Melbourne: Melbourne University Press, 1993.

Bennet, Gillian. "Geologist and Folklorists: Cultural Evolution and the Science of Folklore." *Folklore*. Vol 105. 1994. pp 25–37.

Bennet, Gillian. "Folklore Studies and the English Rural Myth." *Rural History*. Vol 4. 1993. pp 77–91.

Bernal, Martin. *Black Athena*. London: Vintage Books, 1987.

Bloch, Jon. *New Spirituality, Self and Belonging: How Neo-Pagans and New Agers Talk about Themselves*. Westport: Praeger. 1998.

Bishop, Cat. "Embarrassed by our Origins." *The Pomegranate*. No 12. May 2000.

Bonewitz, Isaac. *The Druids Chronicles*. Berkley: Drunmeton Press, 1976.

Bonewits, Isaac. *Real Magic : An Introductory Treatise on the Principles of Yellow Magic*. London: Open Gate Publishing, 1972.

Bonewitz, Isaac. "Why and What is Reformed Druidism in the 1970s." *The Green Egg*. Vol 7. No 75. 1971.

Bonewits, Isaac (Ed.). *Real Magic : An Introductory Treatise on the Principles of Yellow Magic*. London: Open Gate Publishing, 1972.

Bonewits, Isaac. *Witchcraft: A Concise History*. New York: Pocket PC Press, 2000.

Bowman, M. "The Noble Savage and the Global Village: Cultural Evolution in New Age and Neo-Pagan thought." *Journal of Contemporary Religion*. 10(2). 1995.

Bracelin, J. *Gerald Gardner: Witch*. London: Octagon Press, 1960.

Briggs, Robin. *Witches and Neighbors: The Social and Cultural context of European Witchcraft*. London: Harper Collins, 1996.

Brooke, Elizabeth. *A Woman's Book of Shadows: Witchcraft: A Celebration*. London: Women's Press, 1993.

Brown, Mary Ellen (Ed.). *Neo-Paganism: A Search for Religious Alternatives*. Bloomington: Indiana University Women's Studies Program. 1988.

Buckland, Raymond. *Buckland's Complete Book of Witchcraft*. Minneapolis: Llewellyn Publishers, 1986.

Buckland, Raymond. *Witchcraft from the Inside*. Minneapolis: Llewellyn Publishers, 1995.

Budapest, Zsuzsanna. *The Holy Women's Book of Mysteries*. Oakland: Wingbow Press, 1989.

Cabot, Laurie. *The Power of the Witch*. New York: Arkana/Penguin, 1993.

Callinicos, Alex. *Against Postmodernism: A Marxist Critique*. Cambridge: Polity Press, 1989.

Campbell, Joseph. *The Portable Jung*. New York: Penguin Books, 1976.

Carter, Cassandra. *The Old Religion in the New Age*. Lecture Given to the C.G Jung Society. 20 November 1992.

Castle, Leila. *Earthwalking Skydancers: Women's Pilgrimages to Sacred Places*. Berkley: Frog publishers, 1996.

Clark, Stuart. *Thinking With Demons: The Idea of Early Modern Witchcraft in Early Modern Europe*. New York: Oxford University Press, 1997.

Cohn, Norman. *Europe's Inner Demons*. London: Sussex University Press, 1975.

Cohen, Stanley. *Folk Devils and Moral Panics: The Creation of the Mods and Rockers*. Robertson: Oxford, 1980.

Collinson, P. "No Popery: The Myth of a Protestant Nation." *The Tablet*. March 25. 1995.

Conway, D.J. *Celtic Magic*. New York: Llewellyn Press, 1990.

Coward, Rosalind. *The Myth of Alternative Health*. New York: Faber Publishing, 1989.

Cox, Harvey. *The Feast of Fools*. Cambridge: Harvard University Press, 1969.

Cranston, Sylvia. *Helene Blavatsky Unveiled*. G.P. Putnam: London. 1993.

Crowley, Aleister. *Magick Without Tears*. Phoenix: Falcon Press, 1991.

Crowley, Aleister. *The Confessions of Aleister Crowley: An Auto hagiography*. London: Routledge, 1979.

Crowley, Vivian. *The Old Religion in the New Age*. New York: Harper Collins, 1989.

Cunningham, Scott. *Wicca: A Guide for the Solitary Practitioner*. New York: Llewellyn publications, 1988.

Daly, Mary. *Gyn/Ecology*. London: Women's Press, 1979.

Davies, Owen. "Witchcraft: The Spell that didn't break". *History Today*. Vol 49. Issue 8. Aug 1999. pp 7–16.

Douglas, Mary. *Witchcraft Confessions and Accusations.* London: Cambridge University, 1970.

Doyle, William. *The Oxford History of the French Revolution.* Oxford: Oxford University Press, 1989.

Drury, N. *Exploring the Labyrinth: Making Sense of the New Spirituality.* St Leonards: Allen & Unwin, 1999.

Dworkin, Andrea. *Women Hating.* New York: Dutton, 1974.

Eagleton, Terry. *The Illusion of Postmodernism.* Oxford: Blackwell Publishers, 1996.

Echols, Alice. "We Gotta Get Out of this Place: Notes Towards Remapping the Sixties." *Socialist Review.* Vol 22. No 2. April/June, 1992. pp 9–33.

Evans, I. *Woodcraft and World Service.* London: Douglas Press, 1930.

Evans, Richard. *The German Underworld: Deviants and Outcasts in German History.* London: Routledge, 1988.

Ezzy, Doug. "The Commodification of Witchcraft." *Australian Religious Review.* Volume 14, No 1. 1998. pp 31–44.

Farrar, Janet & Stuart. *A Witch's Bible: The Complete Witch's Handbook.* Washington: Pheonix Publishing, 1996.

Fichte, Johann Gotlieb. *Foundations of Transcendental Philosophy.* Breazeale, Daniel (Trans). New York: Cornell University Publications, 1992 (1796).

Foucault, Michel. *Discipline and Punish: The Birth of the Prison.* New York: Random House Publishing, 1977.

Fox, Selena. *Pagan Spirit Alliance Newsletter.* No. 37. Spring 2000.

Frazer, J.G. *The Golden Bough: A Study in Magic and Religion.* London: MacMillan Press, 1974 (1922).

Friedberg, Anne. "Cinema and the Post-modern Condition." *PMLA,* Issue106: 3, 1991. pp 419–431.

Frere, Howard. *Visitations, Articles and Injunctions of the Period of the Reformation.* Vol 2. London: Aluin, 1963.

Gardner, Gerald. *Witchcraft Today.* London: Rider Press. 1954.

Gare, Arran. *Post-Modernism and the Environmental Crisis.* London: Routledge, 1995.

George, Janet and Davis Alan. *States of Health.* 3rd ed. Melbourne: Wesley & Longman, 1997.

Gijswift-Hoffa, Marijke. "Controversy c.1680–1800." In Ankarloo, Bengt & Clark, Stuart (Ed.) *Witchcraft and magic in Europe: The Eighteenth and*

Nineteenth Centuries. Athlone History of Witchcraft. Vol 5. London: Athlone Press, 1999.

Gildea, Robert. *Barricades and Borders: Europe 1800–1914.* New York: Oxford University Press, 1987.

Ginzberg, Carlo. *Ecstasies: Deciphering the Witch's Sabbath.* London: Penguin Books, 1992.

Ginzberg, Carlo. *The Night Battles: Witchcraft and Agrarian Cults in the Sixteenth and Seventeenth Centuries.* London: Oxford University Press, 1983.

Clifton, Chas. *Her Hidden Children: The Rise of Wicca and Paganism in America.* Alta Mira Press: New York, 2006.

Godwin, Jocelyn. *The Theosophical Enlightenment.* New York: State Library of New York Press, 1994.

Gouldner, Alvin. *For Sociology: Renewal and Critique in Sociology Today.* London: Allen Lane, 1973.

Greenwood, Susan. "The British Occult Sub-culture" in Lewis, James (Ed.) *Magical Religion and Modern Witchcraft.* New York: State University of New York Press, 1996.

Gregory, C.A. *Gifts and Commodities.* London: Academic Press, 1982.

Griggs, Barbara. *The New Green Pharmacy.* New York: Random House Publishing, 1997.

Grimmasi, Raven. "Interview with Oberon." *Ravens Call.* Obtained via personal communication with Raven Grimmasi. 3-23-2001.

Guale, J. *Select Cases of Conscience touching Witches and Witchcraft.* London: Oxford University Press, 1973 (1646).

Guskin, Phyllis. "The Context of English Witchcraft: The Case of Jane Wenham." *Eighteenth Century Studies.* Vol 15. 1981–1982.

Gynne, S.C. "I Saluted a Witch: An Army base in Texas becomes the hotbed for earth goddess worshipers called Wiccans." *Time Magazine.* Time Warner Publications, July 5 1999.

Hammill, John. *The Rosicrucian Seer.* Wellingborough: Aquarian Press, 1986.

Hammill, John. *The Craft: A History of English Freemasonry.* London: Aquarian Press, 1986.

Hanegraff, W. New Age Spiritualities as Secular Religion. *Social Compass.* Issue 46. 1999. pp 145–160.

Hansen, Thomas. "Inside the Romanticist Episteme." *Thesis Eleven.* no 48. London: SAGE, February 1997. pp 21–41.

Harker, Richard & Mahar, Cheleen & Wilkes, Chris. *An Introduction to the Work of Pierre Bourdieu: The Practice of Theory*. London: MacMillan Press, 1990.

Harley, David. "Historians as Demonologists: The Myth of the Midwife Witch." *Journal for the Society of the Social History of Medicine*. vol 3, 1990. pp 1–26.

Hebdidge, Dick. *Subculture: The Meaning of Style*. London: Methuen, 1981.

Heelas, Paul. "The New Age in Cultural Context: The Premodern, the Modern and the Postmodern." *Religion*. Vol 23, 1993. pp 103–116.

Heelas, Paul. *The New Age Movement*. Oxford: Blackwell Publishers: Oxford, 1996.

Henningsen, G. "Ladies from Outside." In Ankarloo, B. & Henningsen, G. *Early Modern European Witchcraft*. Oxford: Clarendon Press, 1990.

Heselton, Philip. *Wiccan Roots: Gerald Gardner and the Modern Pagan Revival*. Berkshire: Cheively, 2001.

Hill, Christopher. *Puritanism and Revolution*. New York: Schocken Books, 1964.

Hill, Christopher. *Some Intellectual Consequences of the English Revolution*. Madison: University of Wisconsin Press, 1980.

Hillgarth, J.N. *Ramon Lull and Lullism in Fourteenth Century France*. London: Oxford University Press, 1972.

Hobbes, Thomas. *Leviathan*. New York: Viking Press. 1982 (1657).

Hobsbawm, Eric. *The Invention of Tradition*. New York: Cambridge University Press, 1983.

Hobsbawm, Eric. *Primitive Rebels: A Study of Archaic Social Movements*. London: Manchester Press, 1959.

Holman, Keith W. "Obituary for a Neo-Pagan Pioneer." *The Green Egg*. Vol IV. No 45 Feb, 1972. pp 33–34.

Holmes, Clive. "Women: Witnesses and Witches." *Past and Present*. Issue 140, 1993.

Holmes, Clive (Ed.). *The Suffolk Committee for Scandalous Ministers 1644–46*. Vol 13. Suffolk Publications: Suffolk, 1970. pp 45–79.

Hopkins, M. *The Discovery of Witches*. Microfilm held at the University of Melbourne. Woodbridge: Research Publications, 1983.

Hume, David. *Enquiries concerning Human Understanding and Concerning the Principles of Morals*. London: Methuen Press, 1777 (1977).

Hume, David. *A Treatise Concerning Human Nature*. London: Penguin Books, 1984 (1739).

Hutchinson, Francis. *A historical essay concerning Witchcraft: With observations of matters of fact, tending to clear the Texts of the sacred Scriptures and confute the Vulgar Errors about that point.* London: AMS Press, 1982 (1712).

Hutcheon, Linda. *A Poetics of Post-Modernism: History, Theory, Fiction.* New York: Routledge, 1987.

Hutcheon, Linda. *Irony, Nostalgia and the Post-Modern.*

http://www.library.utoronto.ca/utel/criticism/hutchinp.html 17/8/2002.

Hutton, Ronald. *Pagan Religions of the British Isles: Their Nature and Legacy.* Blackwell: Oxford University Press, 1991.

Hutton, Ronald. *Triumph of the Moon: A History of Modern Pagan Witchcraft.* Oxford: Oxford University Press, 1999.

Hutton, Ronald. "Finding a Folklore." *The Pomegranate: A Journal of Neo-Pagan Thought.* Issue 12. May 2000. pp 4–15.

Hutton, Ronald. "The Background to Pagan Witchcraft." In Ankarloo, Bengt and Clark, Stuart. *Witchcraft and Magic in Europe: The Twentieth Century.* The Athlone history of Witchcraft. Vol 6. London: Athlone Press, 1999. pp 18–75.

Jackson, Cecile. "Women/Nature or Gender/History? A Critique of Eco-feminist Development." *Journal of Peasant Studies.* Vol 20. No 3, April 1993. pp 389–418.

Jackson, Gerald. *The Inner Executive.* Simon & Shuster: New York. 1989.

James, Roberta. *Spirit Shifts: Erlebnis, Physics and the persuasive passionate minutiae of women's spirituality rituals.* University of New South Wales: Annual Australian Anthropological Society Annual Conference, July 11, 1999.

Jameson, Fredrik. *Periodizing the Sixties: The Sixties without Apology.* Minneapolis: University of Minnesota Press, 1984.

Jameson, Fredrik. *Post-Modernism or the Cultural Logic of Late Capitalism.* Druham: Duke University Press, 1999.

Johnson, Pauline. "The Quest for the Self: Feminism's appropriation of Romanticism." *Thesis Eleven.* Vol 41. London: SAGE, 1995. pp 76–93.

Jones, Colin & Newitt, Malyn & Roberts, Stephen. *Politics and People in Revolutionary England: Essays in Honour of Ivan Roots.* London: Oxford University Press, 1986.

Jones, Edwin. *The English Nation: The Great Myth.* Gloucestershire: Sutton Press, 1998.

Jung, Carl. *Symbols of Transformation.* Princeton: Princeton University Press, 1990.

Kant, Immanuel. *Critique of Pure Reason.* London: Everyman's Library Press, 1993 (1781).

Kearney, Richard. *The Wake of Imagination Towards a Postmodern Culture.* Minneapolis: University of Minnesota Press, 1988.

Kelly, Andy. "English Kings and the Fear of Sorcery," *Mediaeval Studies.* 39 (1977). pp 206–238.

Kephart. M J. "Rationalists vs Romantics among Scholars of Witchcraft." In Marwick, Max (Ed.) *Witchcraft & Sorcery.* London: Penguin Books, 1970.

Kevin, Robin. "Magical Emasculation and the Limits of Popular Anti-Clericism in Early Modern Europe." *Journal of Social History.* Vol 31. No 1. Fall 1997.

Kieckhefer, Richard. *European Witch trials: their foundations in popular and learned culture, 1300–1500.* Berkeley: University of California Press, 1976.

King, Francis. *Ritual Magic in England.* London: Neville Spearman, 1970.

Klein, Naomi. *No Logo: No Space, No Choice, No Jobs.* London: Harper-Collins, 2001.

Knapp, Stephen. "Collective Memory and the Actual Past." *Representations.* No' 26, Spring 1989. pp 123–149.

Lathrop, Gordon. *Holy Things: A Liturgical Theology.* Minneapolis: Ausburg Fortress, 1993.

Leach, Edmund. "Golden Bough or Gilded Twig." *Daedalus,* Spring 1961. pp 371–386.

Lehmberg, Stanford. *The Later Parliament of King Henry VIII.* London: Cambridge, 1977.

Leland. Charles. *Aradia Or the Gospel of the Witches.* London: Phoenix Publishing, 1990.

Lewis, James (Ed.). *Magical Religion and Modern Witchcraft.* New York: State University of New York Press. 1996.

Luhrmann, Tanya. *Persuasions of the Witch's Craft: Ritual Magic in Contemporary England.* London: Harvard University Press. 1989.

Lyon, D. *Jesus in Disneyland: Religion in Post-Modern Times.* Cambridge: Polity Press, 2000.

McAdam, Doug. *Freedom Summer.* London: Oxford University Press, 1988.

MacFarlane, Alan. *Witchcraft in Tudor and Stuart England: A regional and comparative Study.* London: Harper and Row, 1970.

MacFarlane, Alan. *Witchcraft Prosecutions in Essex, 1560–1680: A Sociological Analysis.* London: Oxford University Press, 1967.

MacKenzie, Norman. *Secret Societies.* London: Aldis Books, 1997.

Maple, Eric. *The Dark World of Witches.* New York: Castle Books, 1964.

Marland, Hillary (Ed.). *The Art of Midwifery: Early Modern Midwives in Europe.* London: Routledge, 1993.

Marron, Kevin. *Witches, Pagans and Magic in the New Age.* Toronto: Seal Books, 1989.

Marsh, Jan. *Back to the Land: The Pastoral Impulse in England from 1880 to 1914.* London: Quartet publishing, 1982.

Marwick, Max (Ed.). *Witchcraft & Sorcery.* London: Penguin Books, 1970.

Marx, Karl. *Capital.* Vol 1. London: Harmondsworth. 1976.

Marx, Karl. *Grundrisse.* Harmondsworth: Penguin, 1973.

Maus, Marcel. *The Gift.* London: Routledge, 1974.

Michelet, Jules. *La Sorciere.* English Translation. London: Oxford University Press, 1966 (1862).

Miller, David. *The New Polytheism.* New York: Harper & Row, 1974.

Monter, William. "Toads and Eucharists: The Male Witches of Normandy." *Journal of French History.* Vol 20. No 4, Fall 1997. pp 563–595.

Moore, R. *Selling God: American Religions in the Market Place of Culture.* New York: Oxford University Press. 1994.

Morgan, Robin. *Going too Far: The Personal Chronicle of a Feminist.* New York: Vintage Books, 1978.

Morgan, Robin. *Lady of the Beasts: Poems.* Random House: New York, 1976.

Morgan, Robin. *The Demon Lover: On the sexuality of Terrorism.* London: Methuen Press, 1989.

Moss, Harold. Open Forum. *The Green Egg.* Vol 5. No 51, 1972. pp 2–7.

Mulcock, Jane. "(Re)Discovering out Indigenous Selves: The Nostalgic Appeal of Native Americans and Other Generic Indigenes." *Australian Religious Studies.* Volume 14, No 1. 1998. pp 45–63.

Mulcock, Jane. "Creativity and Politics in the Cultural Supermarket: Synthesizing indigenous identities for the r/evolution of spirit." *Continuum: Journal of Media and Cultural Studies.* Vol 15. No 2, 2001. pp 169–185.

Murphy, Peter. "Romantic Modernism and the Greek Polis." *Thesis Eleven,* Number 34, 1993. pp 42–65.

Murray, Margaret. *The Witch Cult in Western Europe.* Oxford: Clarendon Press, 1962 (1921).

Musgrove, Frank. *Ecstasy and Holiness.* London: Methuen, 1974.

Neville, Richard. *Playpower.* London: Granada Publishing, 1971.

Newton, Janice. "Aborigines, Tribes and Counterculture." *Social Analysis.* No 23, August 1988. pp 53–71.

Niebuhr, Richard H. *The Meaning of Revelation.* New York: Macmillan, 1941.

Noll, Richard. *The Jung Cult: The Origins of a Charismatic Movement.* New York: Princeton University Press, 1994.

Nottestein, Wallis. *A History of Witchcraft from 1558–1718.* London: Barnes and Noble, 1968.

Outram, Dorinda. *The Enlightenment.* New York: Cambridge University Press. 1995.

Plant, J. (Ed.). *Healing the Wounds: The Promise of Eco-Feminism.* Philadelphia: New Society Publishers, 1987.

Principia Discordia, 4th ed, (privately published and distributed set of principles for the Discordian Society) 1970. Courtesy of the Australian Pagan Information centre (3-2-2000).

Pritchard, Evans. "Sorcery and Native Opinion." *Africa,* Vol 4, no 1. 1931.

Purkiss, Diane. *The Witch in History: Early Modern and Twentieth Century Interpretations.* London: Routledge, 1996.

Rainbow, P. (Ed.). *The Foucault Reader.* Penguin: New York, 1984.

Rajan,Tilottama. *The Dark Interpreter: The discourse of Romanticism.* New York: Cornell University Press, 1980.

Randolph, Vance. *Ozark Superstition.* New York: Columbia University Press, 1947.

Reid, Stan. "Witch Wars: Factors Contributing to Conflict in Canadian Neo-Pagan Communities." *Pomegranate.* No 11, February 2000. pp 10–21.

Rex, Richard. *Henry VIII and the English Reformation.* London: Palgrave, 1993.

Richardson, Alan. *Priestess: The Life and Times of Dion Fortune.* Wellingborough: Aquarian Press, 1987.

Rigby, Kate. "Women and Nature Revisited: Ecofeminist Reconfigurations Of an Old Association." *Arena Journal.* No. 12, 1998. pp 143–169.

Robins, Kevin. "Magical Emasculation and the Limits of Popular Anti-Clericism in Early Modern Europe." *Journal of Social History.* Vol 31. No 1, Fall 1997. pp 61–83.

Robinson, John. *Honest to God.* London: Billing and Sons, 1963.

Rojek, Chris & Turner, Bryan. *Forget Baudrillard.* London: Routledge, 1993.

Rose, Elliot. *A Razor for a Goat.* Toronto: University of Toronto Press, 1962.

Roszak, Theodore. *The Making of a Counter-Culture.* New York: Doubleday Books, 1973.

Roszak, Theodore. *Where the wasteland ends: politics and transcendence in post-industrial society.* New York: Anchor Books, 1973.

Rountree, Kathryn. "The New Witch of the West: Feminists Reclaim the Crone." *Journal of Popular Culture,* Vol 30(4), Spring 1997. pp 215–229.

Rountree, Kathryn. "The Politics of the Goddess: Feminist Spirituality and the Essentialism Debate." *Social Analysis,* Issue 43(2), July 1999. pp 138–165.

Rubin, Jerry. *Do It! Scenarios of the Revolution.* New York: Simon and Schuster, 1970.

Ruether, Rosemary. *Sexism and God-talk: Towards a Feminist Theology.* New York: Beacon Press, 1983.

Runes, Dagobert. A *Dictionary of Philosophy.* New York: Philosophical Library, 1942.

Russell, Jeffrey. *A History of Witchcraft: Sorcerers, Heretics, and Pagans.* London: Thames and Hudson, 1980.

Russell, Steve. *Foucault Genealogy and Witchcraft.* School of Humanities. Monash University Gippsland. Obtained via personal communication 31-1-2000.

St John, Graham. *Alternative Culture Heterotopia: Confest as Australia's Marginal Centre.* http://www.angelfire.com/pq/edgecentral/contents.html 10-12-2001.

Schelling, Friedrich Wilhelm. *Ideas for a Philosophy of Nature as Introduction to the Study of this Science.* Cambridge: Cambridge University Press, 1988 (1797).

Schelling, Freidrich Wilhelm Joseph. *The System of Transcendent Idealism.* Richmond: Virginia University Press, 1978 (1800).

Schermer, Michael. *Why People Believe Weird Things.* Freeman: New York, 1997.

Scholem, Gershom. *Major Trends in Jewish Mysticism.* Jerusalem: Schocken Books, 1941.

Seabrook, William. *Witchcraft: Its Power in the World Today.* New York: Harcourt & Brace, 1940.

Sharpe, J.A. *Instruments of Darkness: Witchcraft in Early Modern England.* Pennsylvania: University of Pennsylvania Press, 1996.

Singer, Andre & Lynette. *Divine Magic: The World of the Supernatural.* London: Boxtree Publishing, 1995.

Singer, C. *The Legacy of Israel.* Oxford: Oxford University Press, 1927.

Skinner, Stephen. *Divination by Geomancy.* London: Routledge, 1980.

Smyth, Frank. *Modern Witchcraft.* London: MacDonald Press, 1970.

Sommerville, C. *The Secularization of Early Modern England.* London: Oxford University Press, 1992.

Spretnak, Charlene ed. *The Politics of Women's Spirituality: Essays on the Rise of Spiritual Power within the Feminist Movement.* New York: Doubleday, 1982.

Starhawk (Simos, Miriam). *The Fifth Sacred Thing.* New York: Harper-Collins Publishers, 1994.

Starhawk (Simos, Miriam). *The Spiral Dance: 10th Anniversary Edition.* New York: Harper-Collins Press, 1989.

Starhawk (Simos, Miriam). *Dreaming the Dark.* Chicago: Llewellyn Publishers, 1986.

Starhawk. *Truth or Dare.* San Francisco: Harper and Row, 1987.

Stearne, John. *A Confirmation and Discovery of Witchcraft.* Exeter: University of Exeter Press, 1985 (1644).

Stephen's Julie. *Anti-disciplinary protest: Sixties radicalism and Post-modernism.* London: Cambridge University Press, 1998.

Stevenson, David. *The First Freemasons.* Aberdeen: Aberdeen University Press, 1988.

Stevenson, David. *The Origins of Freemasonry.* Cambridge: Cambridge University Press, 1990.

Stewart, Pamela J and Strathern, Andrew. *Witchcraft, Sorcery, Rumours and Gossip.* Cambridge University Press: Cambridge, 2004.

Strmiska, Michael. Lecturer in History and Comparative Religion

Miyazaki International College. "Natrel-L" newsgroup. 29-11-2000.

Sykes, Karen. *Arguing with Anthropology: An Introduction to Critical Theories of the Gift.* London: Routledge, 2005.

Symonds, John. *The Great Beast.* London: MacDonald Press, 1971.

Tamas, Richard. *The Passion of the Western Mind.* London: Pinicuto Press, 1996.

Thomas, Keith. *Religion and the Decline of Magic: Studies in Popular Belief in Sixteenth and Seventeenth Century England.* Harmondsworth: Penguin Books, 1971.

Thorndike, Lynn. *A History of Magic and Experimental Science.* Vol ii. Columbia: Columbia University Press, 1934.

Trevor-Roper, Hugh. "Witches and Witchcraft: a Historical Essay." *Encounter,* vol 28. no 6, 1967. pp 4–30.

Twilgus, Neal. "An Interview with Anton Wilson." *Science Fiction Review.* Vol 5. No 2, 1976. pp 32–33.

Valiente, Doreen. *An ABC of Witchcraft Past and Present.* New York: St Martin's Press, 1973.

Valiente, D. *The Rebirth of Witchcraft.* Washington: Valkyrie Press, 1989.

Vlastos, Stephen. *Mirror of Modernity: Invented Traditions of Modern Japan.* Berkeley: University of California Press, 1998.

Wafer, Jim. "Gay and Lesbian Alternative Religious Movements: Do you have to have Foundations before you can rock them." *Alternative Culture Seminar.* University of New South Wales: Australian Anthropological Society Annual Conference, 10 July 1999.

Wallis, R. *Neo-Platonism.* New York: Charles Scribner, 1972.

Weber, Max. *The Protestant Ethic and the Spirit of Capitalism.* London: Allen & Unwin, 1976.

Weiner, Martin. *English Culture and the Decline of the Industrial Spirit: 1850–1980.* London: Harmondsworth Press, 1985.

Weisner, Mary. *Women in Gender in Early Modern Europe.* Cambridge: Cambridge University Press, 1993.

Wells, Roy. *The Rise and Development of Organized Freemasonry.* London: A Lewis (Masonic Publishers) LTD, 1986.

Wenegrat, B & Yalom, I. Large Group Awareness Training. *Annual Review of Psychology,* 1982. pp 515–539.

White, Evelyn. *The Journal of William Dowsing of Stratford.* Cambridge: Cambridge University Press, 1970.

Wilby, Emma. *Cunning Folk and Familiar Spirits: Shamanistic Visionary Traditions in Early Modern British Witchcraft and Magic.* Sussex Academic Press: Brighton, 2005.

Williams, Raymond. *The Country and the City.* London: Chatto and Windus, 1973.

Wolf, Naomi. *Fire with Fire: The New Female Power and How it Will Change the 21st Century.* London: Chatto & Windus, 1993.

Yates, Francis. *The Occult Philosophy in the Elizabethan Age.* London: Routledge, 1979.

Yates, Francis. *The Rosicrucian Enlightenment.* St Albans: Granada Publishing, 1975.

York, Michael. "Defining Paganism." *The Pomegranate.* Issue 11, Feb 2000.

York, Michael. *The Emerging Network: A Sociology of the New Age and Neo-Pagan movements.* London: Rowman and Littlefield, 1995.

INDEX